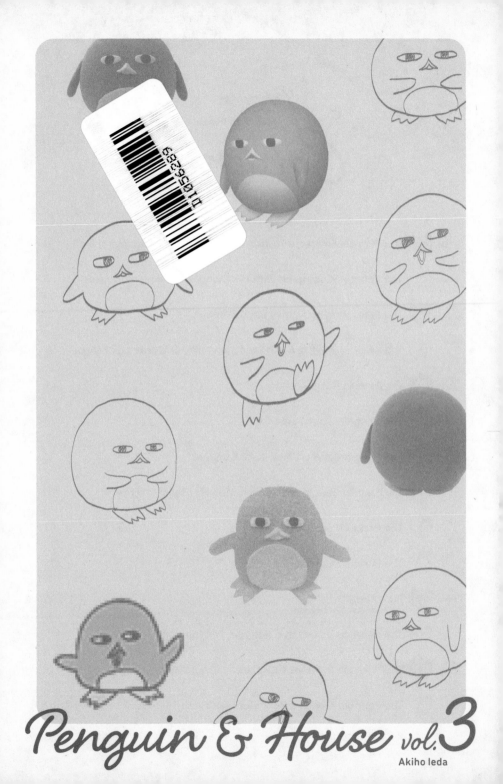

Penguin & House vol. 3

Akiho Ieda

Penguin & House
Contents

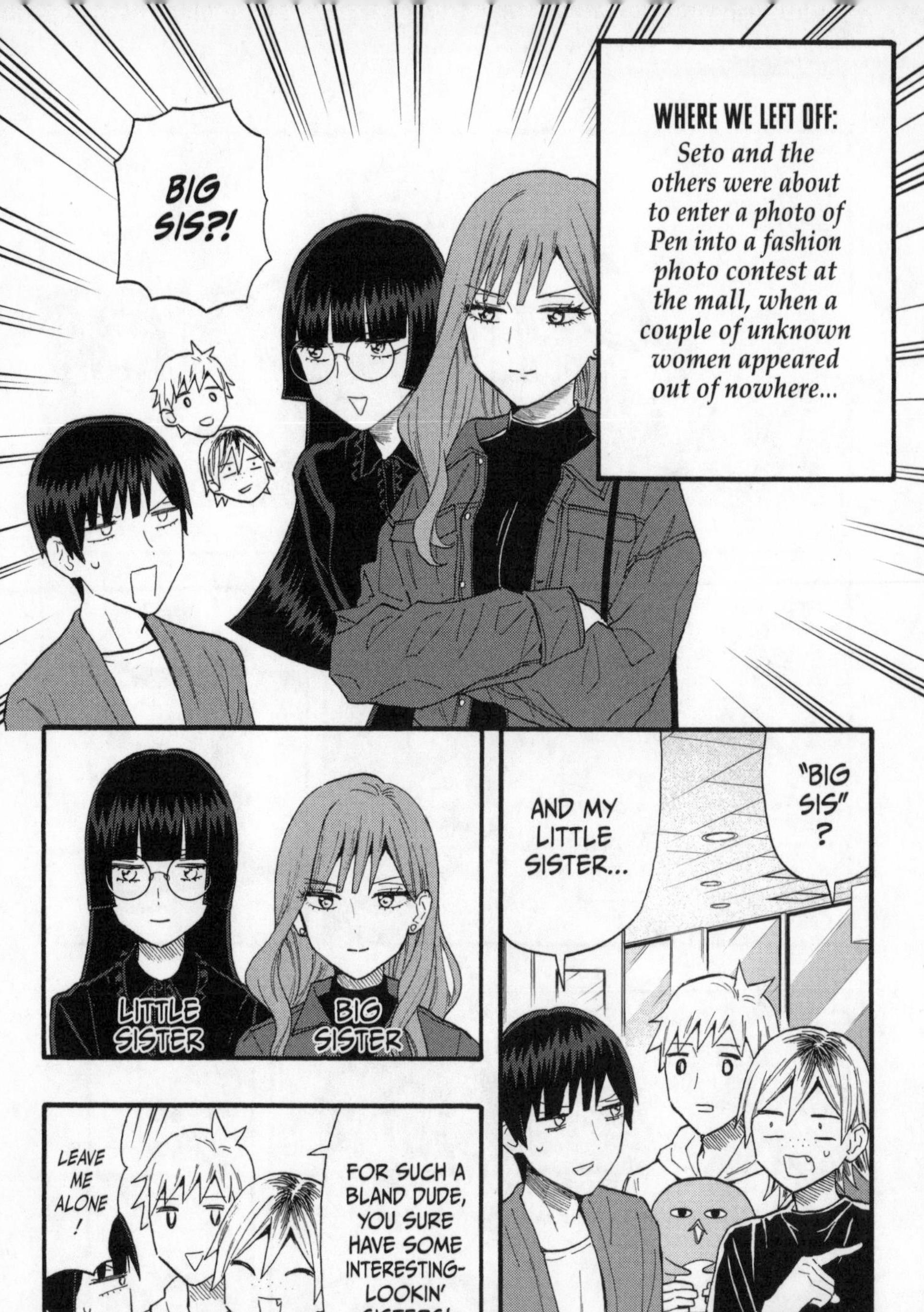
WHERE WE LEFT OFF:
Seto and the others were about to enter a photo of Pen into a fashion photo contest at the mall, when a couple of unknown women appeared out of nowhere...
BIG SIS?!
"BIG SIS"?
AND MY LITTLE SISTER...
BIG SISTER
LITTLE SISTER
FOR SUCH A BLAND DUDE, YOU SURE HAVE SOME INTERESTING-LOOKIN' SISTERS!
LEAVE ME ALONE!

Pen 29 The Penguin Entered a Fashion Photo Contest in a Shopping Mall

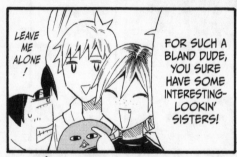

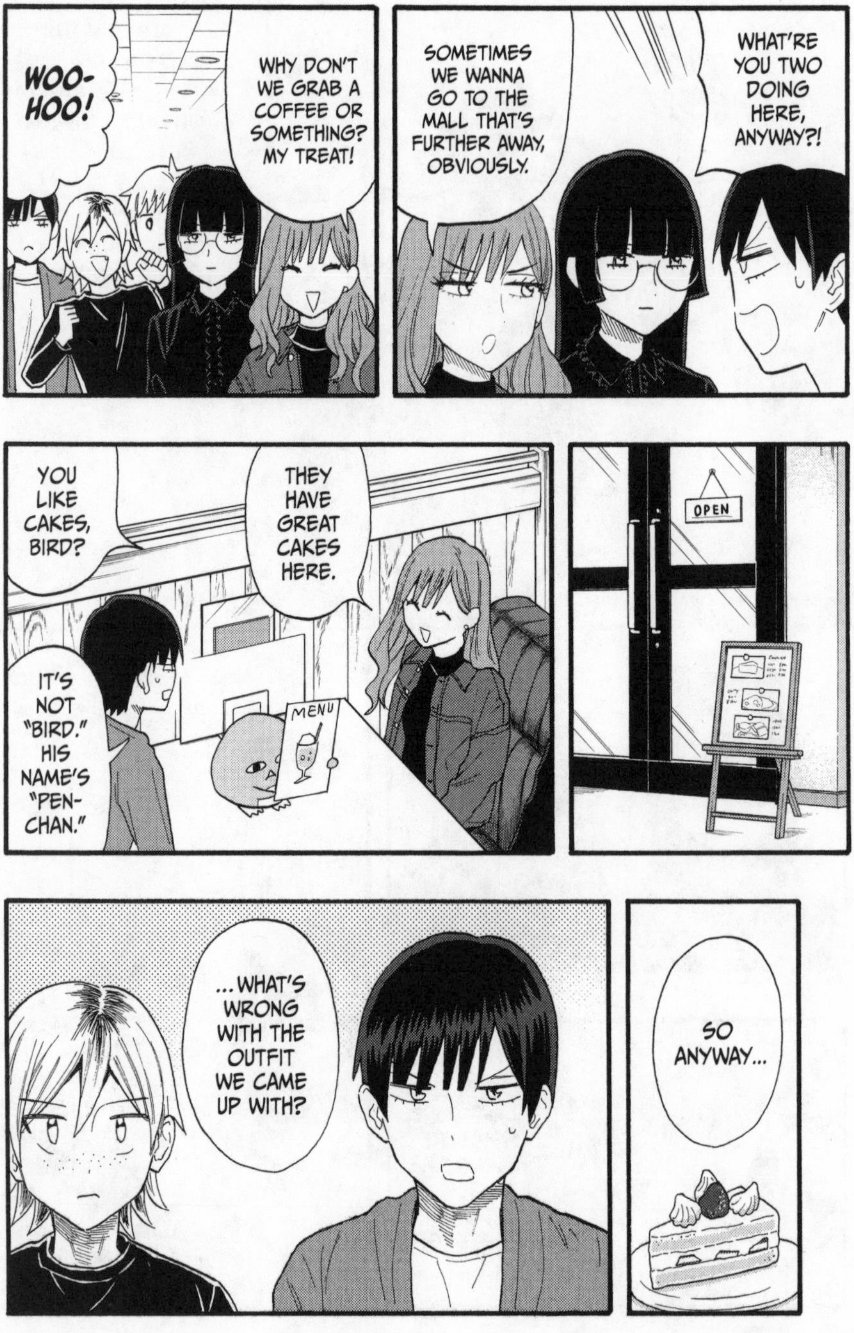
WHAT'RE YOU TWO DOING HERE, ANYWAY?!
SOMETIMES WE WANNA GO TO THE MALL THAT'S FURTHER AWAY, OBVIOUSLY.
WHY DON'T WE GRAB A COFFEE OR SOMETHING? MY TREAT!
WOO-HOO!
OPEN
THEY HAVE GREAT CAKES HERE.
YOU LIKE CAKES, BIRD?
MENU
IT'S NOT "BIRD." HIS NAME'S "PEN-CHAN."
SO ANYWAY...
...WHAT'S WRONG WITH THE OUTFIT WE CAME UP WITH?

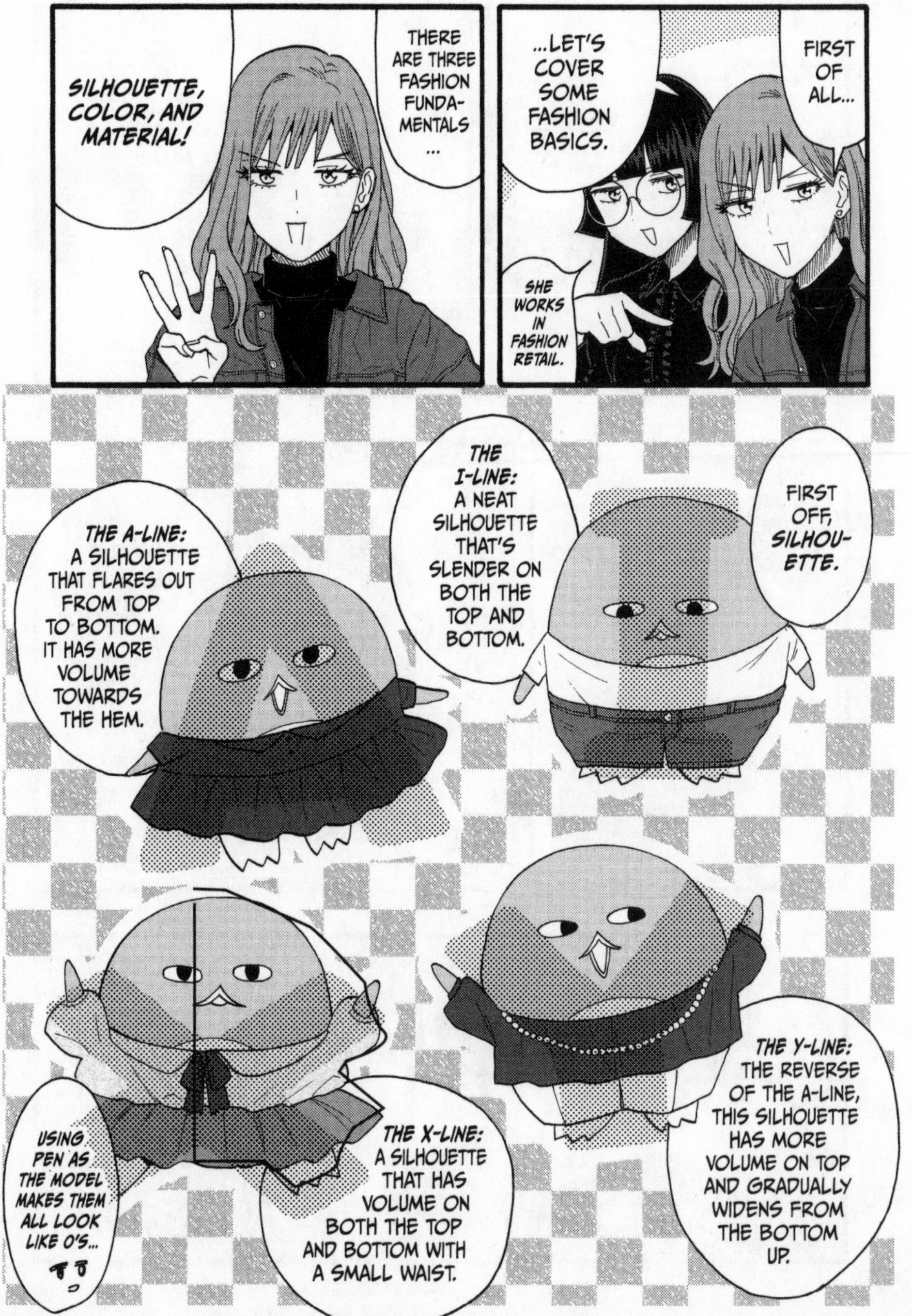
FIRST OF ALL...
...LET'S COVER SOME FASHION BASICS.
SHE WORKS IN FASHION RETAIL.
THERE ARE THREE FASHION FUNDAMENTALS ...
SILHOUETTE, COLOR, AND MATERIAL!
FIRST OFF, SILHOUETTE.
THE I-LINE: A NEAT SILHOUETTE THAT'S SLENDER ON BOTH THE TOP AND BOTTOM.
THE A-LINE: A SILHOUETTE THAT FLARES OUT FROM TOP TO BOTTOM. IT HAS MORE VOLUME TOWARDS THE HEM.
THE Y-LINE: THE REVERSE OF THE A-LINE, THIS SILHOUETTE HAS MORE VOLUME ON TOP AND GRADUALLY WIDENS FROM THE BOTTOM UP.
THE X-LINE: A SILHOUETTE THAT HAS VOLUME ON BOTH THE TOP AND BOTTOM WITH A SMALL WAIST.
USING PEN AS THE MODEL MAKES THEM ALL LOOK LIKE O'S...

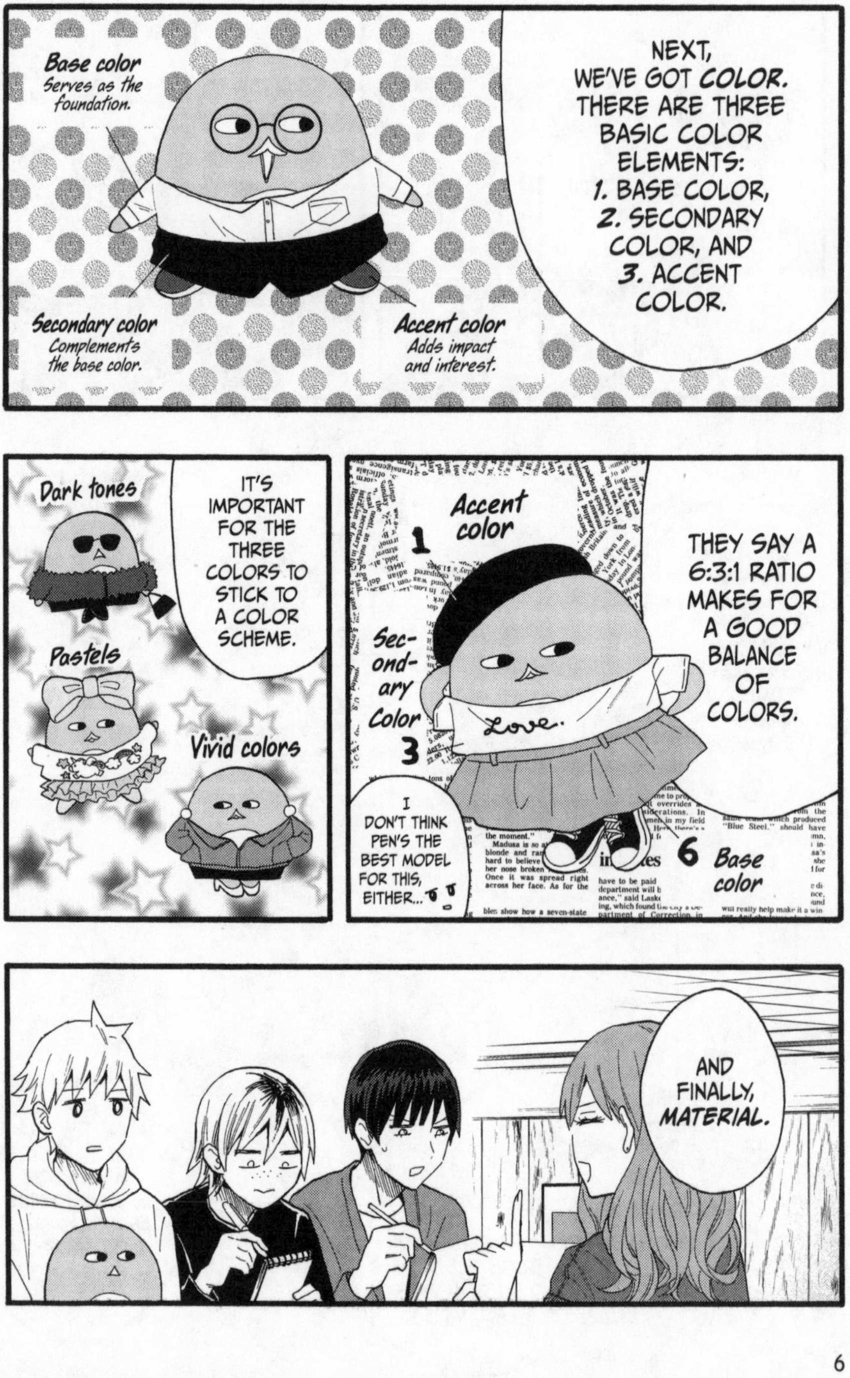
NEXT, WE'VE GOT COLOR. THERE ARE THREE BASIC COLOR ELEMENTS: 1. BASE COLOR, 2. SECONDARY COLOR, AND 3. ACCENT COLOR.
Base color Serves as the foundation.
Secondary color Complements the base color.
Accent color Adds impact and interest.
THEY SAY A 6:3:1 RATIO MAKES FOR A GOOD BALANCE OF COLORS.
Accent color 1
Sec-ond-ary Color 3
6 Base color
Love.
I DON'T THINK PEN'S THE BEST MODEL FOR THIS, EITHER...
IT'S IMPORTANT FOR THE THREE COLORS TO STICK TO A COLOR SCHEME.
Dark tones
Pastels
Vivid colors
AND FINALLY, MATERIAL.

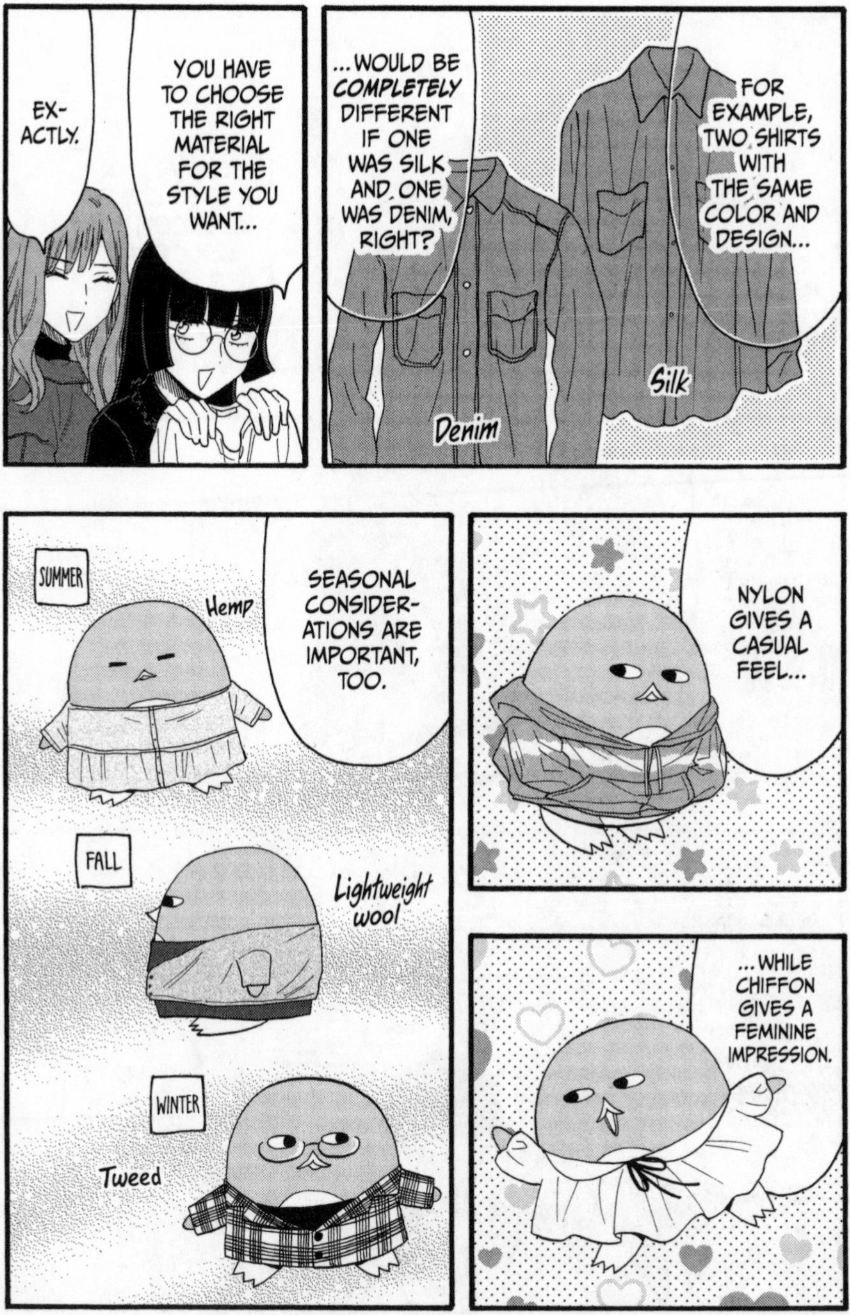
FOR EXAMPLE, TWO SHIRTS WITH THE SAME COLOR AND DESIGN...
...WOULD BE COMPLETELY DIFFERENT IF ONE WAS SILK AND ONE WAS DENIM, RIGHT?
Silk
Denim
YOU HAVE TO CHOOSE THE RIGHT MATERIAL FOR THE STYLE YOU WANT...
EX-ACTLY.
NYLON GIVES A CASUAL FEEL...
...WHILE CHIFFON GIVES A FEMININE IMPRESSION.
SEASONAL CONSIDER-ATIONS ARE IMPORTANT, TOO.
SUMMER
Hemp
FALL
Lightweight wool
WINTER
Tweed

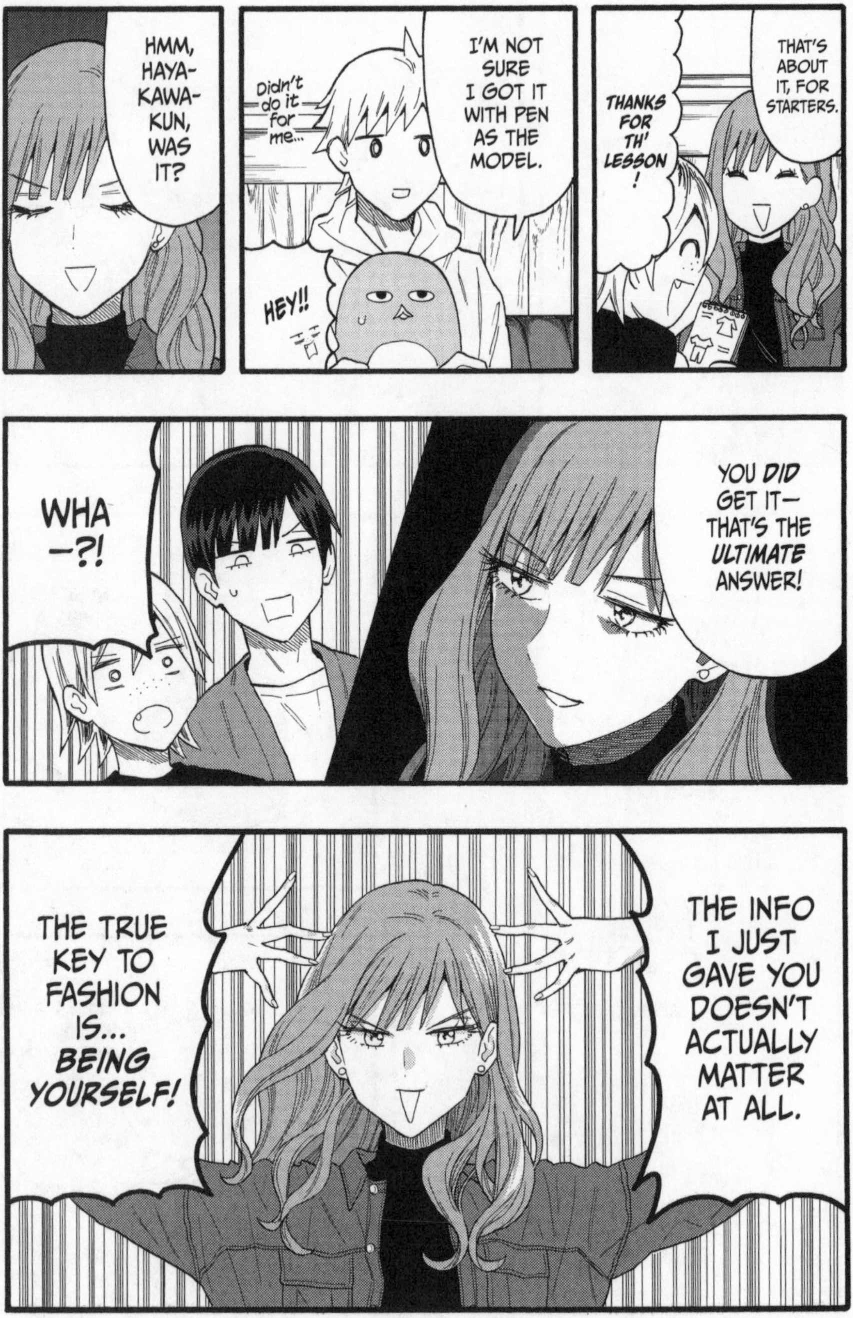
THAT'S ABOUT IT, FOR STARTERS.
THANKS FOR TH' LESSON!
I'M NOT SURE I GOT IT WITH PEN AS THE MODEL.
Didn't do it for me...
HEY!!
HMM, HAYAKAWA-KUN, WAS IT?
YOU *DID* GET IT—THAT'S THE *ULTIMATE* ANSWER!
WHA—?!
THE INFO I JUST GAVE YOU DOESN'T ACTUALLY MATTER AT ALL.
THE TRUE KEY TO FASHION IS... *BEING YOURSELF!*

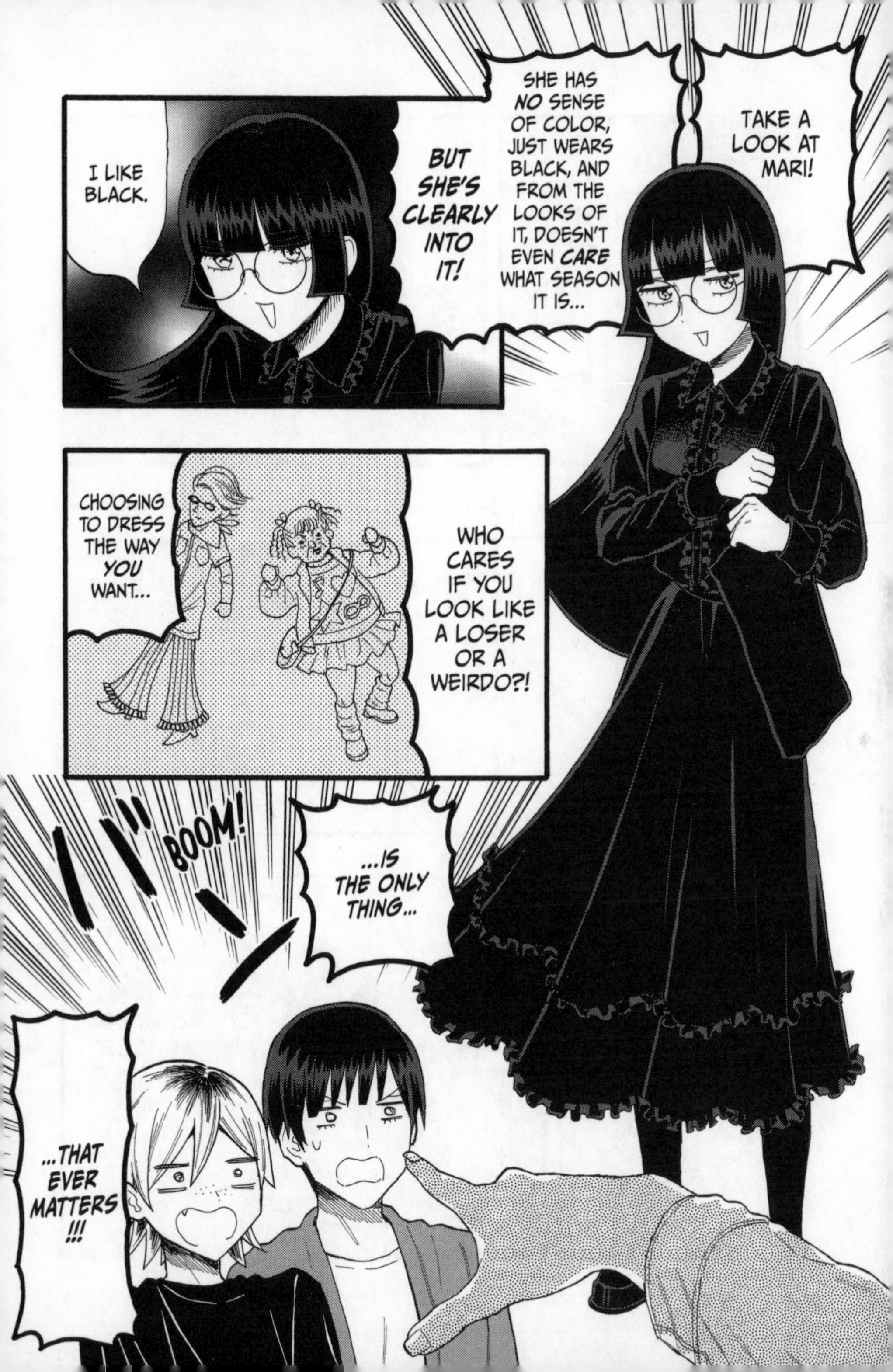
TAKE A LOOK AT MARI!
SHE HAS NO SENSE OF COLOR, JUST WEARS BLACK, AND FROM THE LOOKS OF IT, DOESN'T EVEN CARE WHAT SEASON IT IS...
BUT SHE'S CLEARLY INTO IT!
I LIKE BLACK.
WHO CARES IF YOU LOOK LIKE A LOSER OR A WEIRDO?!
CHOOSING TO DRESS THE WAY YOU WANT...
...IS THE ONLY THING...
BOOM!
...THAT EVER MATTERS!!!

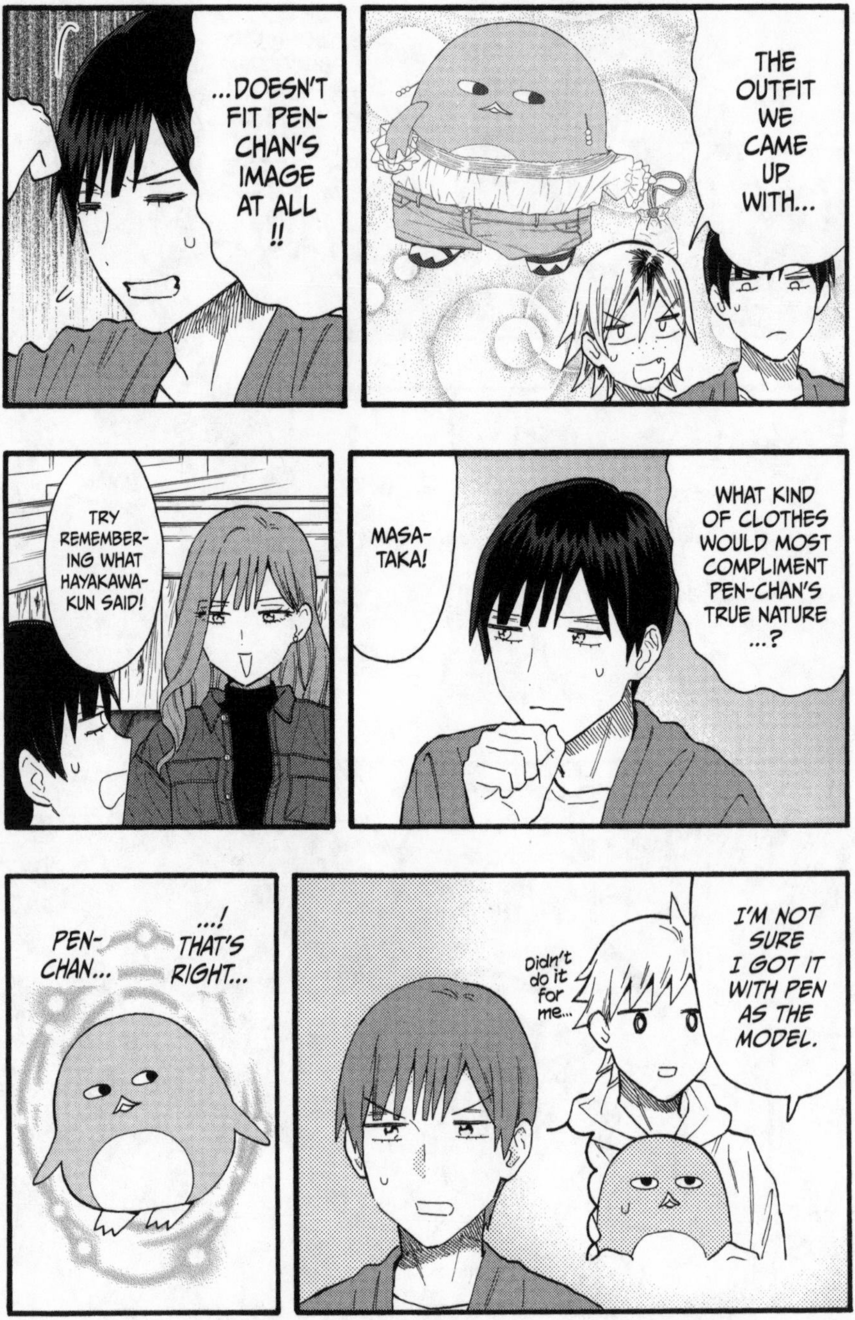
THE OUTFIT WE CAME UP WITH...
...DOESN'T FIT PEN-CHAN'S IMAGE AT ALL !!
WHAT KIND OF CLOTHES WOULD MOST COMPLIMENT PEN-CHAN'S TRUE NATURE ...?
MASA-TAKA!
TRY REMEMBERING WHAT HAYAKAWA-KUN SAID!
I'M NOT SURE I GOT IT WITH PEN AS THE MODEL.
Didn't do it for me...
...! THAT'S RIGHT...
PEN-CHAN...

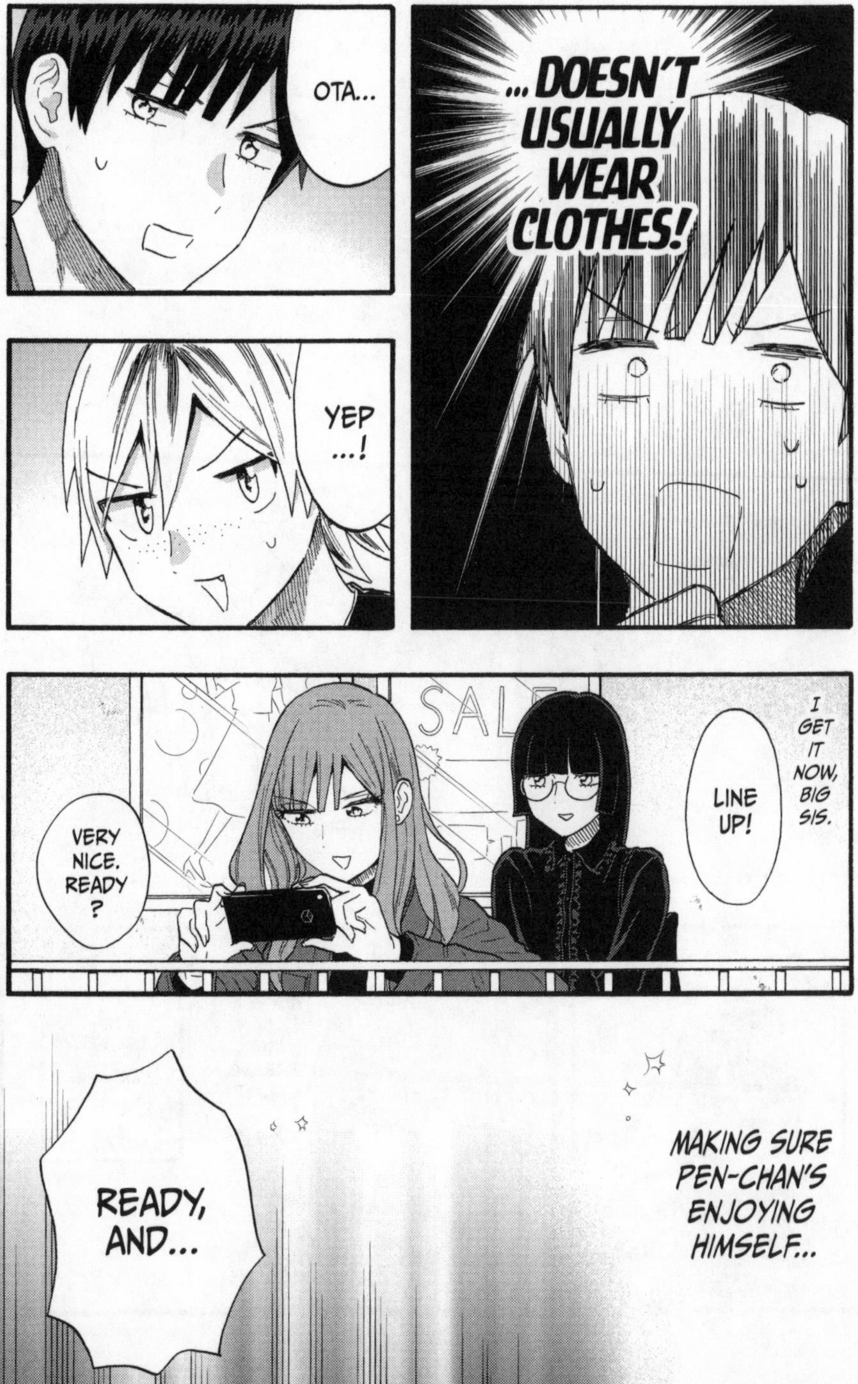
OTA...
YEP ...!
...DOESN'T USUALLY WEAR CLOTHES!
VERY NICE. READY?
LINE UP!
I GET IT NOW, BIG SIS.
READY, AND...
MAKING SURE PEN-CHAN'S ENJOYING HIMSELF...

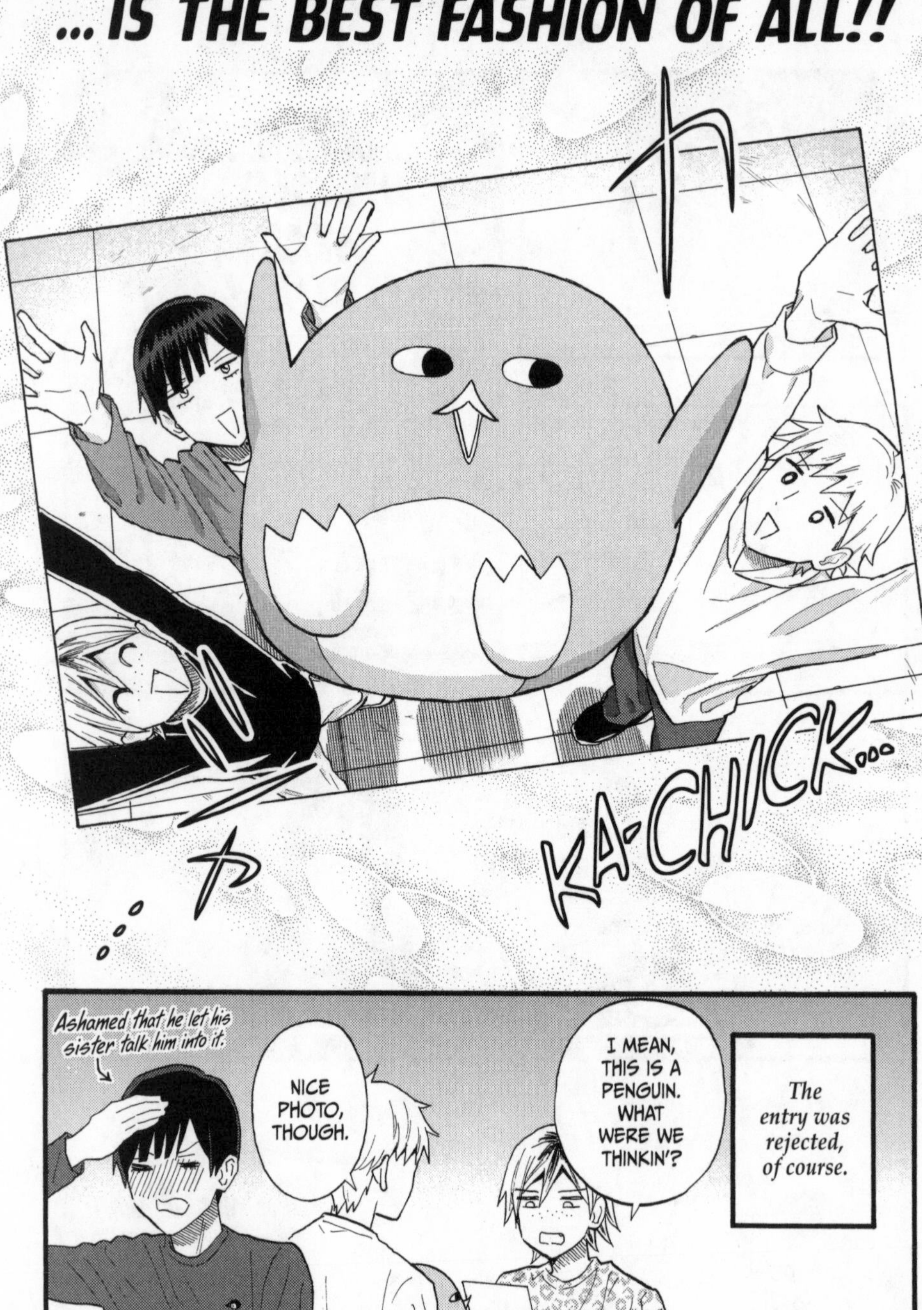
...IS THE BEST FASHION OF ALL!!
KA-CHICK...
The entry was rejected, of course.
I MEAN, THIS IS A PENGUIN. WHAT WERE WE THINKIN'?
NICE PHOTO, THOUGH.
Ashamed that he let his sister talk him into it.

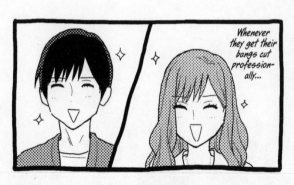

THE CURSE ON THE SETO FAMILY
Unrelated to Pen
Whenever they get their bangs cut profession-ally...
WHY?!
...they always end up like this the next day, for some reason.
MIRROR
MIRROR
Cuts her own bangs
MIRROR

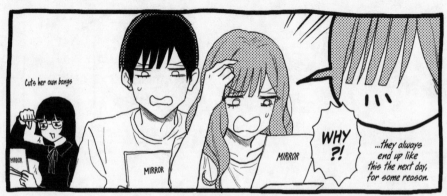

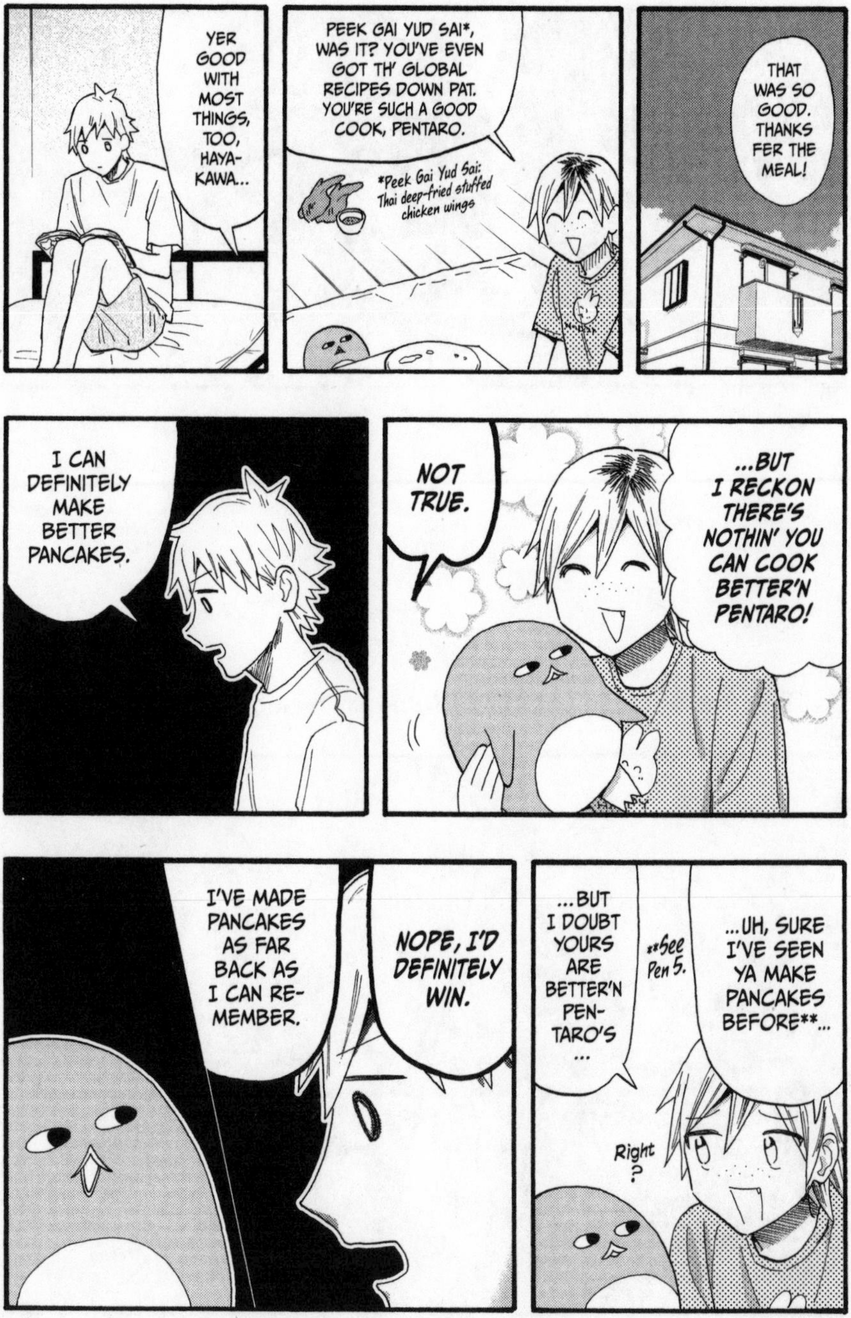
THAT WAS SO GOOD. THANKS FER THE MEAL!
PEEK GAI YUD SAI*, WAS IT? YOU'VE EVEN GOT TH' GLOBAL RECIPES DOWN PAT. YOU'RE SUCH A GOOD COOK, PENTARO.
*Peek Gai Yud Sai: Thai deep-fried stuffed chicken wings
YER GOOD WITH MOST THINGS, TOO, HAYA-KAWA...
...BUT I RECKON THERE'S NOTHIN' YOU CAN COOK BETTER'N PENTARO!
NOT TRUE.
I CAN DEFINITELY MAKE BETTER PANCAKES.
...UH, SURE I'VE SEEN YA MAKE PANCAKES BEFORE**...
**See Pen 5.
...BUT I DOUBT YOURS ARE BETTER'N PEN-TARO'S ...
Right?
NOPE, I'D DEFINITELY WIN.
I'VE MADE PANCAKES AS FAR BACK AS I CAN RE-MEMBER.

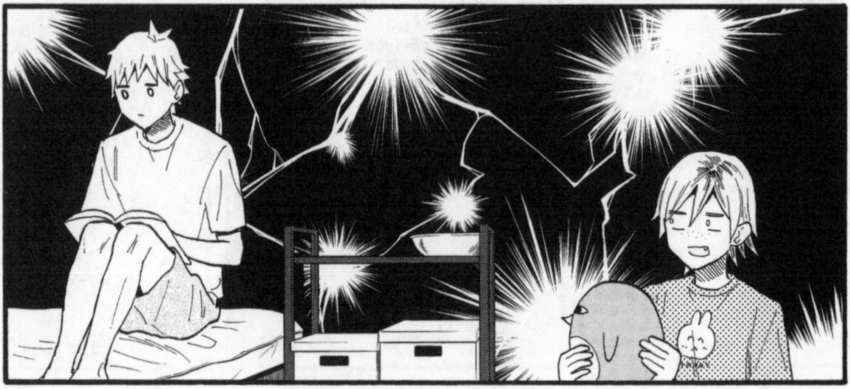

Pen 30 The Penguin Competes With His Owner at Making Pancakes

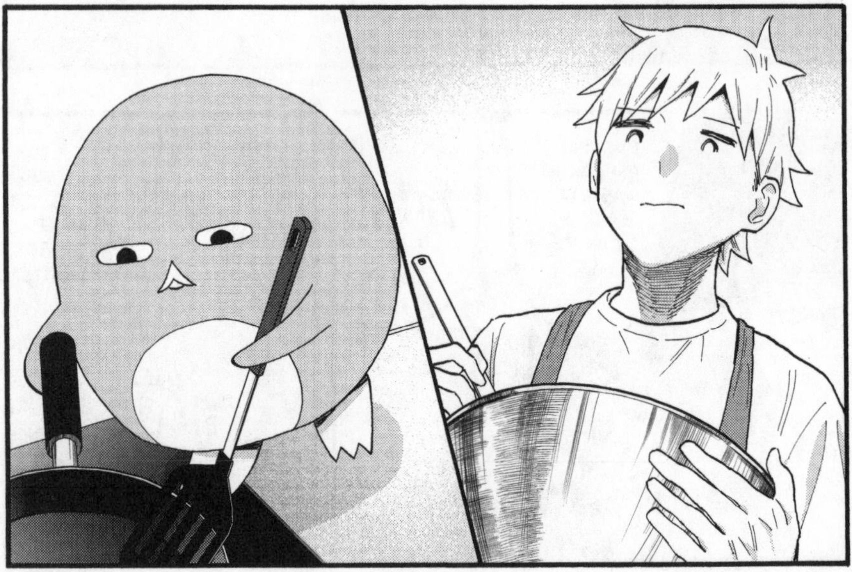

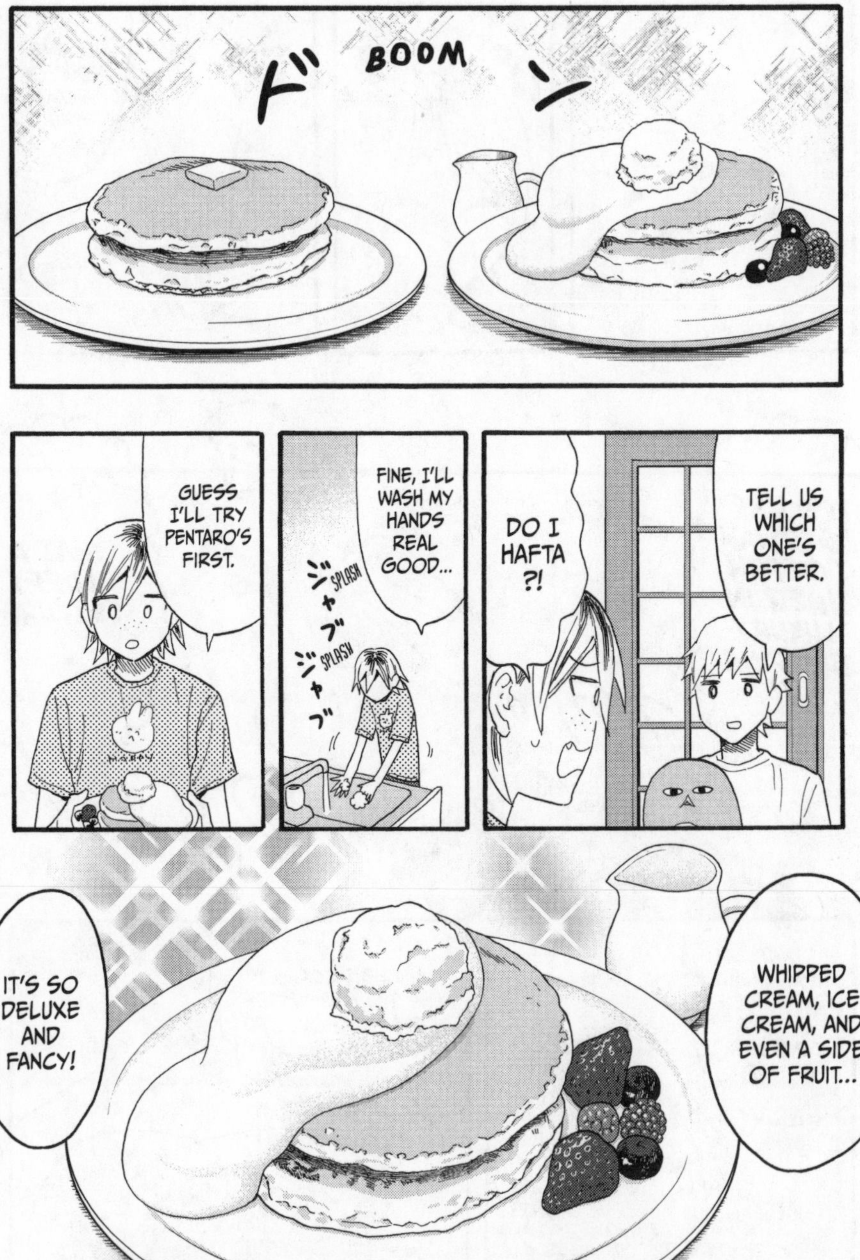
ド BOOM ン
TELL US WHICH ONE'S BETTER.
DO I HAFTA?!
FINE, I'LL WASH MY HANDS REAL GOOD...
ジャブ SPLASH
ジャブ SPLASH
GUESS I'LL TRY PENTARO'S FIRST.
WHIPPED CREAM, ICE CREAM, AND EVEN A SIDE OF FRUIT...
IT'S SO DELUXE AND FANCY!

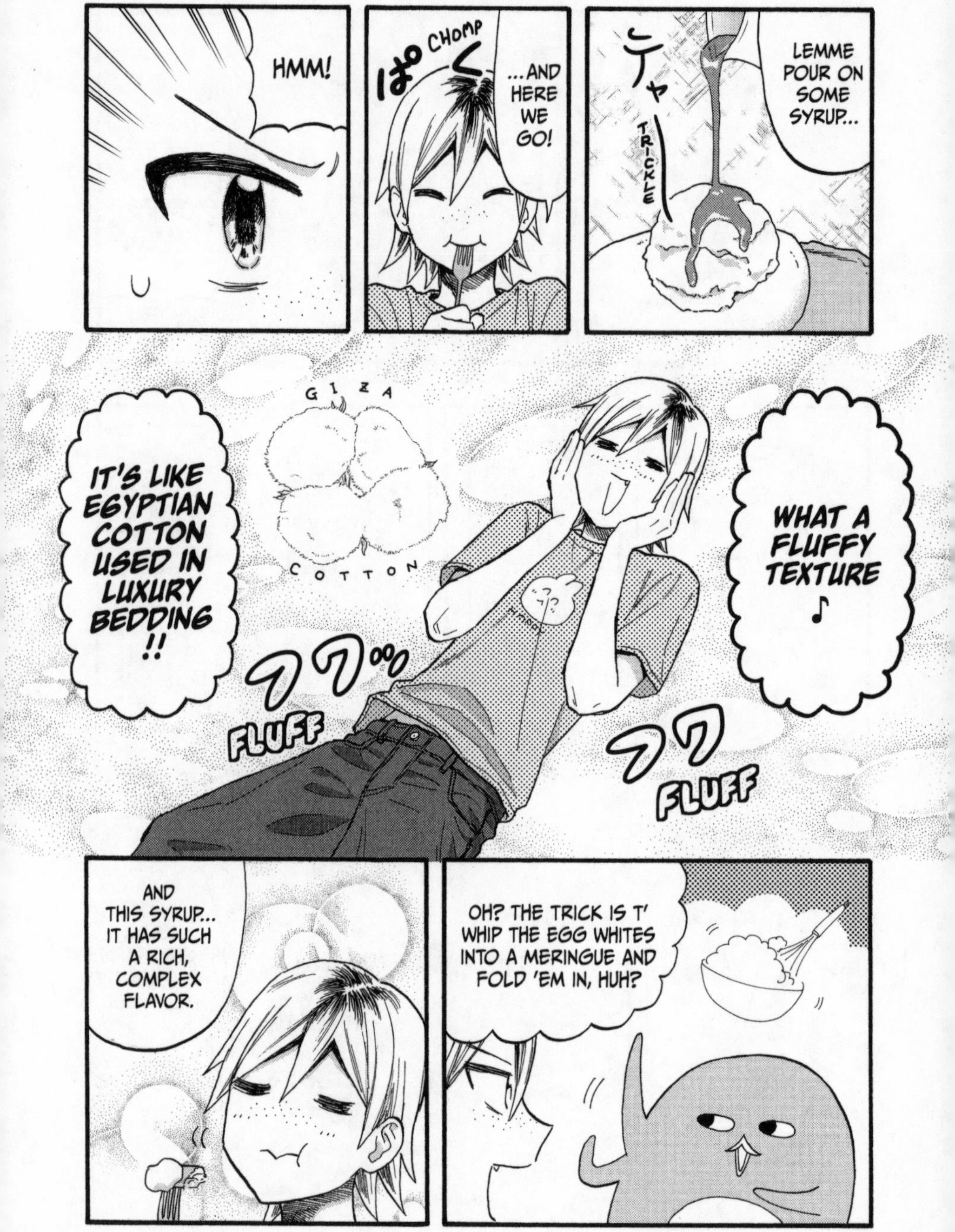

LEMME POUR ON SOME SYRUP...
テャー
TRICKLE
ぱく
CHOMP
...AND HERE WE GO!
HMM!
WHAT A FLUFFY TEXTURE ♪
IT'S LIKE EGYPTIAN COTTON USED IN LUXURY BEDDING!!
GIZA COTTON
フワ
FLUFF
フワ
FLUFF
OH? THE TRICK IS T' WHIP THE EGG WHITES INTO A MERINGUE AND FOLD 'EM IN, HUH?
AND THIS SYRUP... IT HAS SUCH A RICH, COMPLEX FLAVOR.

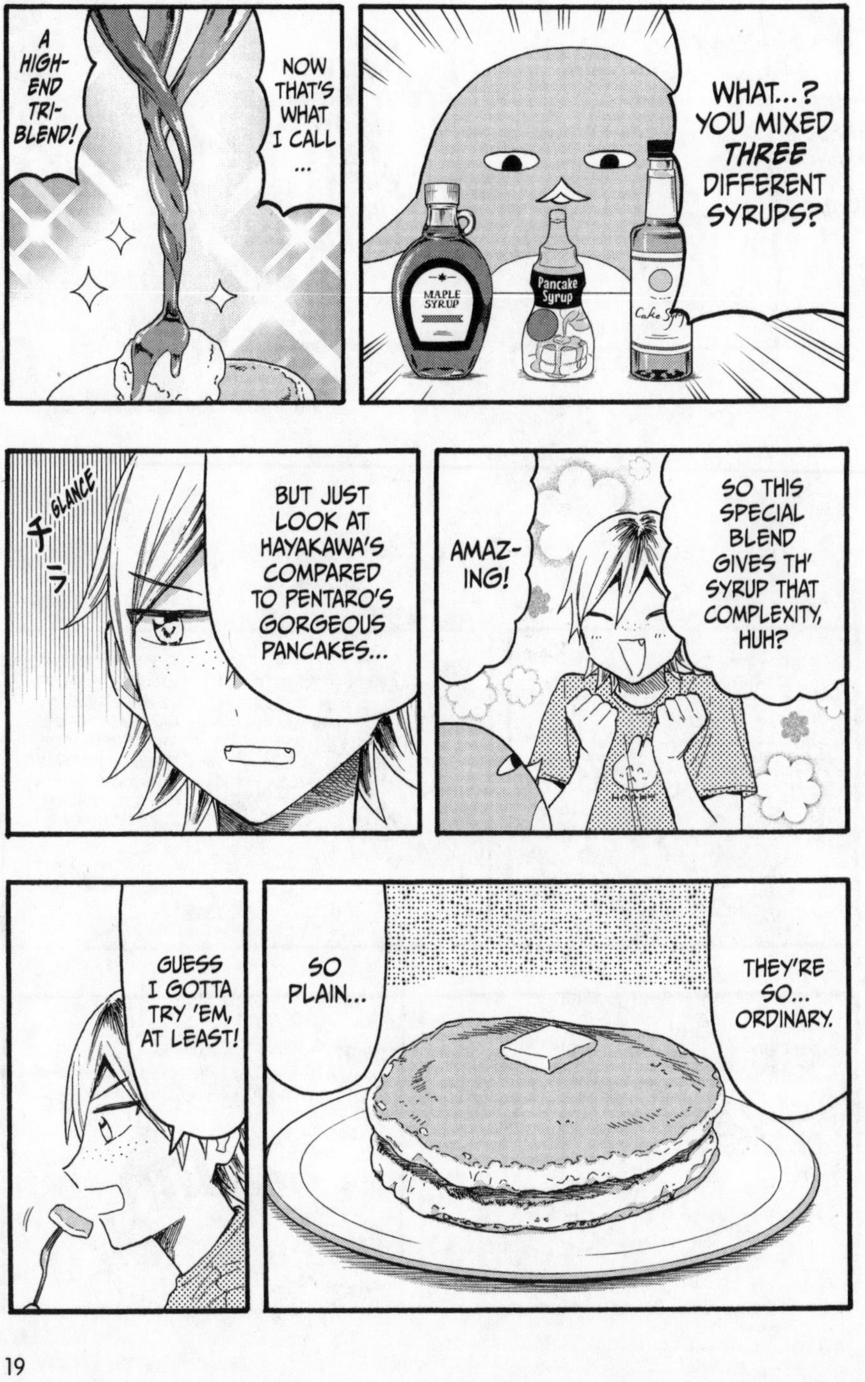
WHAT...? YOU MIXED THREE DIFFERENT SYRUPS?
MAPLE SYRUP
Pancake Syrup
NOW THAT'S WHAT I CALL ...
A HIGH-END TRI-BLEND!
SO THIS SPECIAL BLEND GIVES TH' SYRUP THAT COMPLEXITY, HUH?
AMAZ-ING!
BUT JUST LOOK AT HAYAKAWA'S COMPARED TO PENTARO'S GORGEOUS PANCAKES...
チラ
GLANCE
THEY'RE SO... ORDINARY.
SO PLAIN...
GUESS I GOTTA TRY 'EM, AT LEAST!

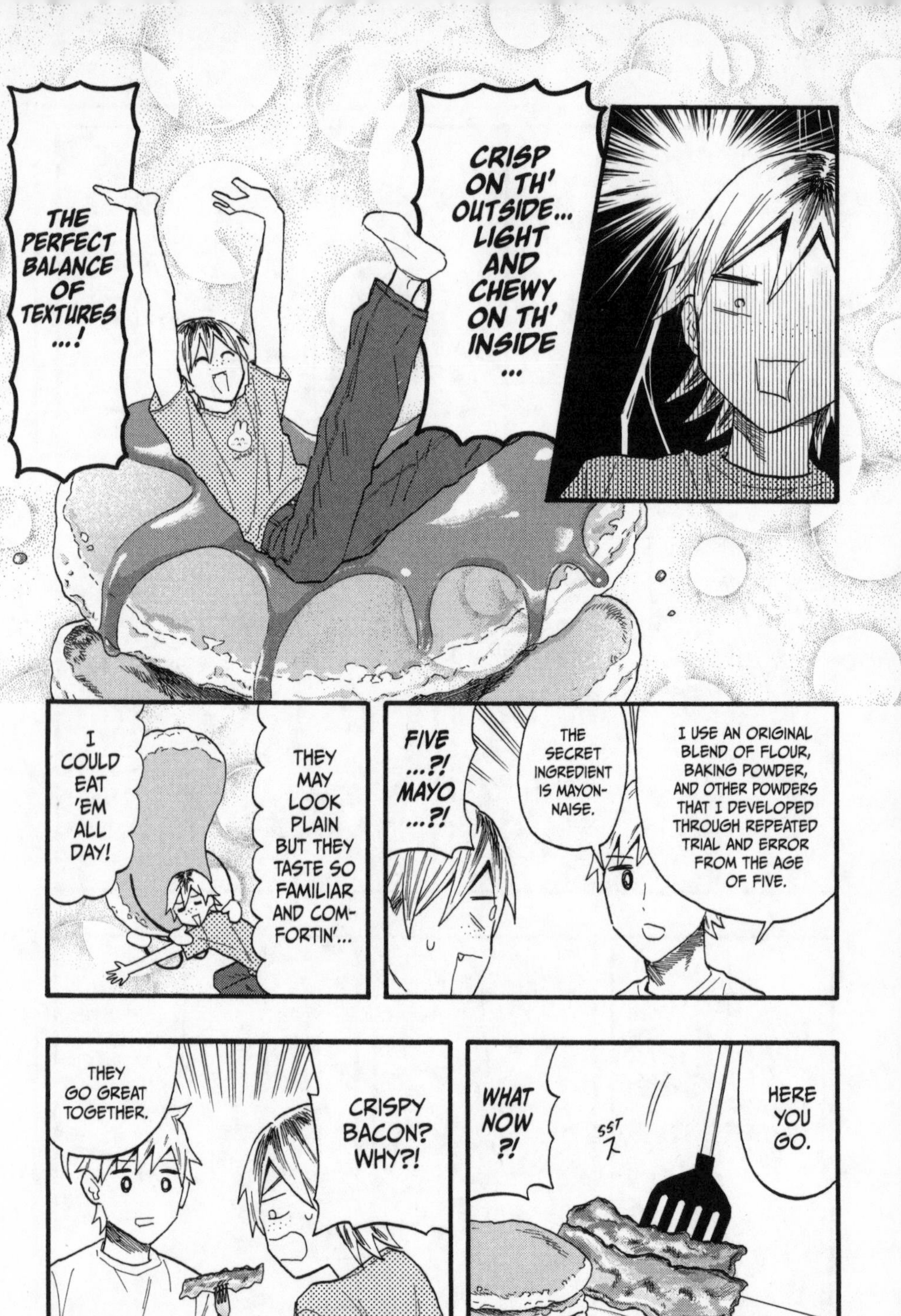
CRISP ON TH' OUTSIDE... LIGHT AND CHEWY ON TH' INSIDE ...
THE PERFECT BALANCE OF TEXTURES ...!
I USE AN ORIGINAL BLEND OF FLOUR, BAKING POWDER, AND OTHER POWDERS THAT I DEVELOPED THROUGH REPEATED TRIAL AND ERROR FROM THE AGE OF FIVE.
THE SECRET INGREDIENT IS MAYON-NAISE.
FIVE ...?! MAYO ...?!
THEY MAY LOOK PLAIN BUT THEY TASTE SO FAMILIAR AND COM-FORTIN'...
I COULD EAT 'EM ALL DAY!
HERE YOU GO.
SST
WHAT NOW ?!
CRISPY BACON? WHY?!
THEY GO GREAT TOGETHER.

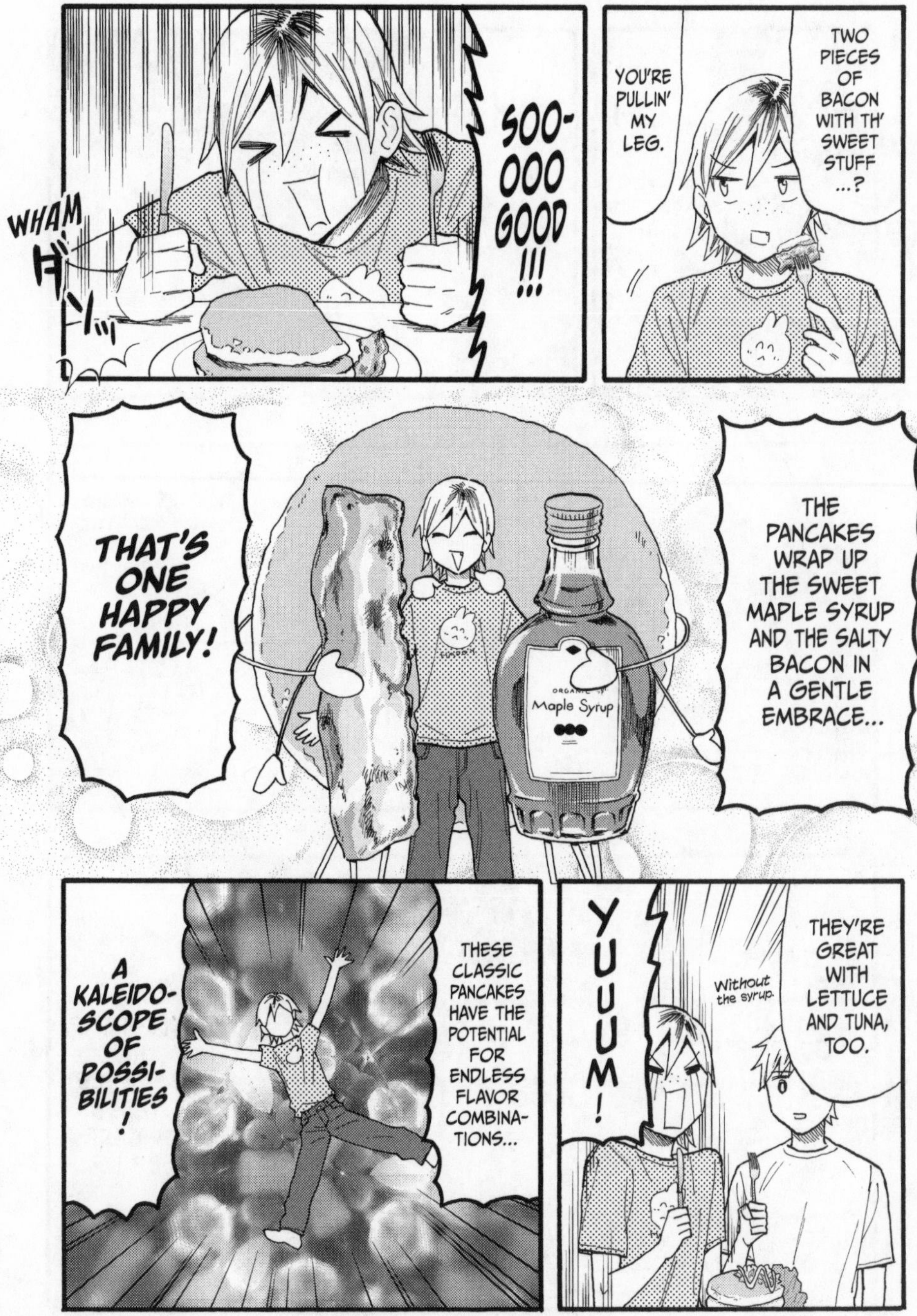

TWO PIECES OF BACON WITH TH' SWEET STUFF ...?
YOU'RE PULLIN' MY LEG.
SOO-OOO GOOD!!!
WHAM
THE PANCAKES WRAP UP THE SWEET MAPLE SYRUP AND THE SALTY BACON IN A GENTLE EMBRACE...
Maple Syrup
THAT'S ONE HAPPY FAMILY!
THEY'RE GREAT WITH LETTUCE AND TUNA, TOO.
Without the syrup.
YUUUM!
THESE CLASSIC PANCAKES HAVE THE POTENTIAL FOR ENDLESS FLAVOR COMBINA-TIONS...
A KALEIDO-SCOPE OF POSSI-BILITIES!

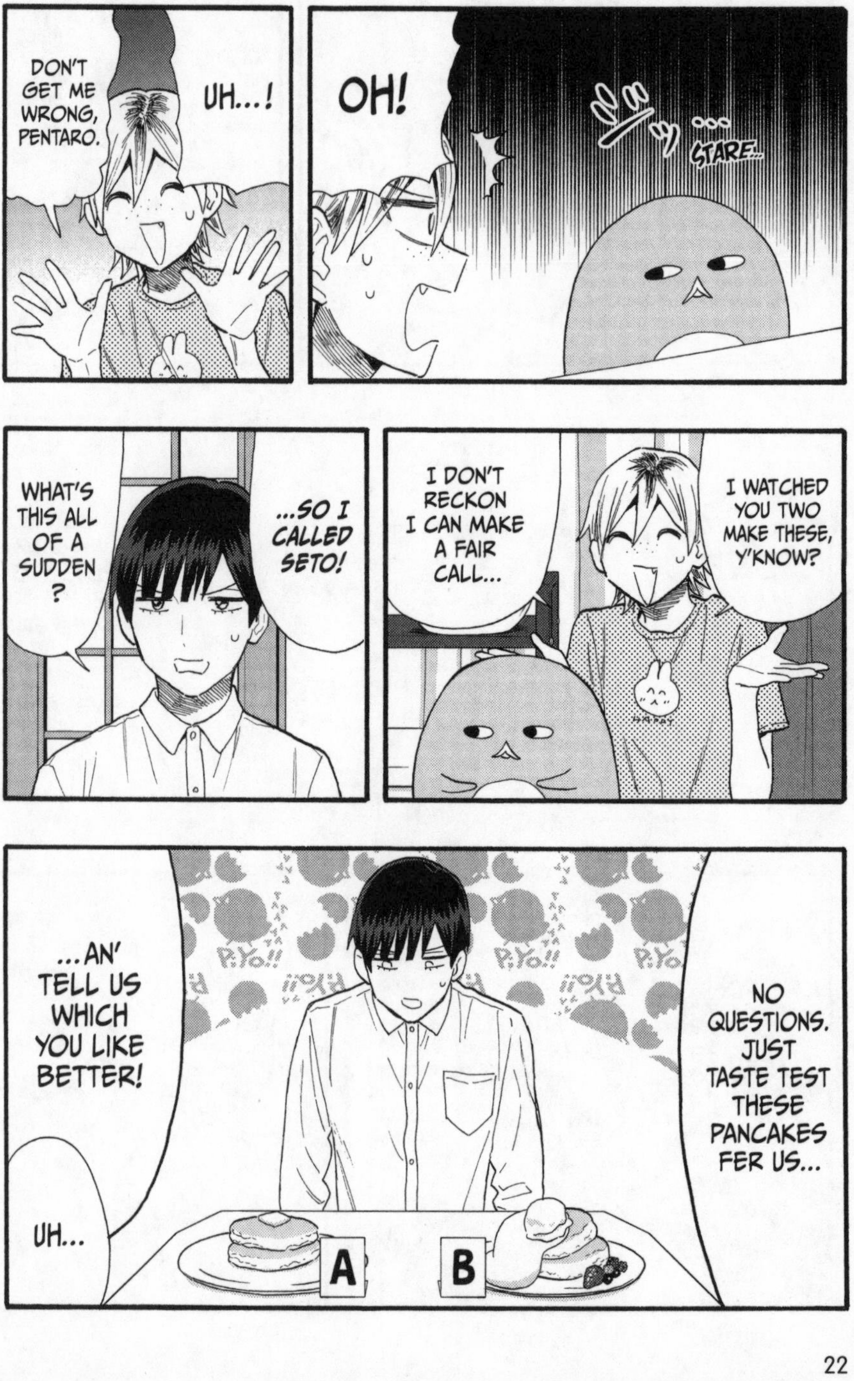
STARE..
OH!
UH...!
DON'T GET ME WRONG, PENTARO.
I WATCHED YOU TWO MAKE THESE, Y'KNOW?
I DON'T RECKON I CAN MAKE A FAIR CALL...
...SO I CALLED SETO!
WHAT'S THIS ALL OF A SUDDEN?
NO QUESTIONS. JUST TASTE TEST THESE PANCAKES FER US...
...AN' TELL US WHICH YOU LIKE BETTER!
UH...
A
B

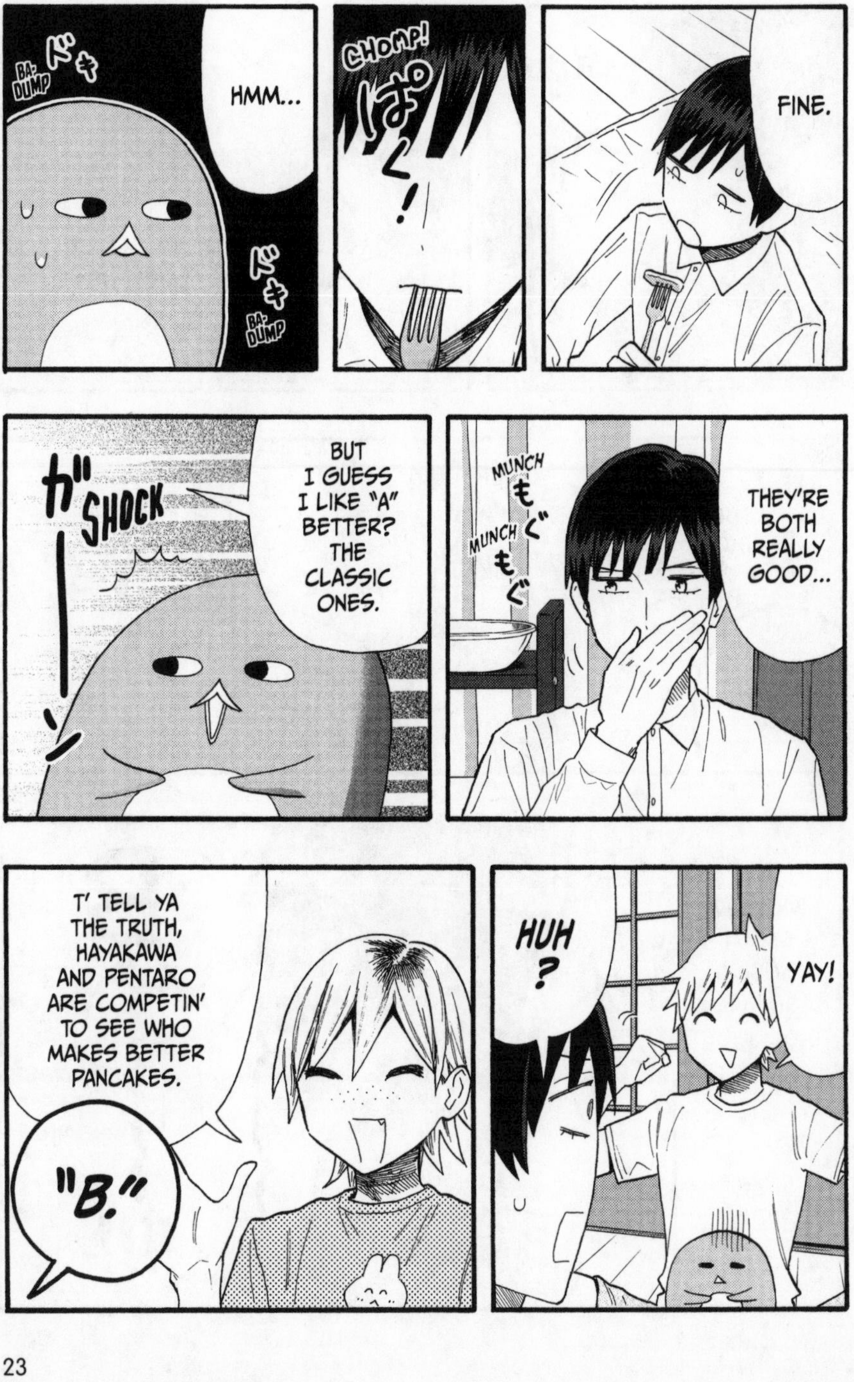
FINE.
CHOMP!
ぱく!
BA-DUMP
ドキ
HMM...
ドキ
BA-DUMP
THEY'RE BOTH REALLY GOOD...
MUNCH
もぐ
MUNCH
もぐ
BUT I GUESS I LIKE "A" BETTER? THE CLASSIC ONES.
が
SHOCK
YAY!
HUH?
T' TELL YA THE TRUTH, HAYAKAWA AND PENTARO ARE COMPETIN' TO SEE WHO MAKES BETTER PANCAKES.
"B."

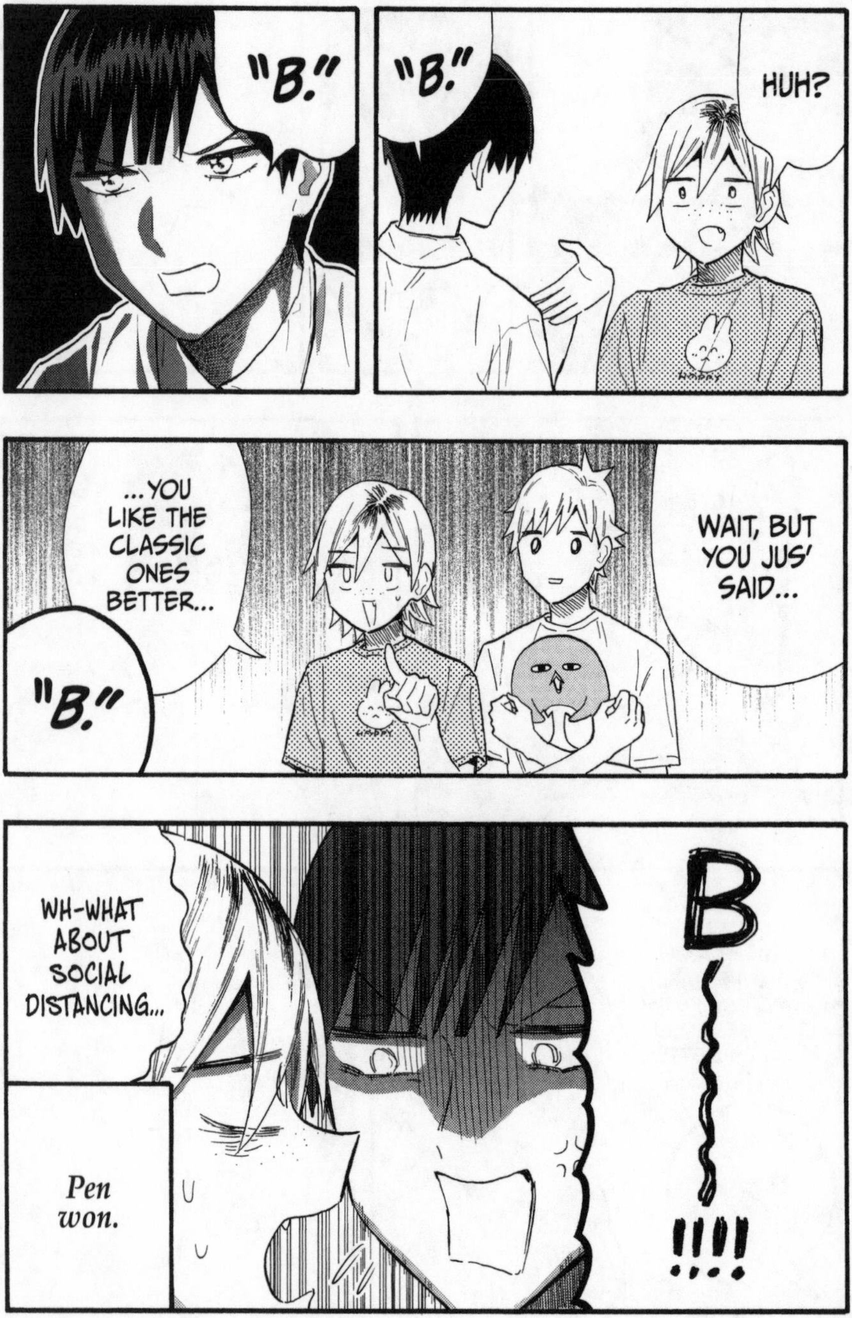
HUH?
"B."
"B."
WAIT, BUT YOU JUS' SAID...
...YOU LIKE THE CLASSIC ONES BETTER...
"B."
B—!!!!
WH-WHAT ABOUT SOCIAL DISTANCING...
Pen won.

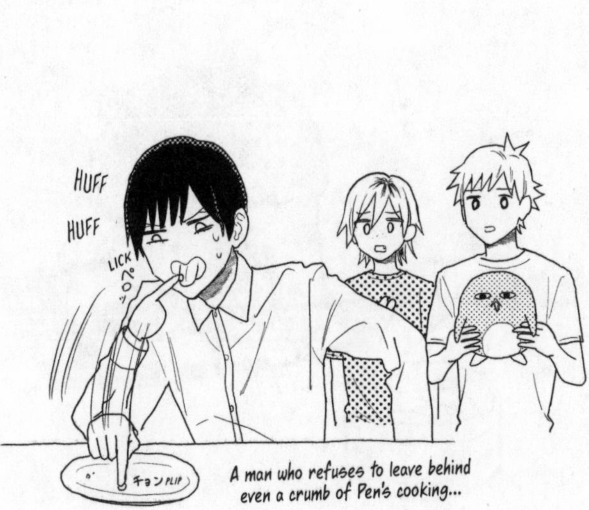
HUFF
HUFF
LICK ペロッ
チョン PLIP

A man who refuses to leave behind even a crumb of Pen's cooking...

IN THIS WEEK'S "EXPLORING COFFEE SHOPS"...

...WE WILL TAKE A LOOK AT SYPHON BREWING.

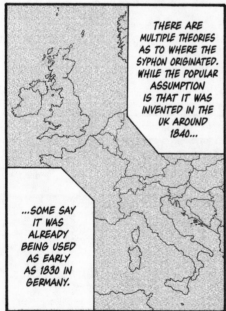

THERE ARE MULTIPLE THEORIES AS TO WHERE THE SYPHON ORIGINATED. WHILE THE POPULAR ASSUMPTION IS THAT IT WAS INVENTED IN THE UK AROUND 1840...

...SOME SAY IT WAS ALREADY BEING USED AS EARLY AS 1830 IN GERMANY.

♪ DA DA DUUUM

Exploring Coffee Shops

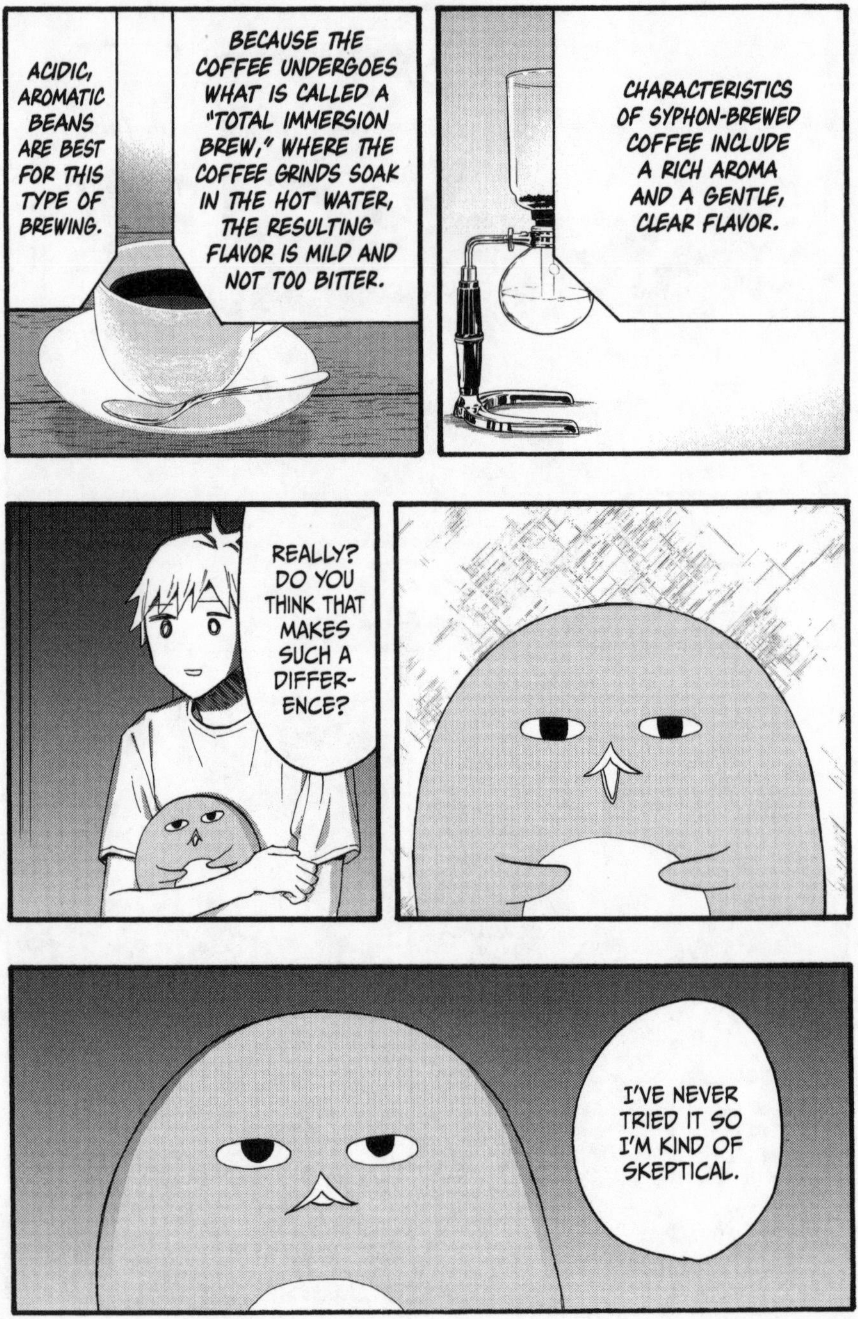
CHARACTERISTICS OF SYPHON-BREWED COFFEE INCLUDE A RICH AROMA AND A GENTLE, CLEAR FLAVOR.
BECAUSE THE COFFEE UNDERGOES WHAT IS CALLED A "TOTAL IMMERSION BREW," WHERE THE COFFEE GRINDS SOAK IN THE HOT WATER, THE RESULTING FLAVOR IS MILD AND NOT TOO BITTER.
ACIDIC, AROMATIC BEANS ARE BEST FOR THIS TYPE OF BREWING.
REALLY? DO YOU THINK THAT MAKES SUCH A DIFFER-ENCE?
I'VE NEVER TRIED IT SO I'M KIND OF SKEPTICAL.

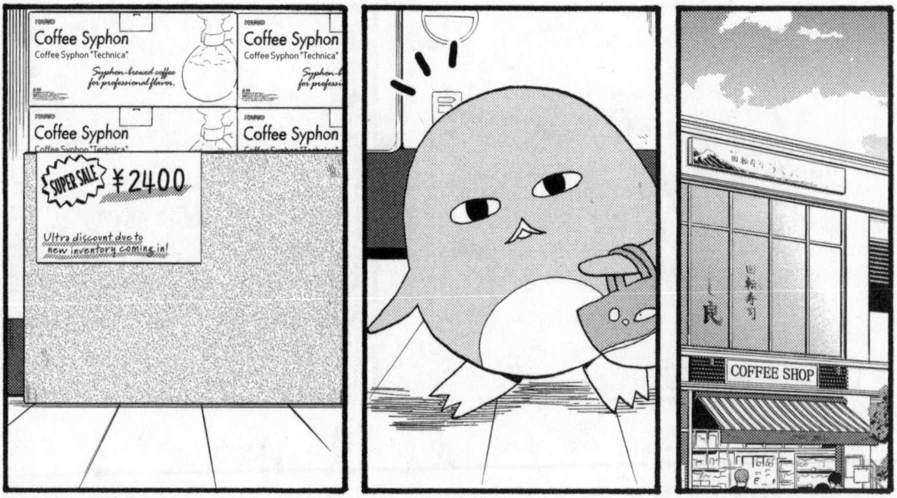
COFFEE SHOP
Coffee Syphon
Coffee Syphon "Technica"
Syphon-brewed coffee for professional flavor.
Coffee Syphon
SUPER SALE ¥2400
Ultra discount due to new inventory coming in!

• ¥2,400 = Approx. $24

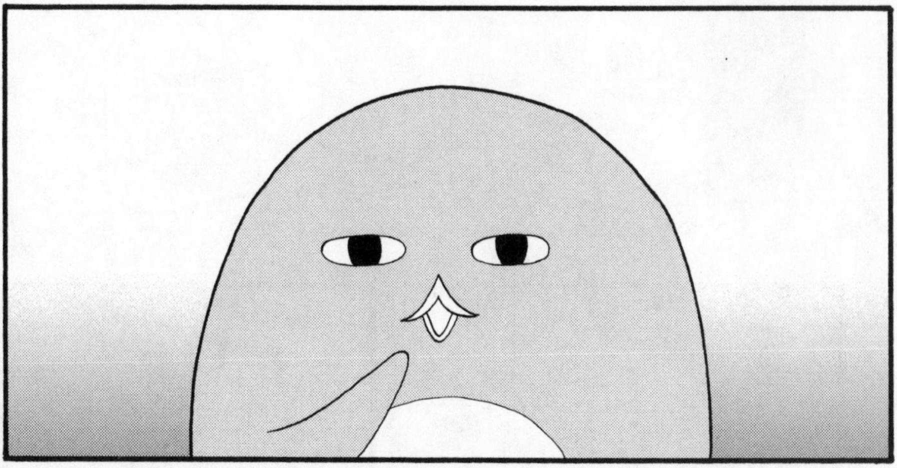

Pen 31 The Penguin Who Knows the Difference

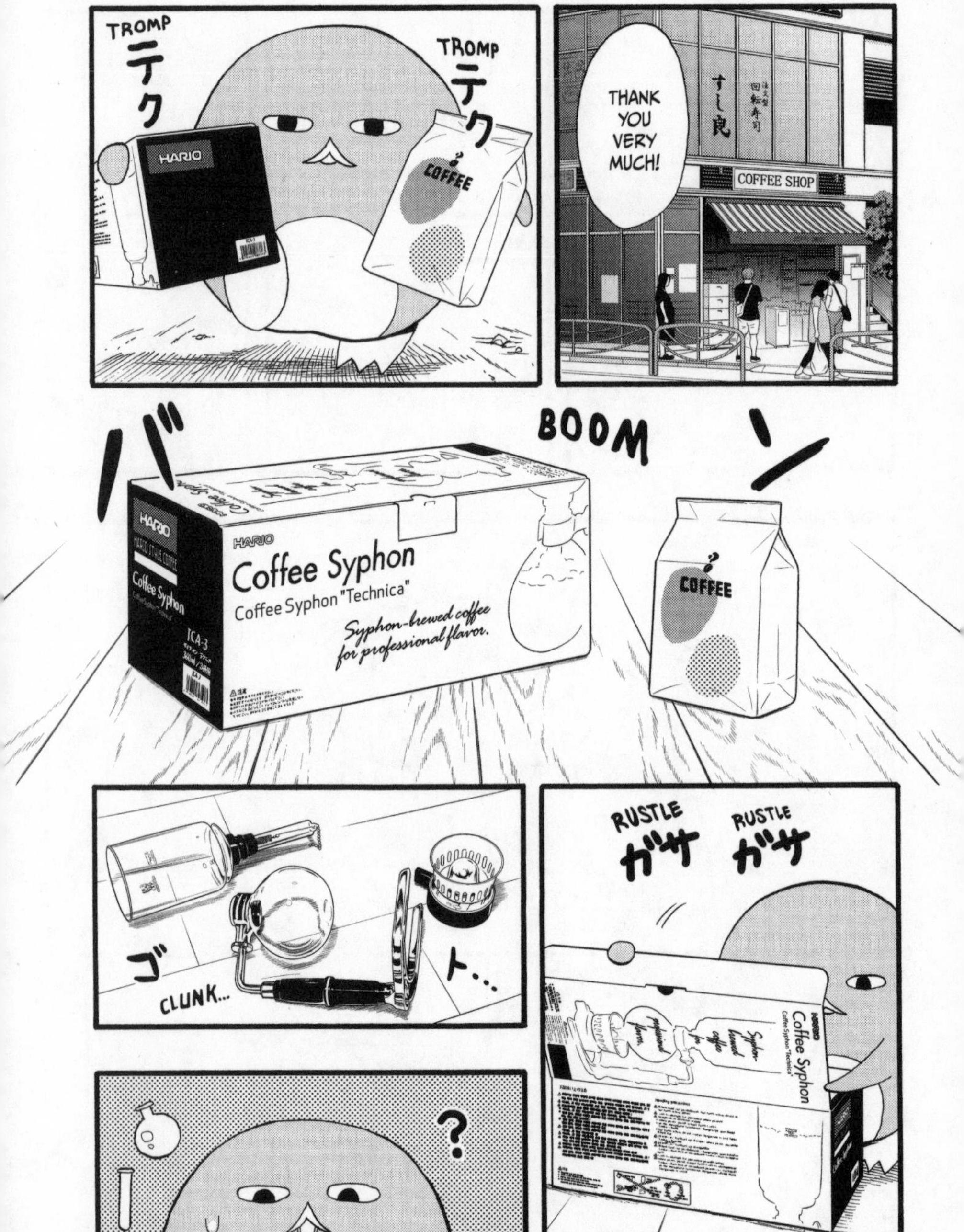

THANK YOU VERY MUCH!
すし良
回転寿司
COFFEE SHOP
TROMP
テク
TROMP
テク
HARIO
COFFEE
BOOM
バン
HARIO
Coffee Syphon
Coffee Syphon "Technica"
Syphon-brewed coffee for professional flavor.
TCA-3
COFFEE
RUSTLE
ガサ
RUSTLE
ガサ
Coffee Syphon
Coffee Syphon "Technica"
ゴト…
CLUNK...
?

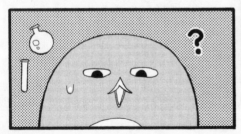

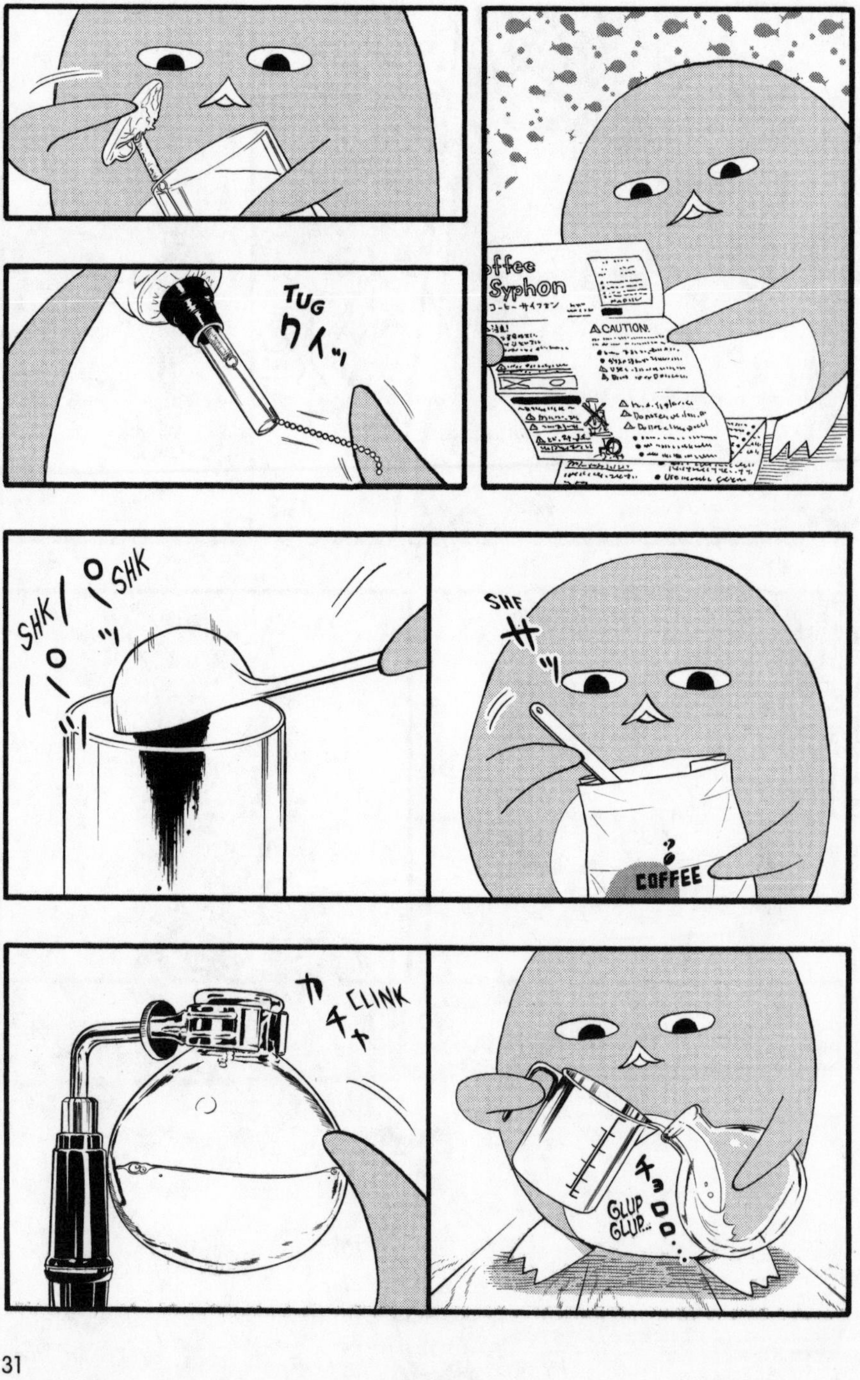
offee
Syphon
コーヒーサイフォン
CAUTION!
TUG
クイッ
SHF
サッ
COFFEE
SHK
パッ
SHK
パッ
GLUP GLUP...
チョロロ...
CLINK
カチャ

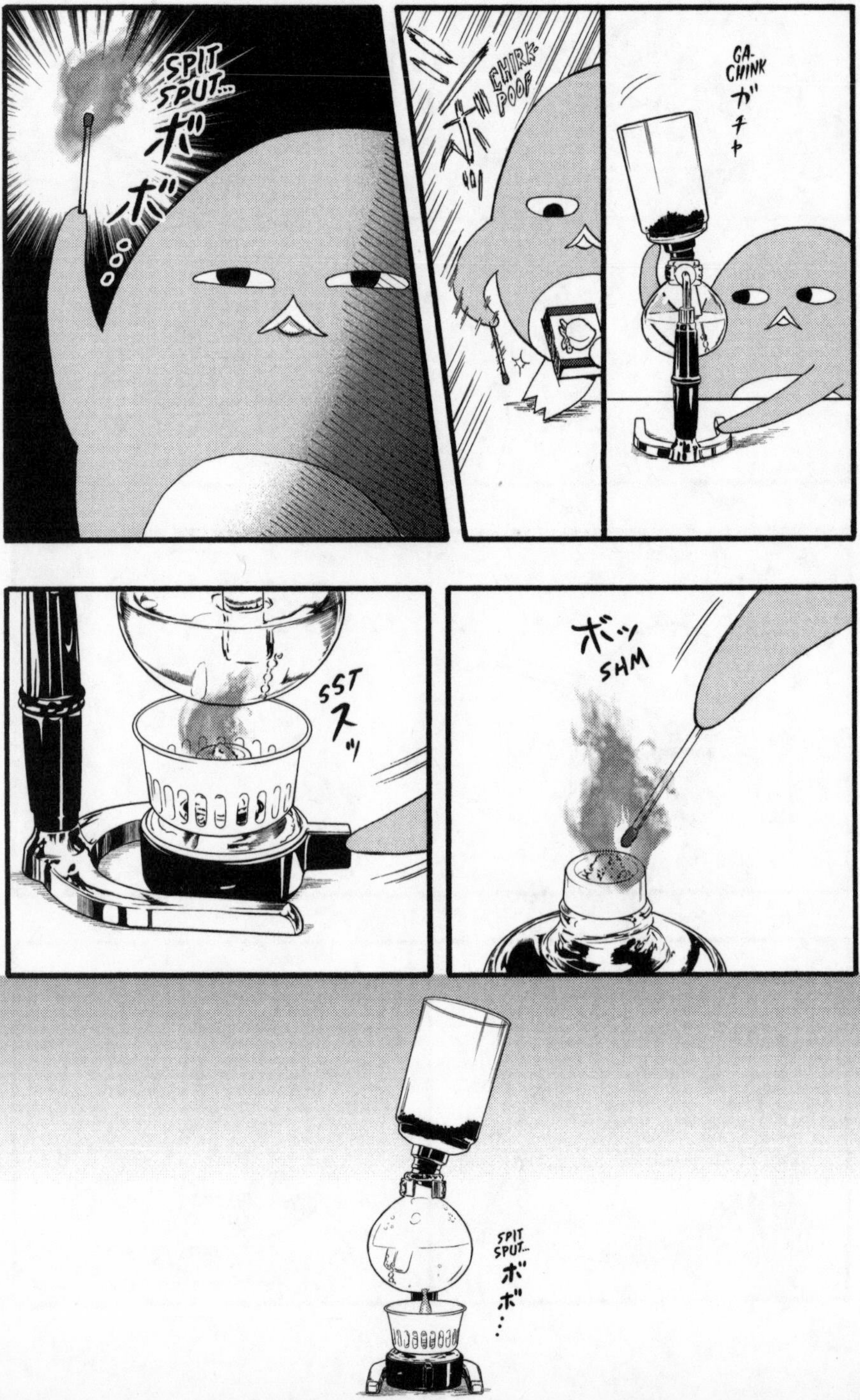
GA-CHINK
ガチャ
CHIRK POOF
ボッ
SPIT SPUT...
ボボボ...
ボッ
SHM
SST
スッ
SPIT SPUT...
ボボ...

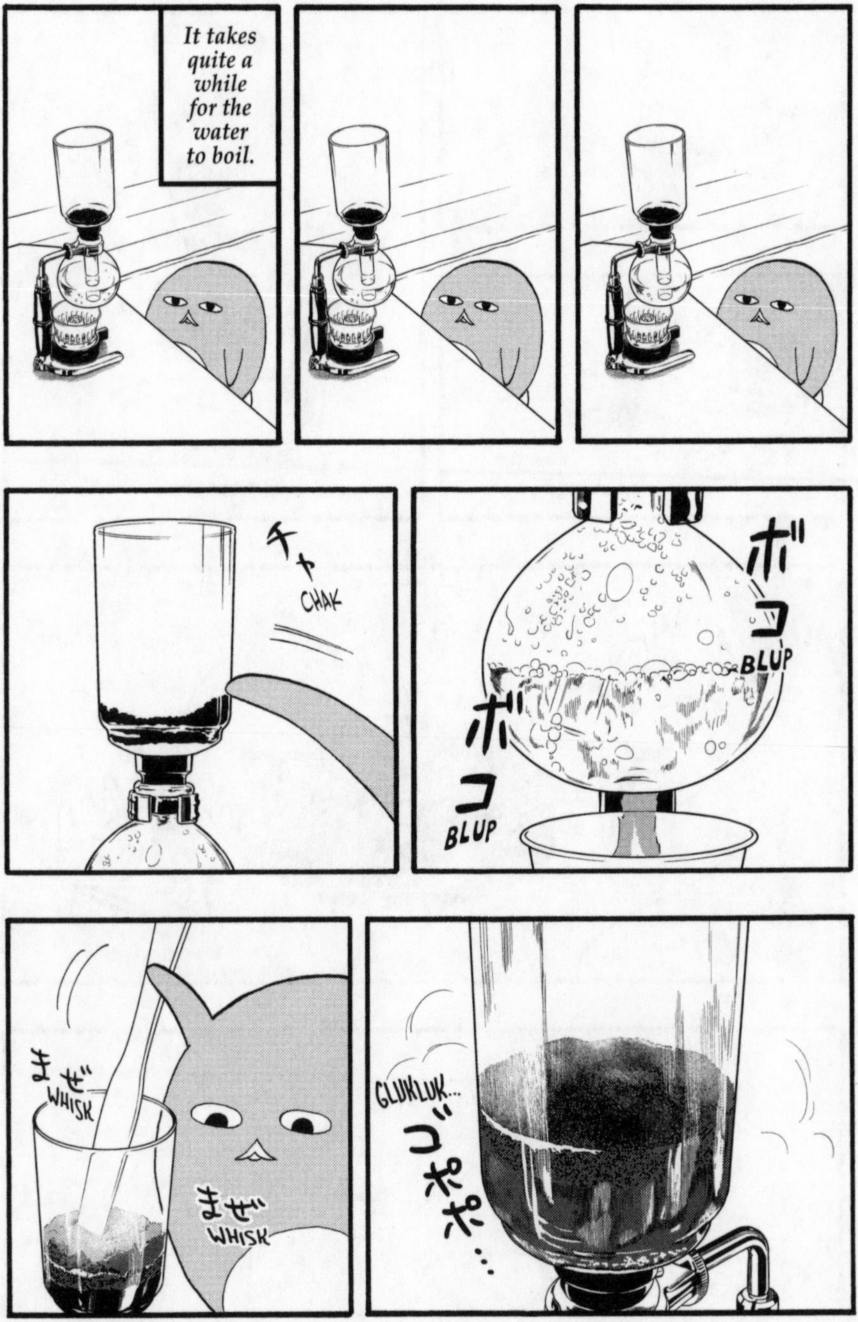
It takes quite a while for the water to boil.
ボコ
BLUP
ボコ
BLUP
チャ
CHAK
GLUKLUK...
ゴポポ…
まぜ
WHISK
まぜ
WHISK

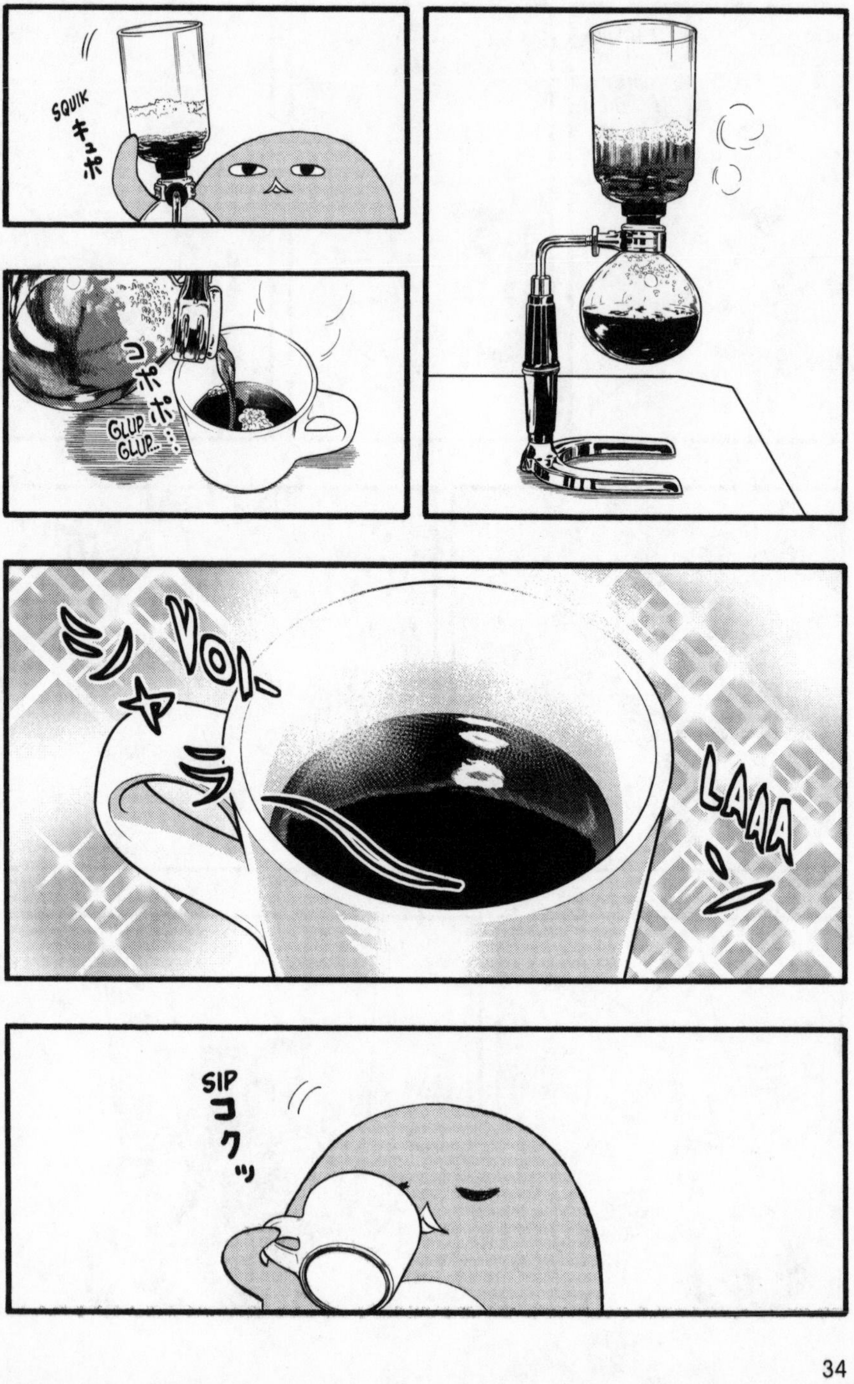
SQUIK
キュポ
GLUP GLUP...
コポポ…
VOI-
LAAA
シャラ
SIP
コクッ

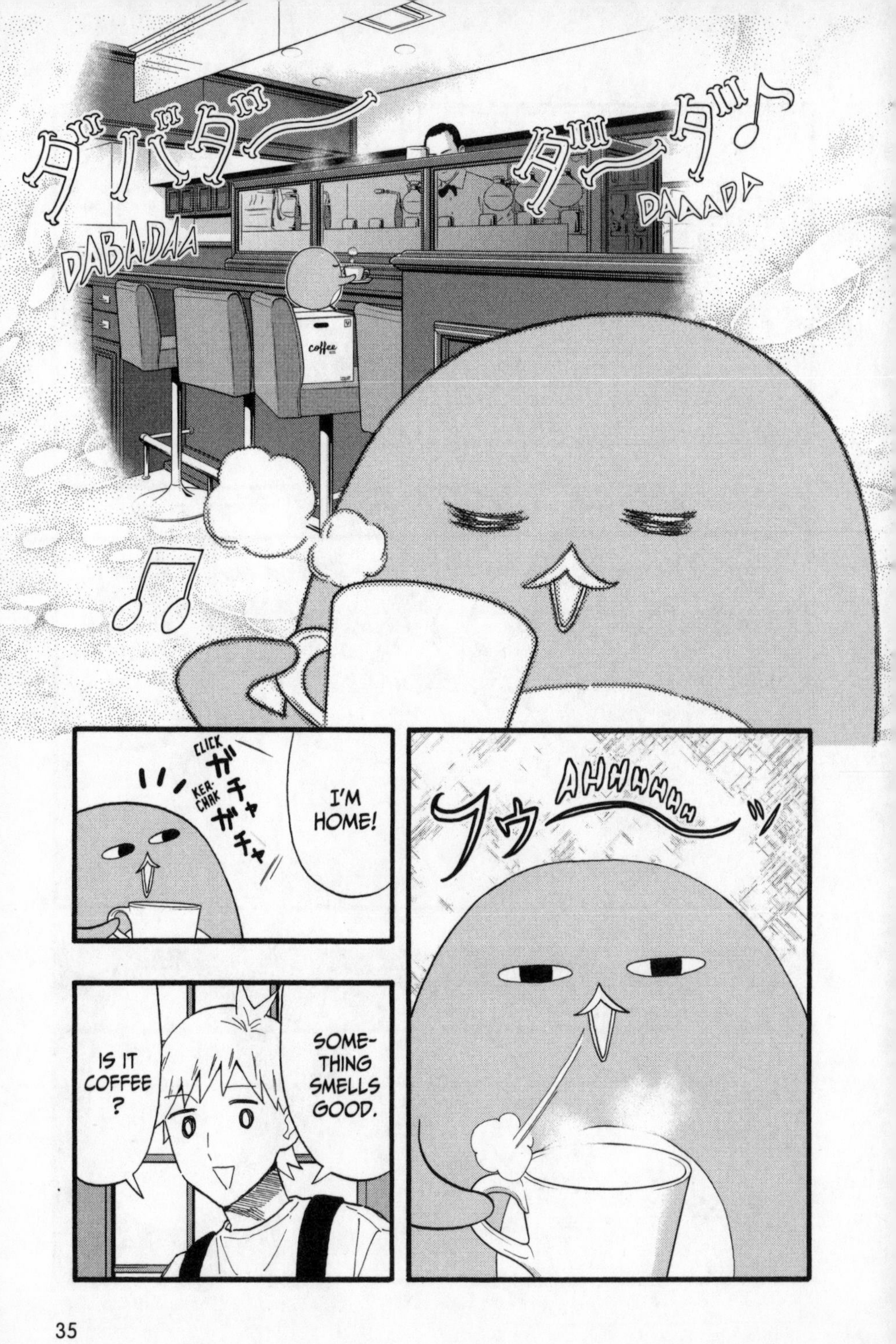
ダバダーー
DABADAA
ダーダ♪
DAAADA
フウ〜〜〜〜ッ
AHHHHHHH
CLICK ガチャ
KER-CHAK ガチャ
I'M HOME!
SOME-THING SMELLS GOOD.
IS IT COFFEE ?

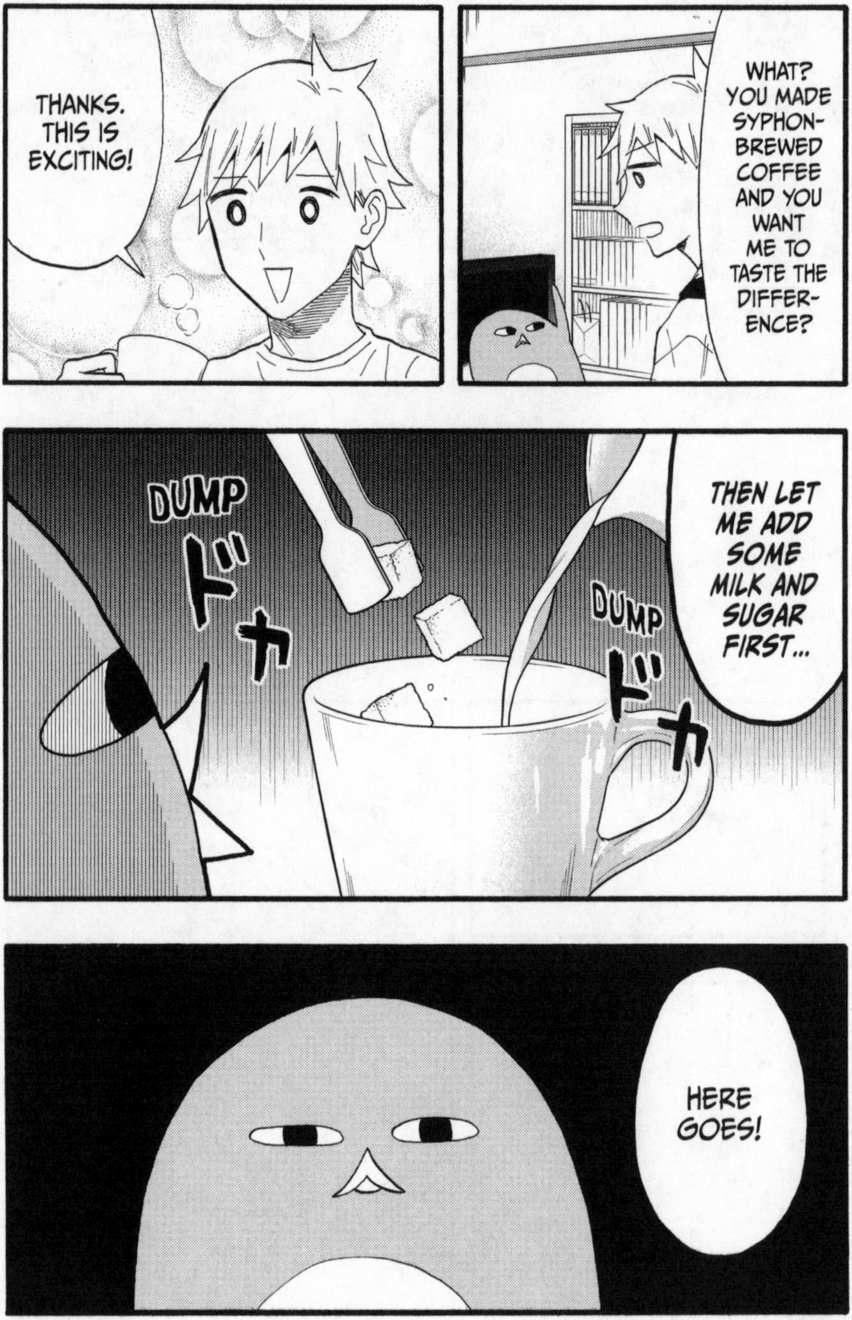
WHAT? YOU MADE SYPHON-BREWED COFFEE AND YOU WANT ME TO TASTE THE DIFFERENCE?
THANKS. THIS IS EXCITING!
THEN LET ME ADD SOME MILK AND SUGAR FIRST...
DUMP
ドカ
DUMP
ドカ
HERE GOES!

Iced coffee

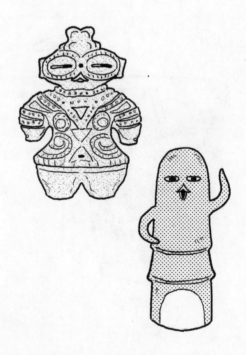

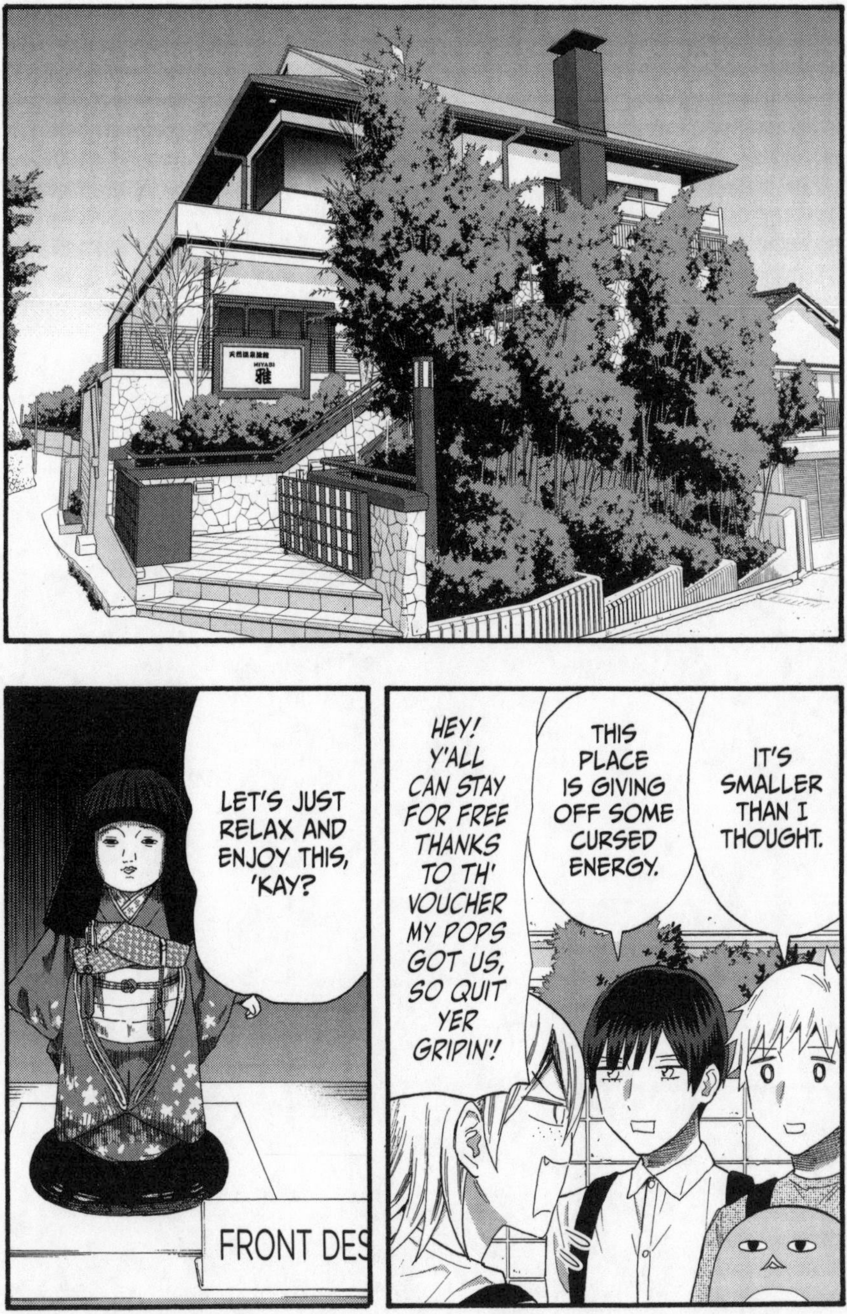
MIYABI
雅
IT'S SMALLER THAN I THOUGHT.
THIS PLACE IS GIVING OFF SOME CURSED ENERGY.
HEY! Y'ALL CAN STAY FOR FREE THANKS TO TH' VOUCHER MY POPS GOT US, SO QUIT YER GRIPIN'!
LET'S JUST RELAX AND ENJOY THIS, 'KAY?
FRONT DES

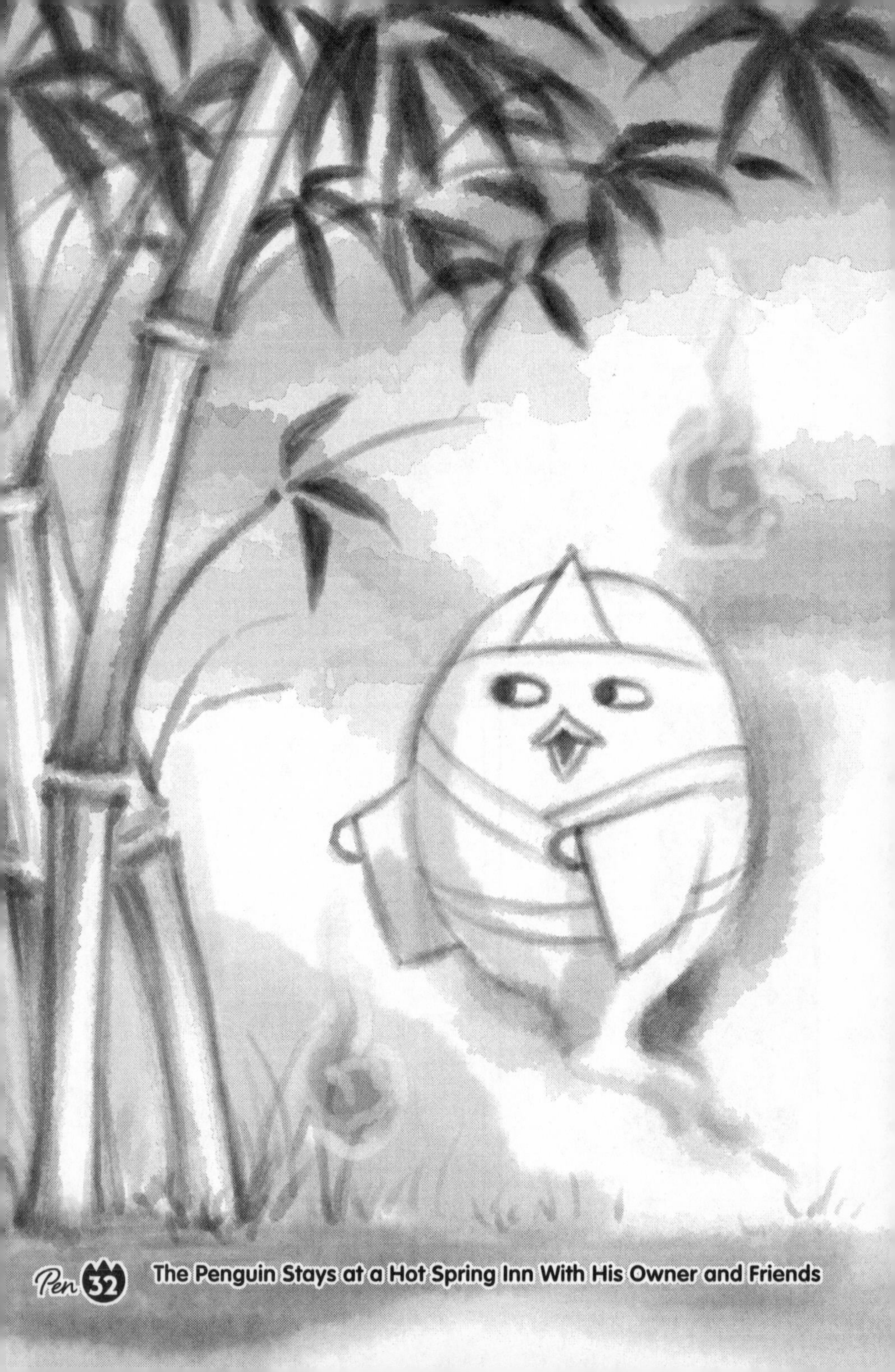

Pen 32 The Penguin Stays at a Hot Spring Inn With His Owner and Friends

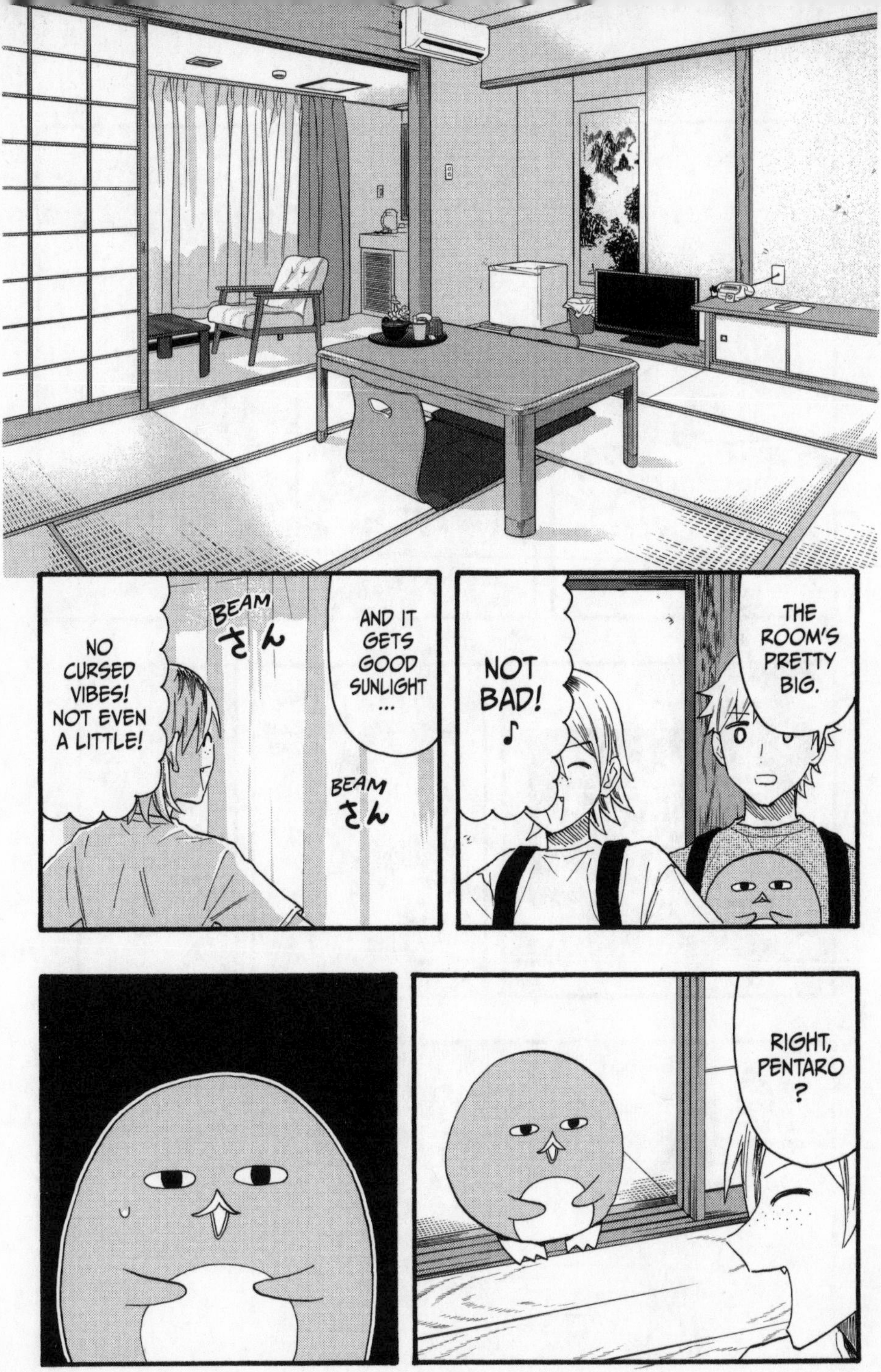
THE ROOM'S PRETTY BIG.
NOT BAD! ♪
AND IT GETS GOOD SUNLIGHT ...
BEAM さん
NO CURSED VIBES! NOT EVEN A LITTLE!
BEAM さん
RIGHT, PENTARO?

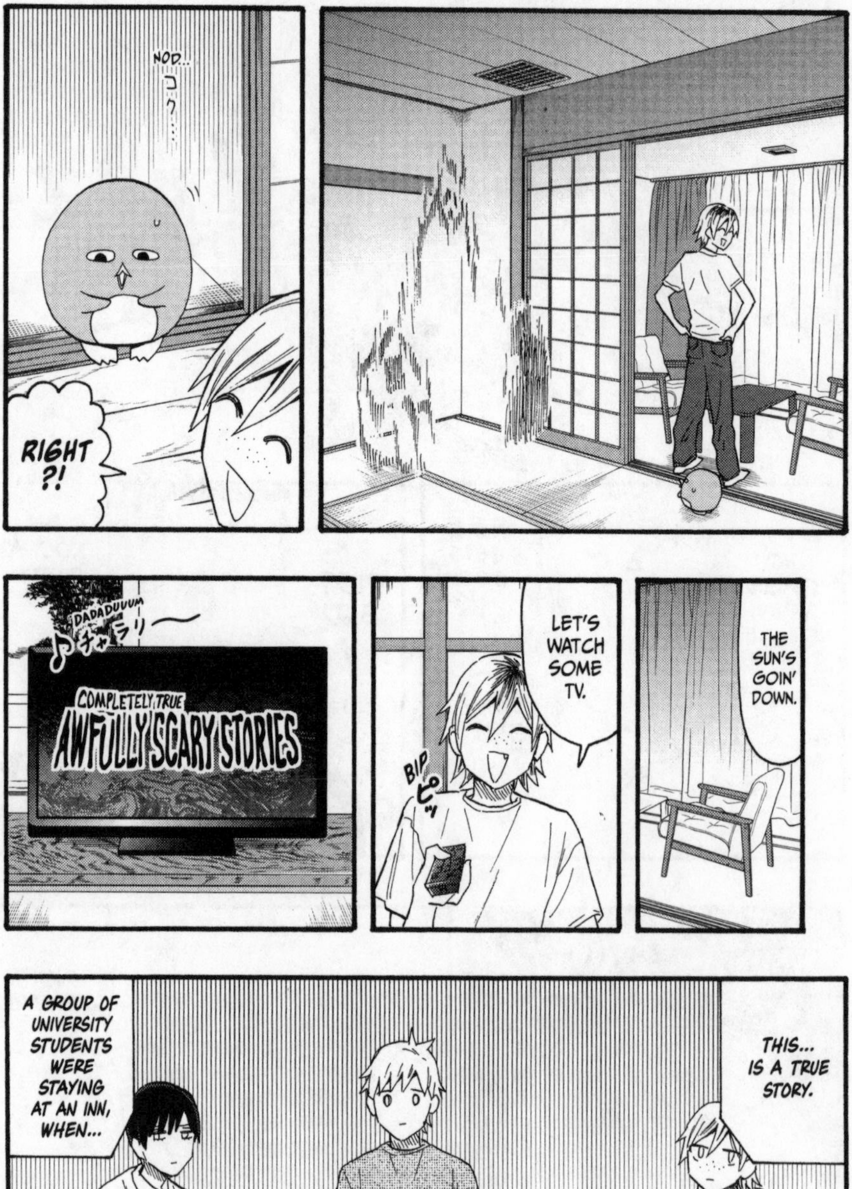
NOD... コク...
RIGHT ?!
THE SUN'S GOIN' DOWN.
LET'S WATCH SOME TV.
BIP ピッ
DADADUUUM チャラリー
COMPLETELY TRUE
AWFULLY SCARY STORIES
THIS... IS A TRUE STORY.
A GROUP OF UNIVERSITY STUDENTS WERE STAYING AT AN INN, WHEN...

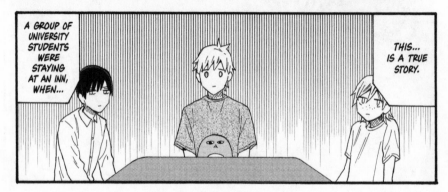

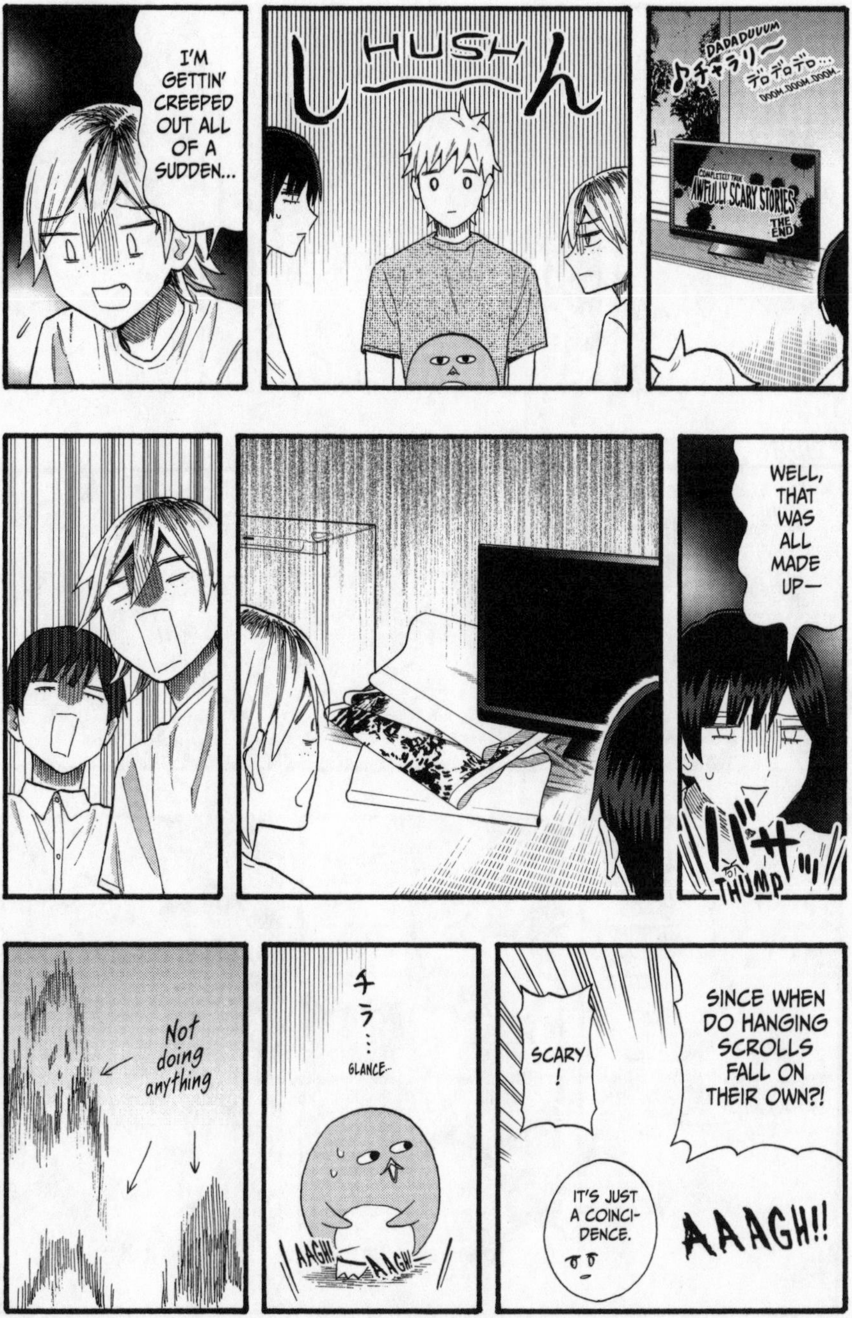
DADADUUUM
♪チャラリ〜
デロデロデロ…
DOOM..DOOM..DOOM..
COMPLETELY TRUE
AWFULLY SCARY STORIES
THE END
HUSH
しーーん
I'M GETTIN' CREEPED OUT ALL OF A SUDDEN...
WELL, THAT WAS ALL MADE UP—
バサッ
THUMP
SINCE WHEN DO HANGING SCROLLS FALL ON THEIR OWN?!
SCARY!
AAAGH!!
IT'S JUST A COINCIDENCE.
チラ…
GLANCE...
AAGH!
AAGH!
Not doing anything

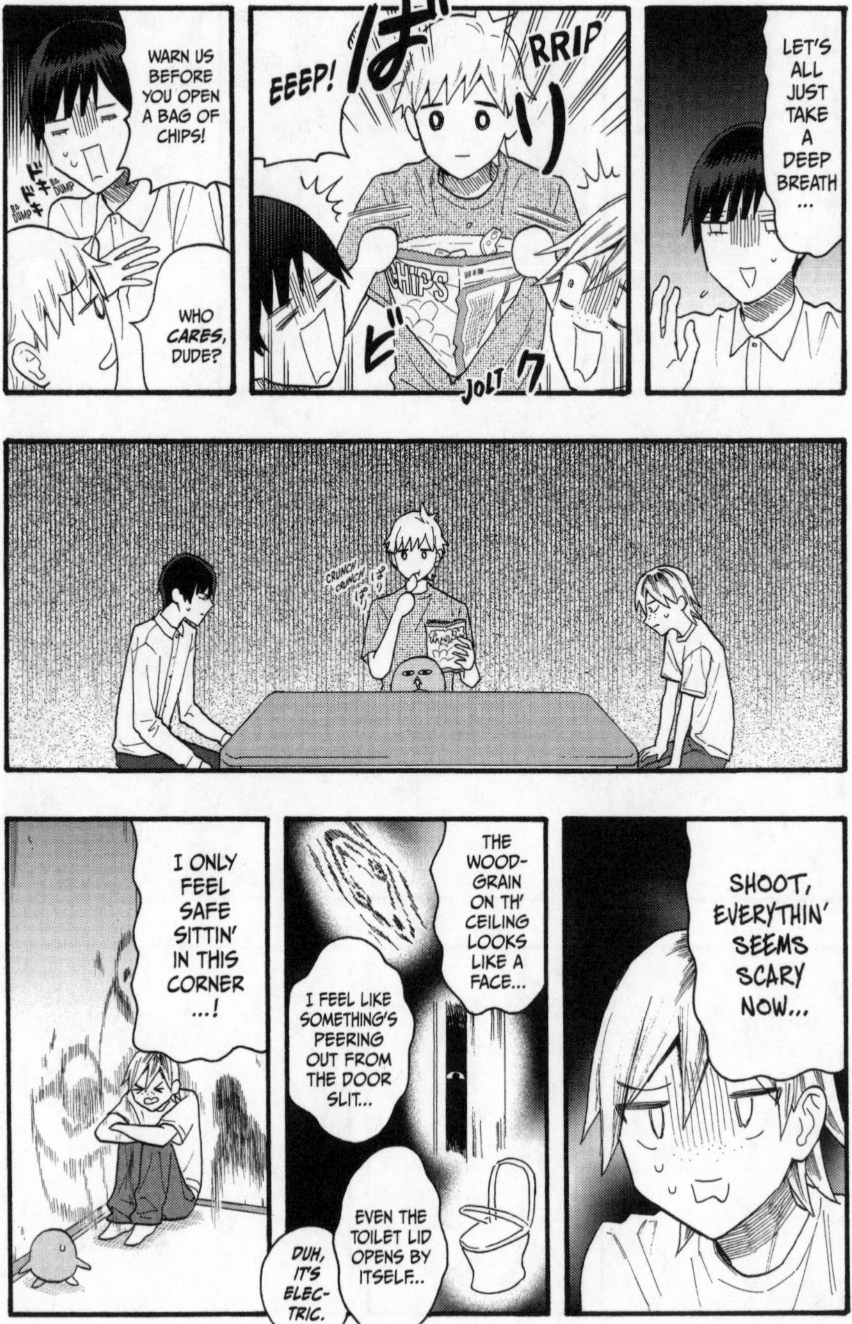
LET'S ALL JUST TAKE A DEEP BREATH ...
RRIP
EEEP!
CHIPS
JOLT
WARN US BEFORE YOU OPEN A BAG OF CHIPS!
BA-DUMP BA-DUMP
WHO CARES, DUDE?
CRUNCH CRUNCH
SHOOT, EVERYTHIN' SEEMS SCARY NOW...
THE WOOD-GRAIN ON TH' CEILING LOOKS LIKE A FACE...
I FEEL LIKE SOMETHING'S PEERING OUT FROM THE DOOR SLIT...
EVEN THE TOILET LID OPENS BY ITSELF...
DUH, IT'S ELECTRIC.
I ONLY FEEL SAFE SITTIN' IN THIS CORNER ...!

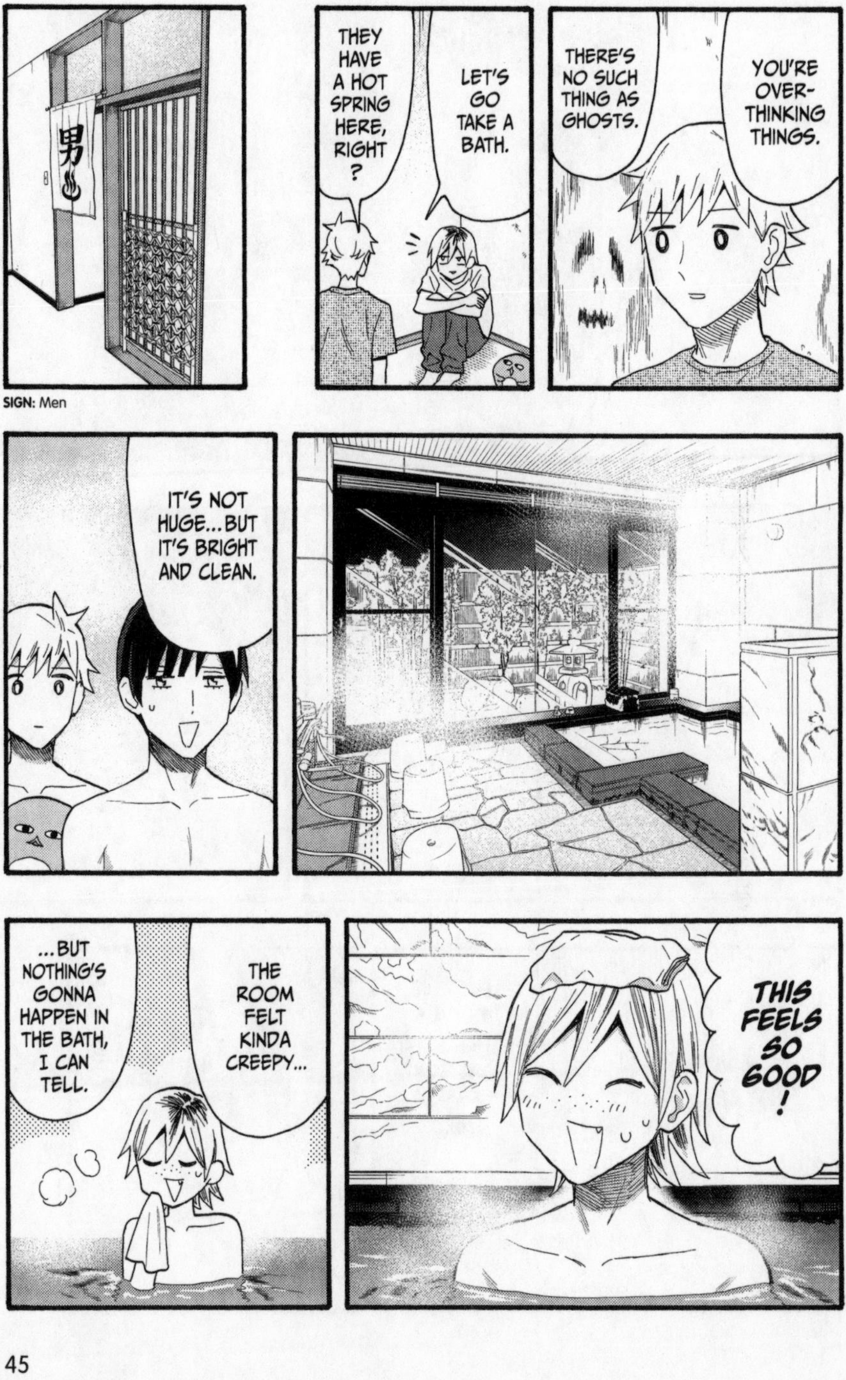
YOU'RE OVER-THINKING THINGS.
THERE'S NO SUCH THING AS GHOSTS.
LET'S GO TAKE A BATH.
THEY HAVE A HOT SPRING HERE, RIGHT?
男
IT'S NOT HUGE...BUT IT'S BRIGHT AND CLEAN.
THIS FEELS SO GOOD!
THE ROOM FELT KINDA CREEPY...
...BUT NOTHING'S GONNA HAPPEN IN THE BATH, I CAN TELL.

SIGN: Men

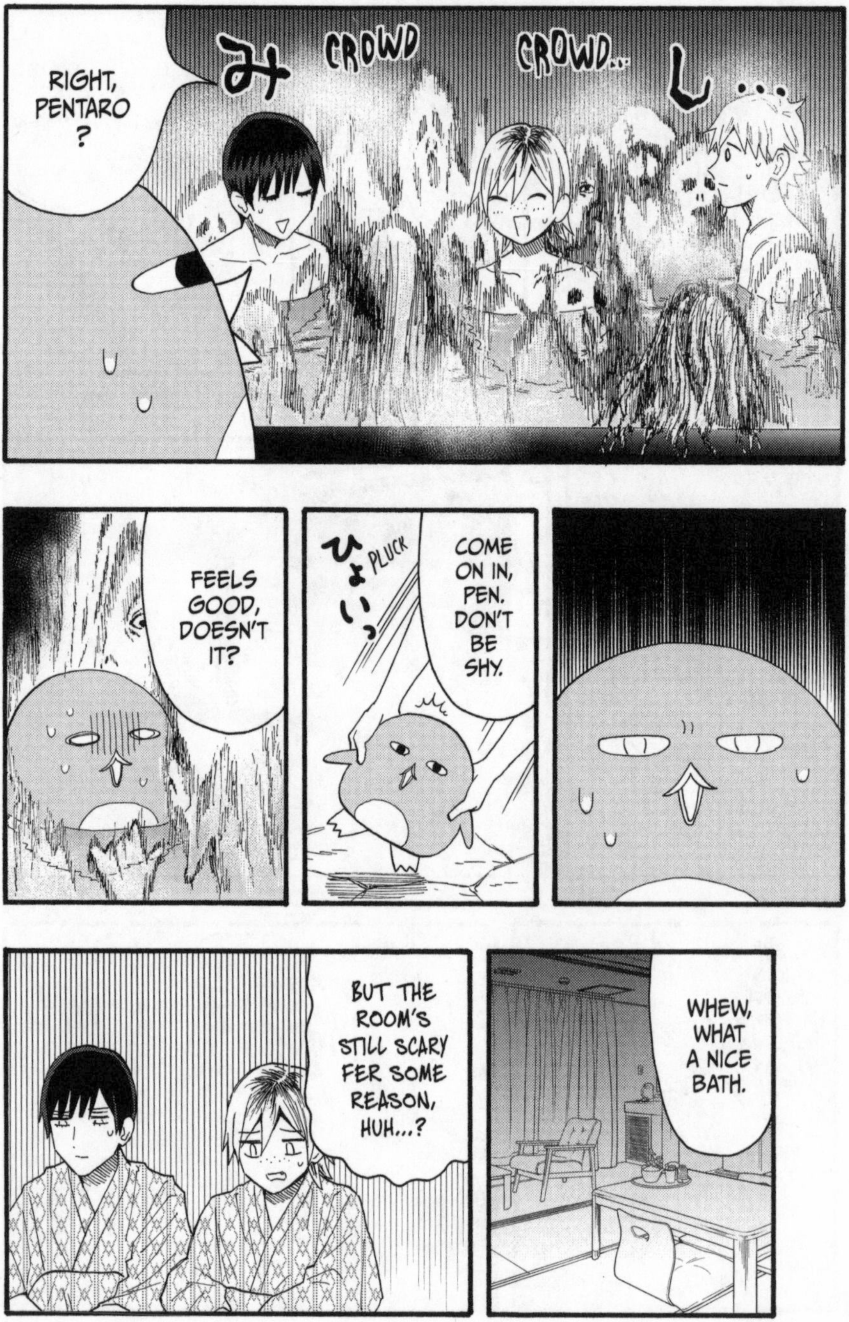
み CROWD CROWD... し ...
RIGHT, PENTARO?
COME ON IN, PEN. DON'T BE SHY.
ひょいっ PLUCK
FEELS GOOD, DOESN'T IT?
WHEW, WHAT A NICE BATH.
BUT THE ROOM'S STILL SCARY FER SOME REASON, HUH...?

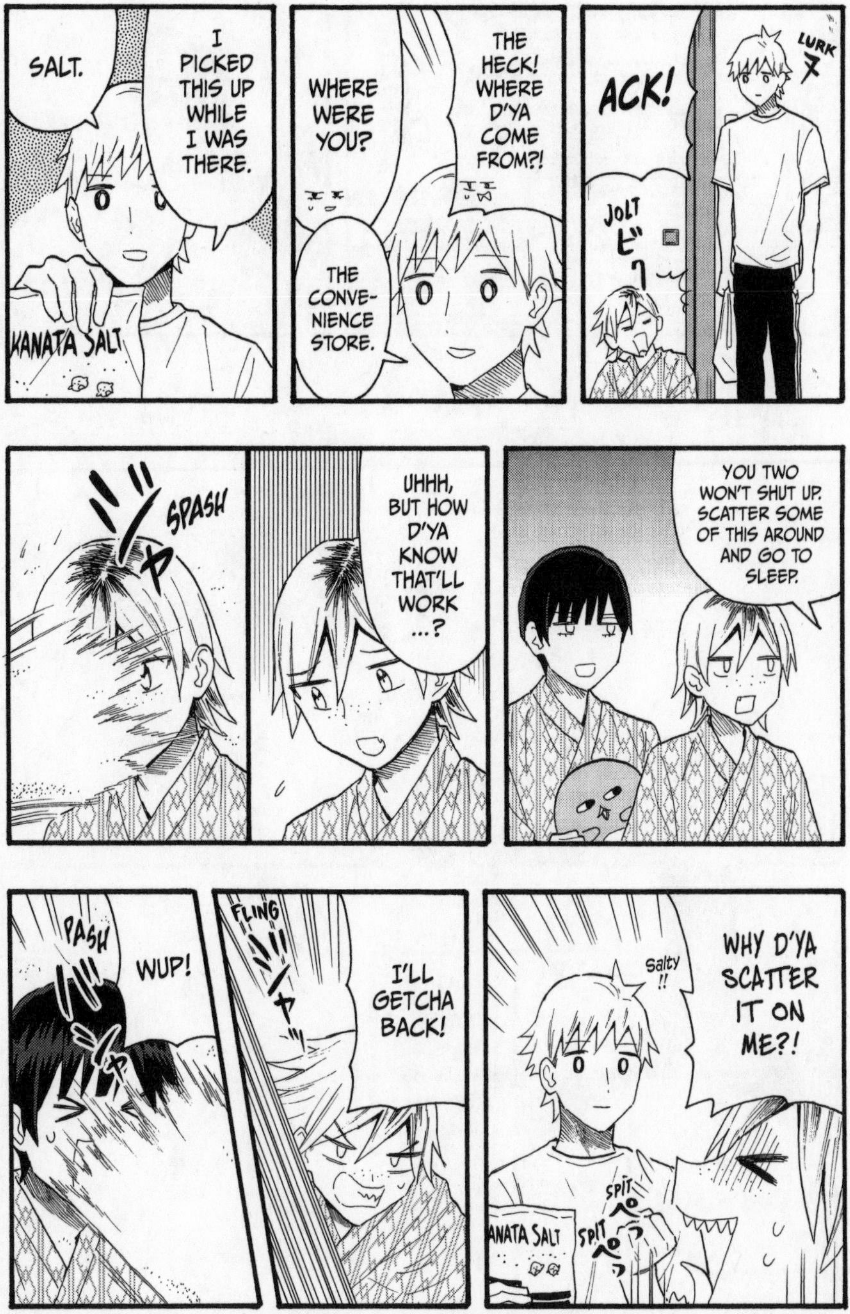
LURK
ACK!
JOLT
THE HECK! WHERE D'YA COME FROM?!
WHERE WERE YOU?
THE CONVENIENCE STORE.
I PICKED THIS UP WHILE I WAS THERE.
SALT.
KANATA SALT
YOU TWO WON'T SHUT UP. SCATTER SOME OF THIS AROUND AND GO TO SLEEP.
UHHH, BUT HOW D'YA KNOW THAT'LL WORK ...?
SPASH
WHY D'YA SCATTER IT ON ME?!
Salty !!
SPIT
SPIT
KANATA SALT
FLING
I'LL GETCHA BACK!
PASH
WUP!

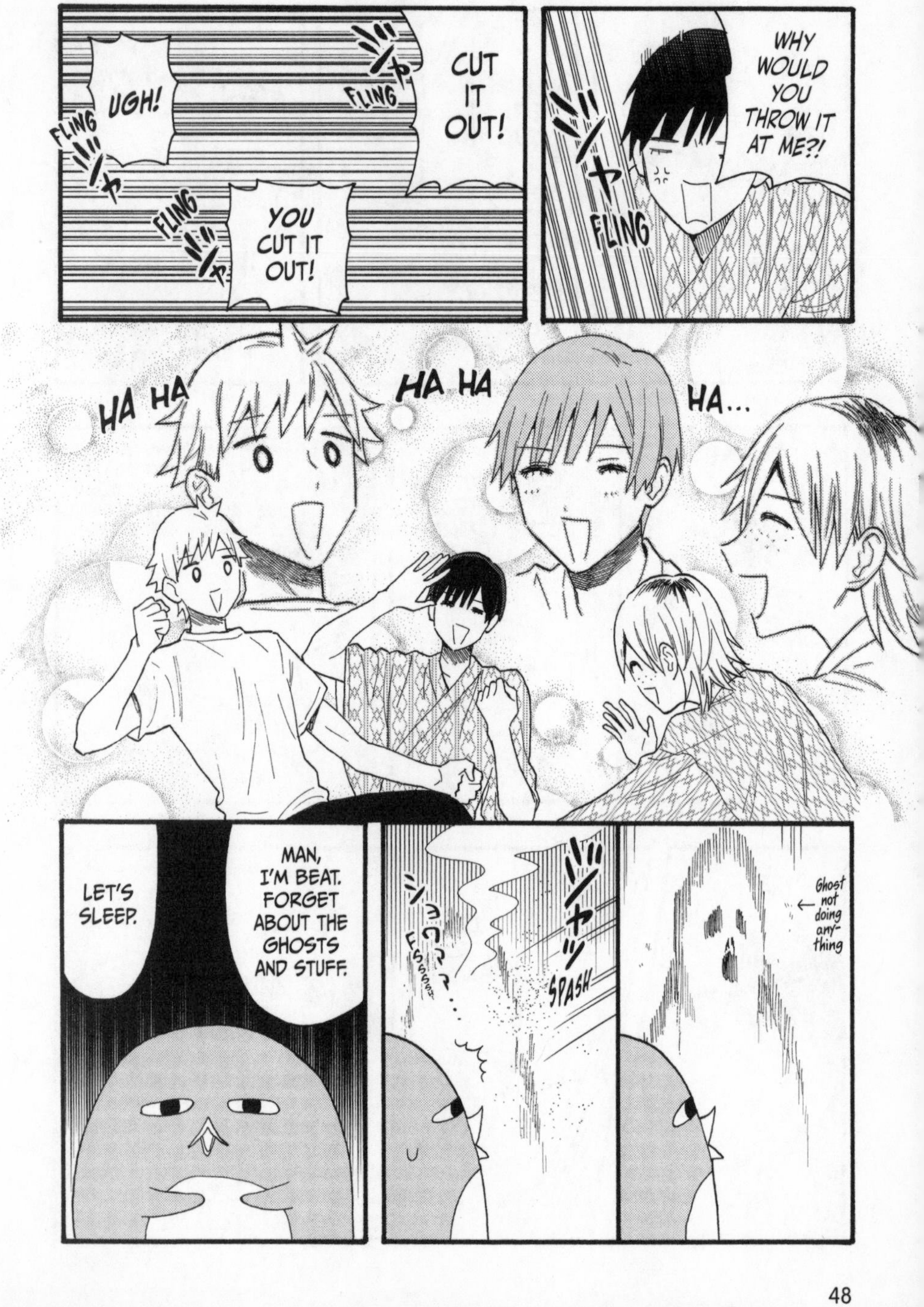
WHY WOULD YOU THROW IT AT ME?!
FLING
FLING
CUT IT OUT!
UGH!
FLING
FLING
YOU CUT IT OUT!
HA...
HA HA
HA HA
Ghost not doing any-thing
SPASH
FSSSSSH
MAN, I'M BEAT. FORGET ABOUT THE GHOSTS AND STUFF.
LET'S SLEEP.

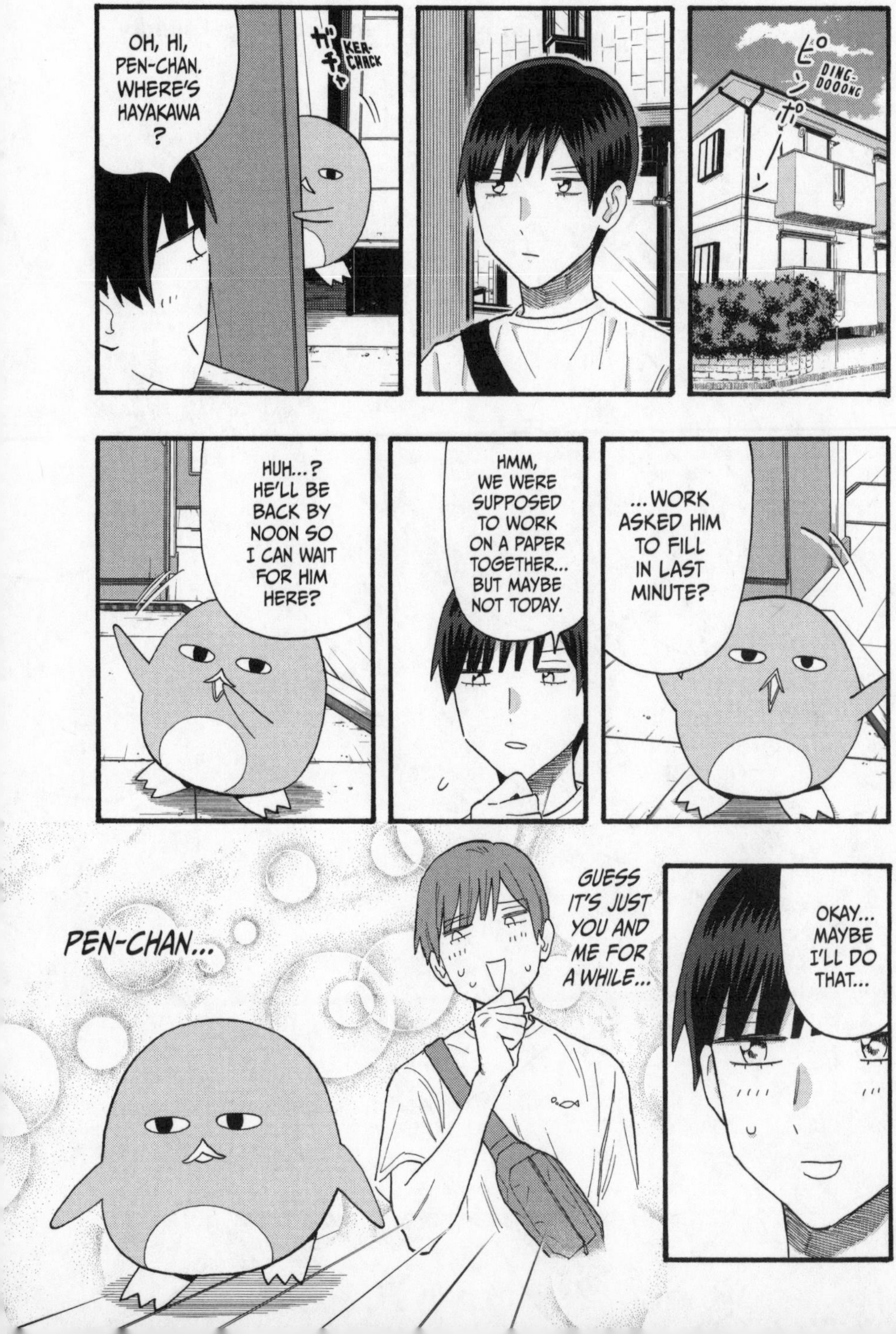
ピンポーン
DING-DOOONG
ガチャ
KER-CHACK
OH, HI, PEN-CHAN. WHERE'S HAYAKAWA?
...WORK ASKED HIM TO FILL IN LAST MINUTE?
HMM, WE WERE SUPPOSED TO WORK ON A PAPER TOGETHER... BUT MAYBE NOT TODAY.
HUH...? HE'LL BE BACK BY NOON SO I CAN WAIT FOR HIM HERE?
OKAY... MAYBE I'LL DO THAT...
GUESS IT'S JUST YOU AND ME FOR A WHILE...
PEN-CHAN...

Pen 33 The Penguin Hangs Laundry

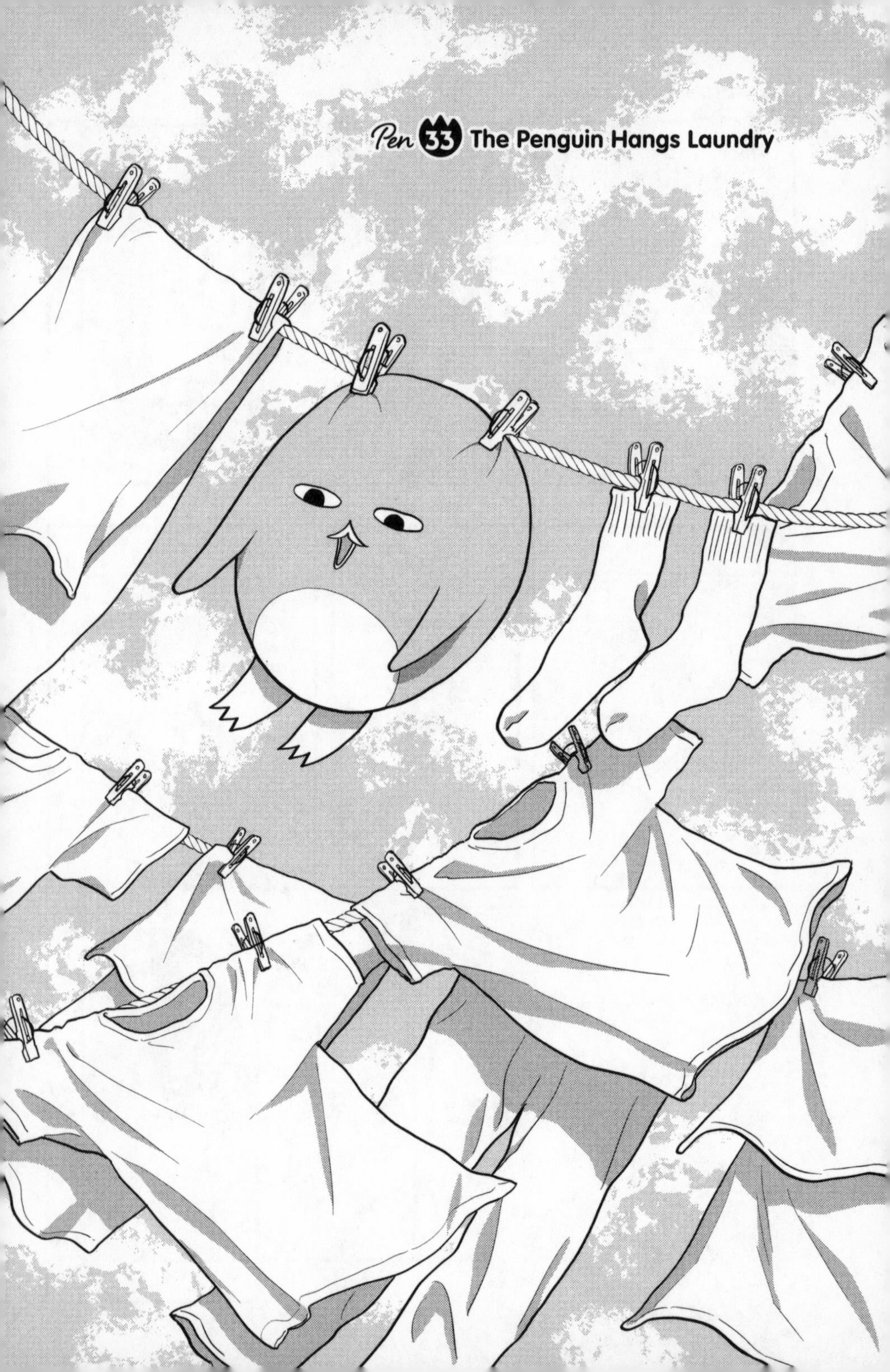

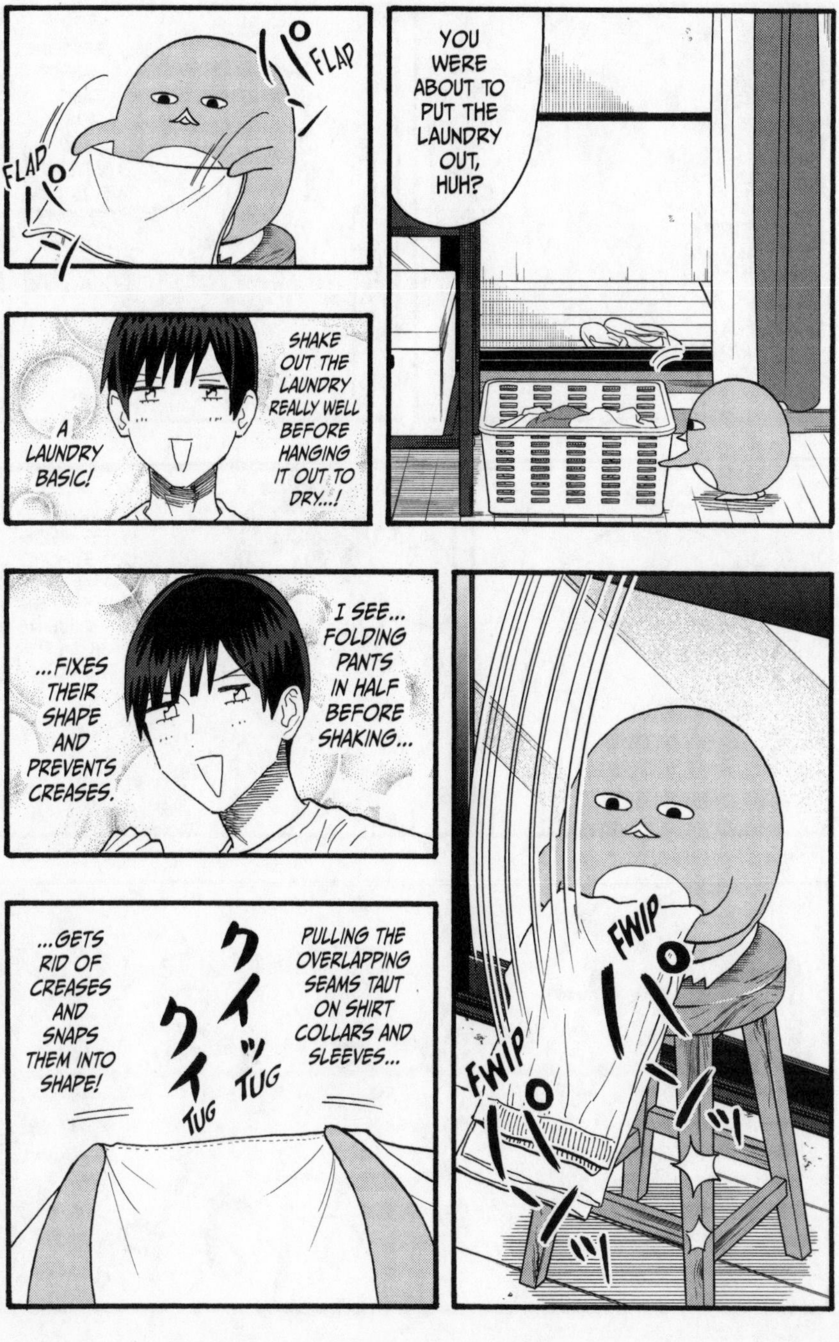
YOU WERE ABOUT TO PUT THE LAUNDRY OUT, HUH?
パ FLAP
パ FLAP
SHAKE OUT THE LAUNDRY REALLY WELL BEFORE HANGING IT OUT TO DRY...!
A LAUNDRY BASIC!
FWIP パ
FWIP パ
I SEE... FOLDING PANTS IN HALF BEFORE SHAKING...
...FIXES THEIR SHAPE AND PREVENTS CREASES.
PULLING THE OVERLAPPING SEAMS TAUT ON SHIRT COLLARS AND SLEEVES...
クイッ TUG
クイ TUG
...GETS RID OF CREASES AND SNAPS THEM INTO SHAPE!

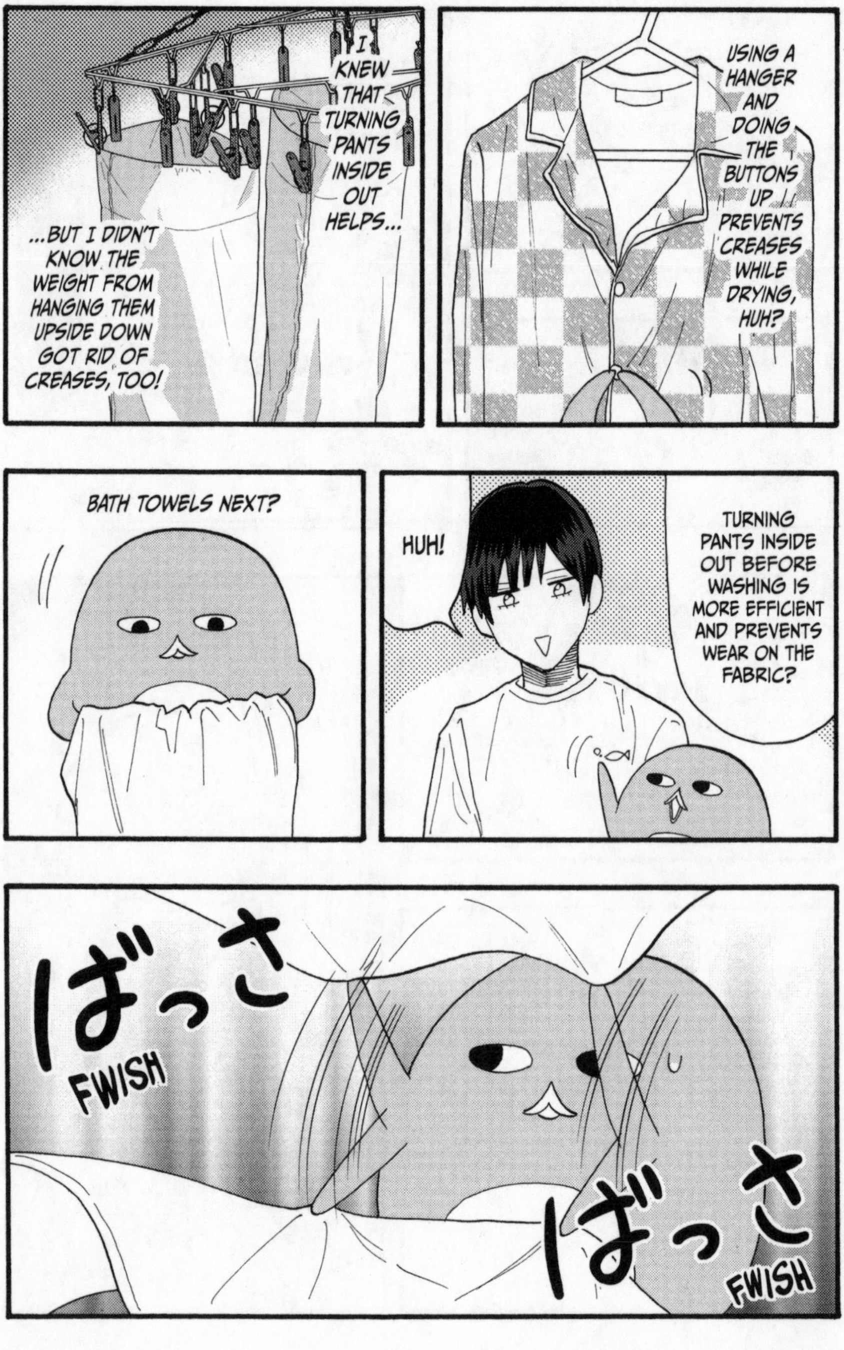
USING A HANGER AND DOING THE BUTTONS UP PREVENTS CREASES WHILE DRYING, HUH?
I KNEW THAT TURNING PANTS INSIDE OUT HELPS...
...BUT I DIDN'T KNOW THE WEIGHT FROM HANGING THEM UPSIDE DOWN GOT RID OF CREASES, TOO!
TURNING PANTS INSIDE OUT BEFORE WASHING IS MORE EFFICIENT AND PREVENTS WEAR ON THE FABRIC?
HUH!
BATH TOWELS NEXT?
ばっさ
FWISH
ばっさ
FWISH

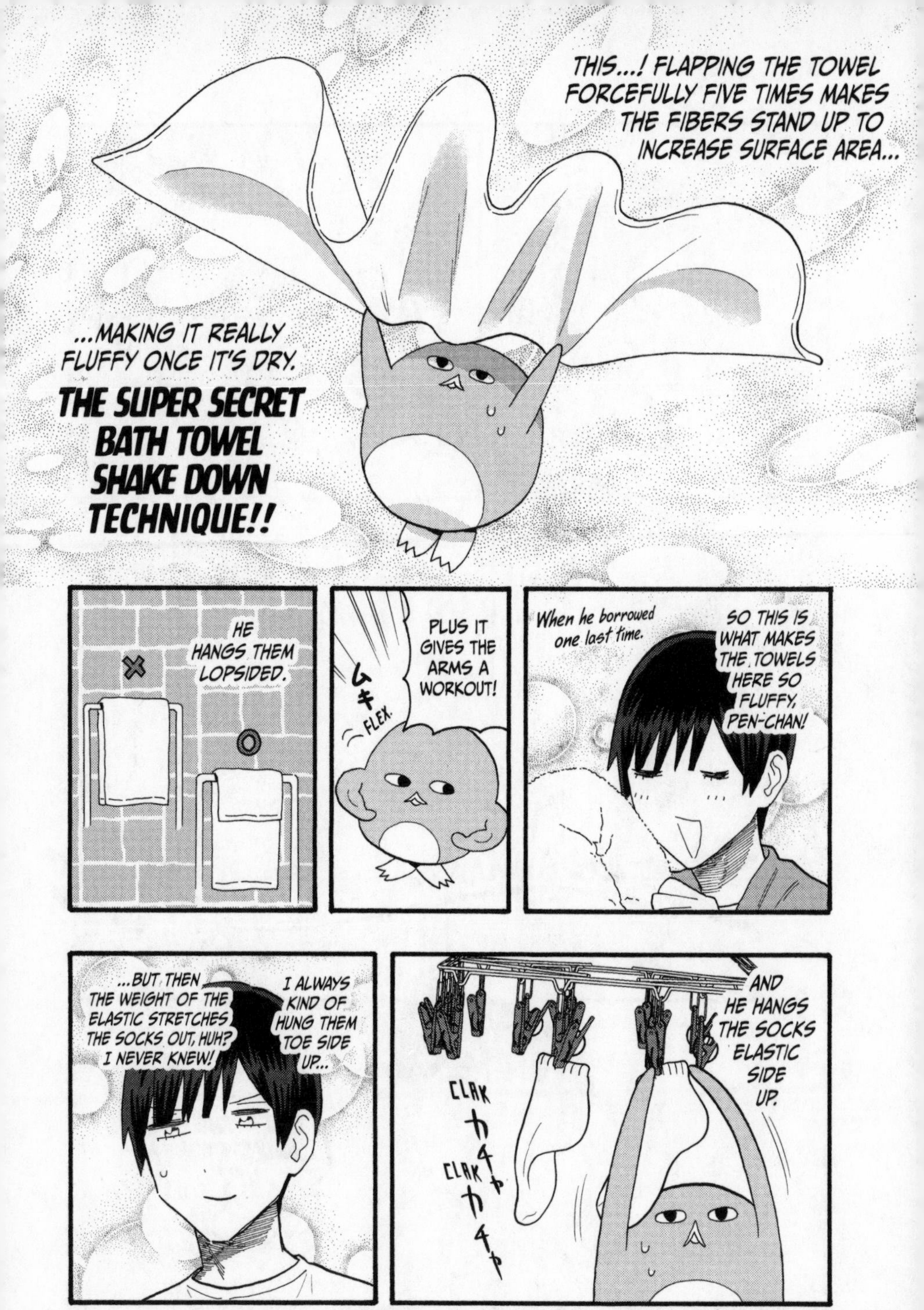
THIS...! FLAPPING THE TOWEL FORCEFULLY FIVE TIMES MAKES THE FIBERS STAND UP TO INCREASE SURFACE AREA...
...MAKING IT REALLY FLUFFY ONCE IT'S DRY.
THE SUPER SECRET BATH TOWEL SHAKE DOWN TECHNIQUE!!
SO THIS IS WHAT MAKES THE TOWELS HERE SO FLUFFY, PEN-CHAN!
When he borrowed one last time.
PLUS IT GIVES THE ARMS A WORKOUT!
ムキ
FLEX.
HE HANGS THEM LOPSIDED.
AND HE HANGS THE SOCKS ELASTIC SIDE UP.
CLAK
カチャ
CLAK
カチャ
I ALWAYS KIND OF HUNG THEM TOE SIDE UP...
...BUT THEN THE WEIGHT OF THE ELASTIC STRETCHES THE SOCKS OUT, HUH? I NEVER KNEW!

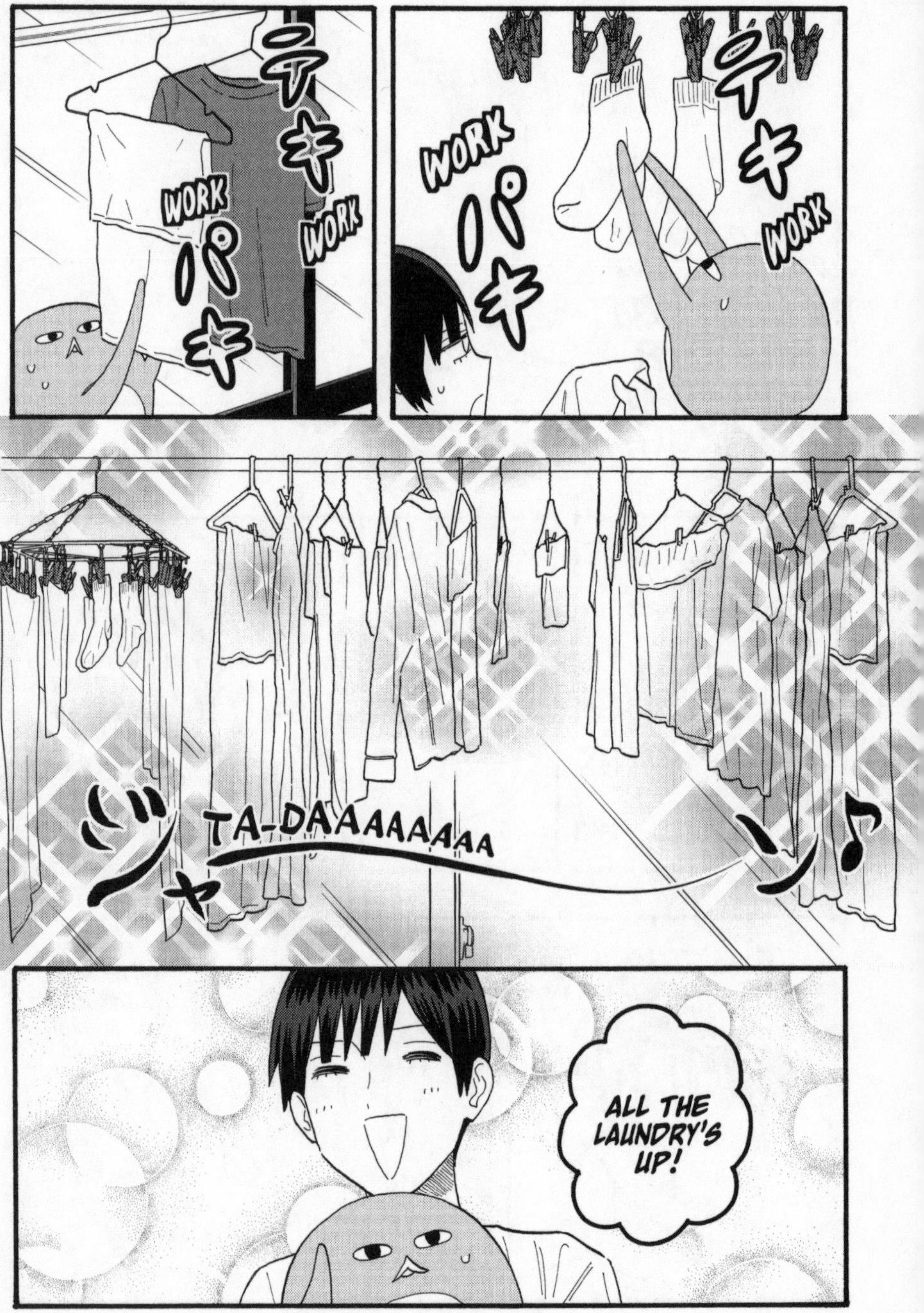
テキ
WORK
パキ
WORK
テキ
WORK
パキ
WORK
ジャーーン♪
TA-DAAAAAAAA
ALL THE LAUNDRY'S UP!

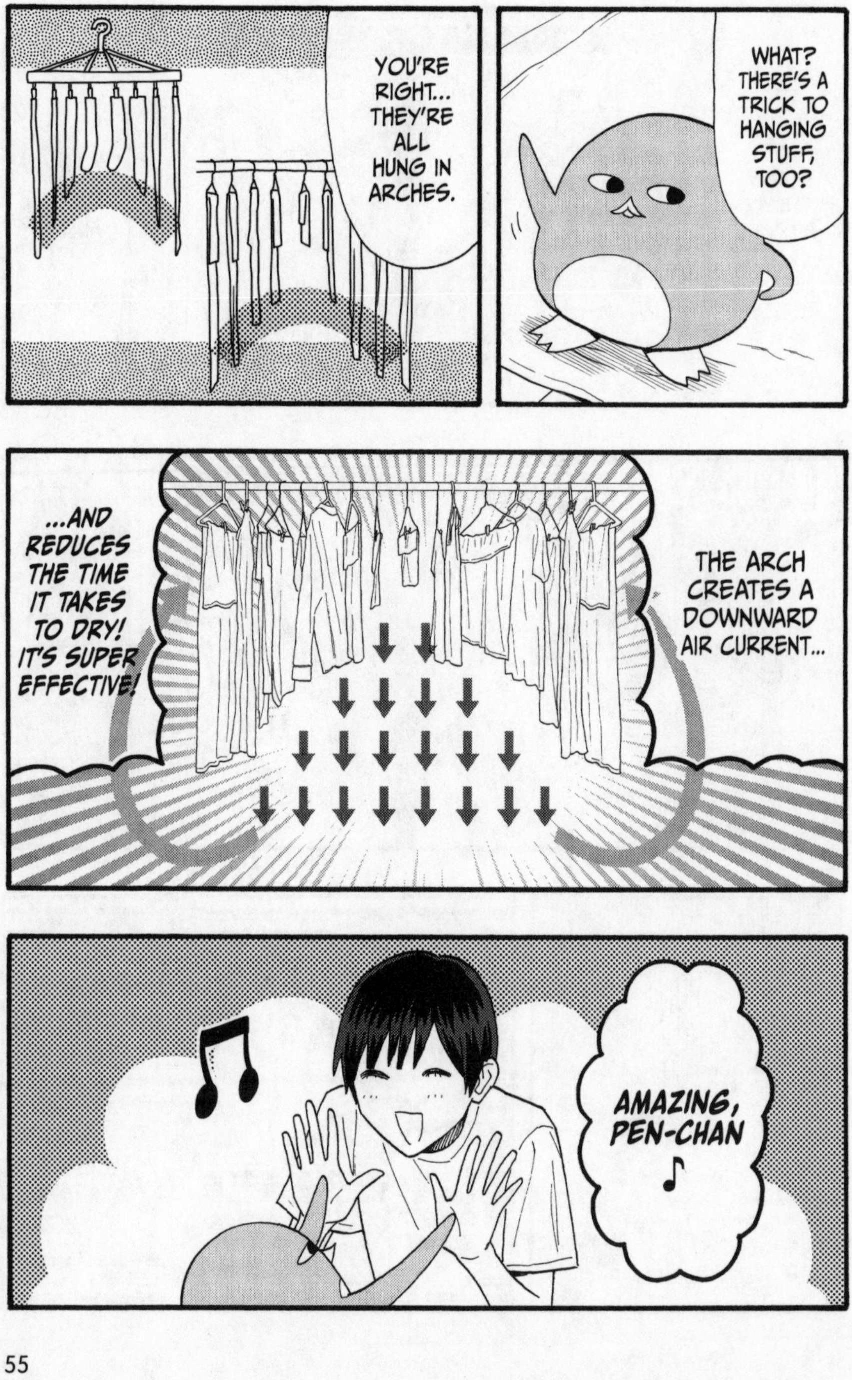
WHAT? THERE'S A TRICK TO HANGING STUFF, TOO?
YOU'RE RIGHT... THEY'RE ALL HUNG IN ARCHES.
THE ARCH CREATES A DOWNWARD AIR CURRENT...
...AND REDUCES THE TIME IT TAKES TO DRY! IT'S SUPER EFFECTIVE!
AMAZING, PEN-CHAN ♪

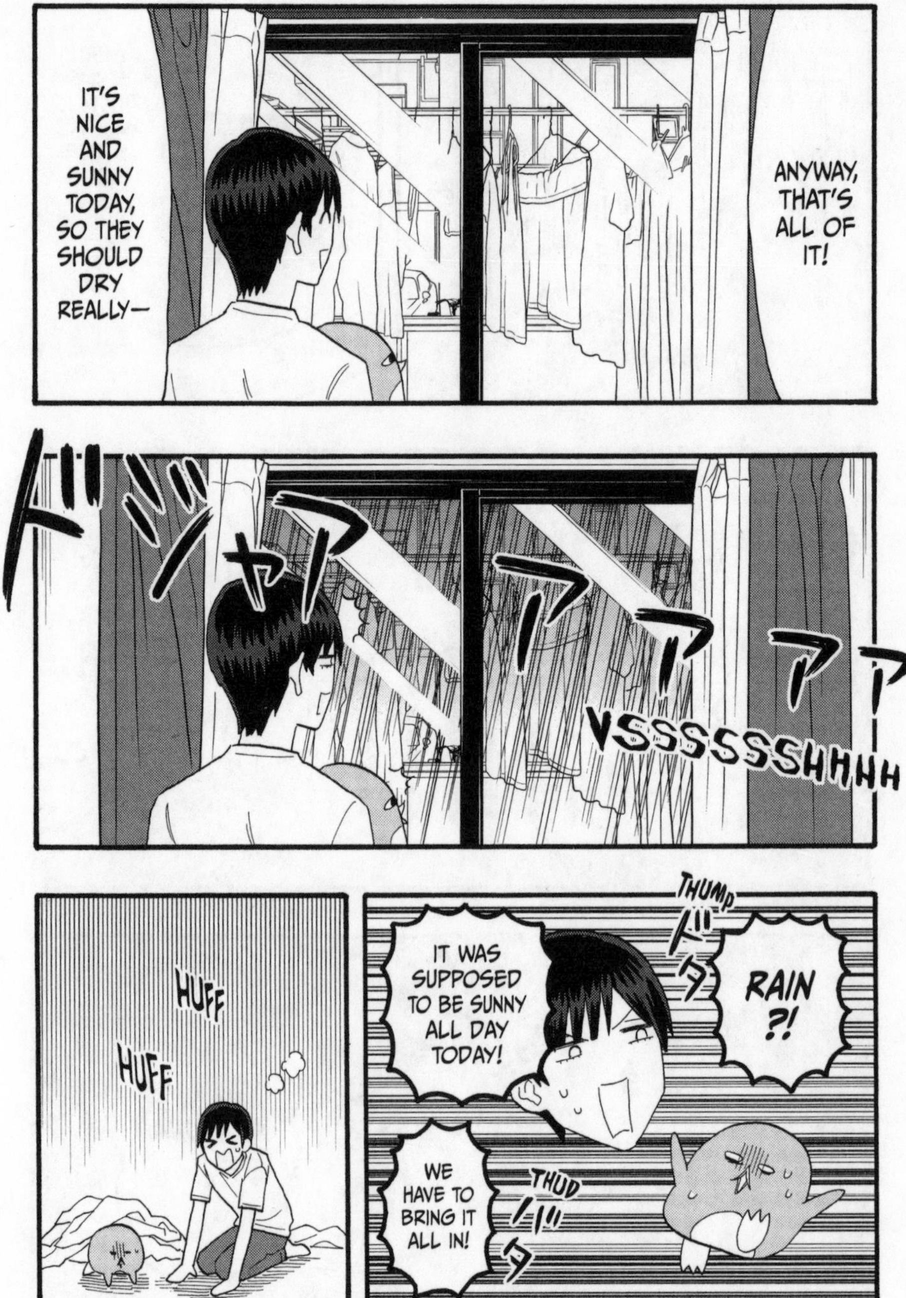
ANYWAY, THAT'S ALL OF IT!
IT'S NICE AND SUNNY TODAY, SO THEY SHOULD DRY REALLY—
ドジャアアア
VSSSSSSSHHHH
THUMP ドタ
RAIN ?!
IT WAS SUPPOSED TO BE SUNNY ALL DAY TODAY!
THUD バタ
WE HAVE TO BRING IT ALL IN!
HUFF
HUFF

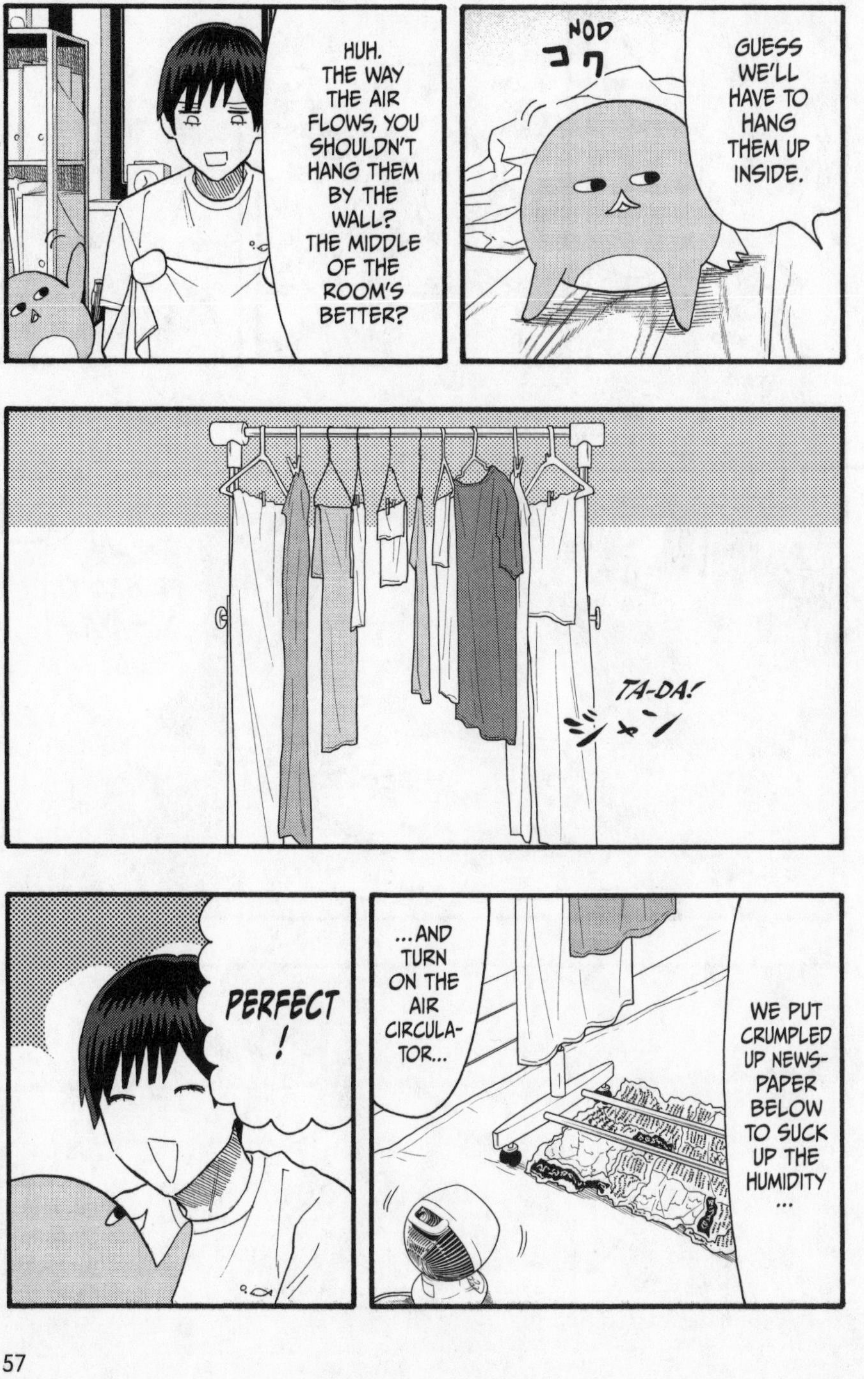
NOD
コク
GUESS WE'LL HAVE TO HANG THEM UP INSIDE.
HUH. THE WAY THE AIR FLOWS, YOU SHOULDN'T HANG THEM BY THE WALL? THE MIDDLE OF THE ROOM'S BETTER?
TA-DA!
ジャーン
WE PUT CRUMPLED UP NEWS-PAPER BELOW TO SUCK UP THE HUMIDITY ...
...AND TURN ON THE AIR CIRCULA-TOR...
PERFECT!

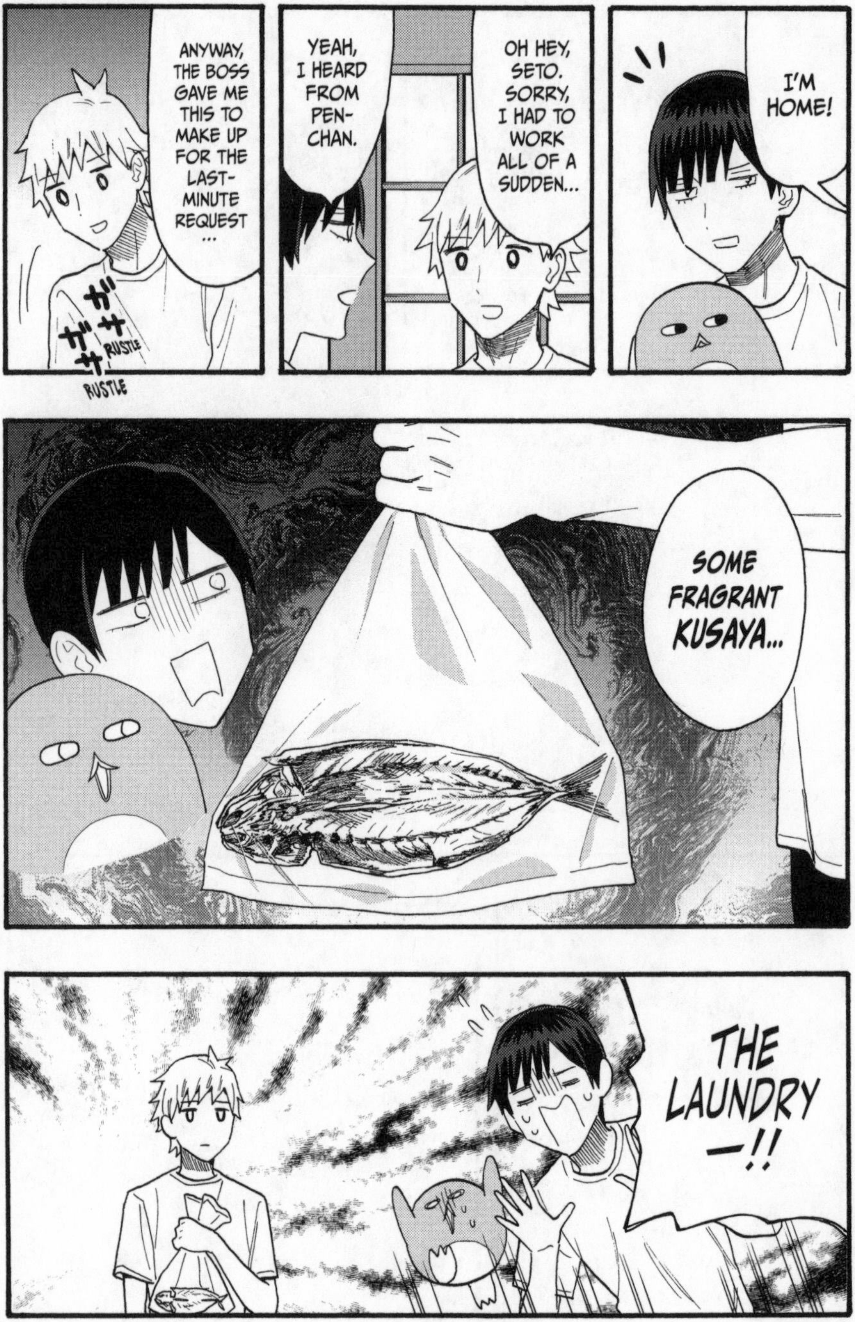
I'M HOME!
OH HEY, SETO. SORRY, I HAD TO WORK ALL OF A SUDDEN...
YEAH, I HEARD FROM PEN-CHAN.
ANYWAY, THE BOSS GAVE ME THIS TO MAKE UP FOR THE LAST-MINUTE REQUEST ...
ガサ RUSTLE
ガサ RUSTLE
SOME FRAGRANT KUSAYA...
THE LAUNDRY —!!

Pen Maria wrapped in a freshly washed towel.

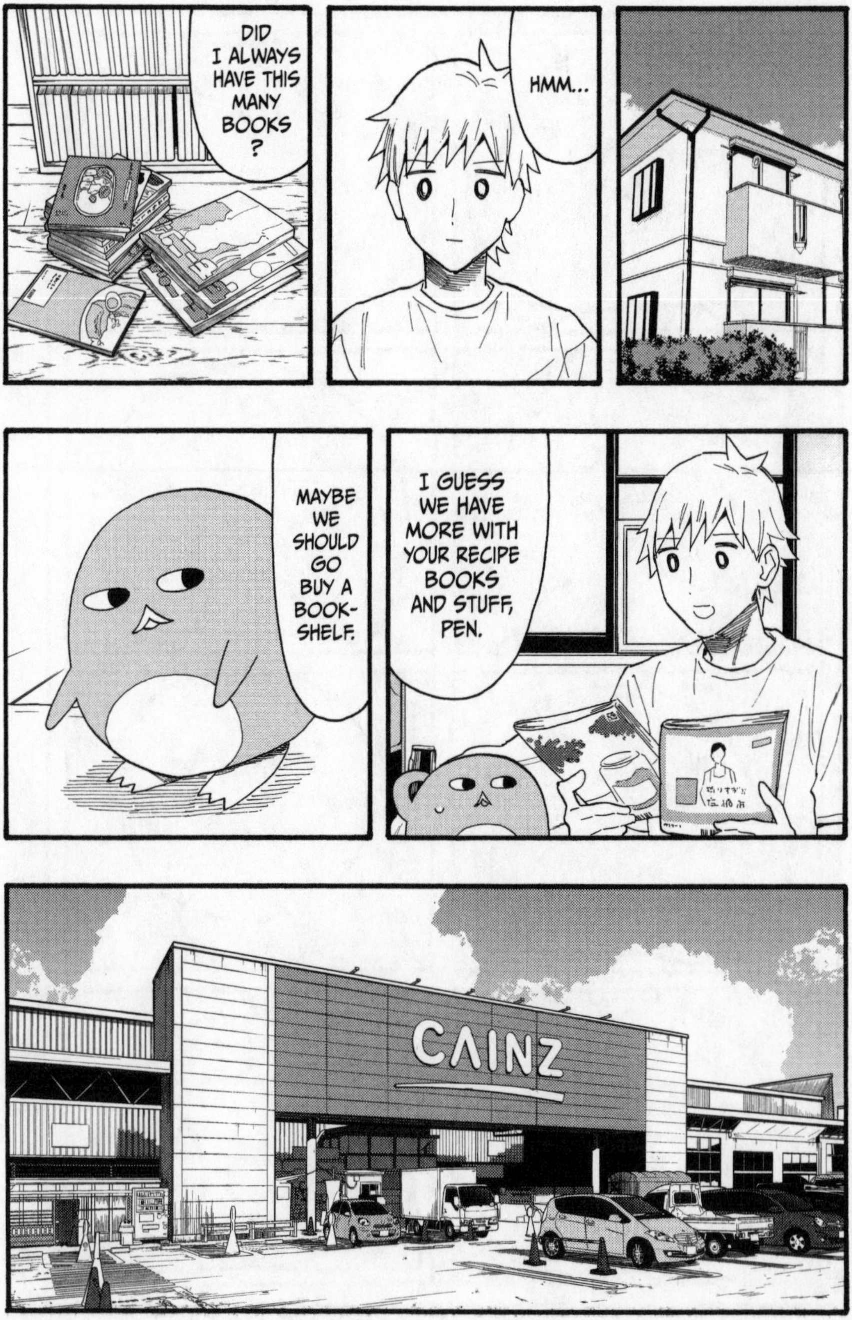
HMM...
DID I ALWAYS HAVE THIS MANY BOOKS?
I GUESS WE HAVE MORE WITH YOUR RECIPE BOOKS AND STUFF, PEN.
MAYBE WE SHOULD GO BUY A BOOK-SHELF.
CAINZ

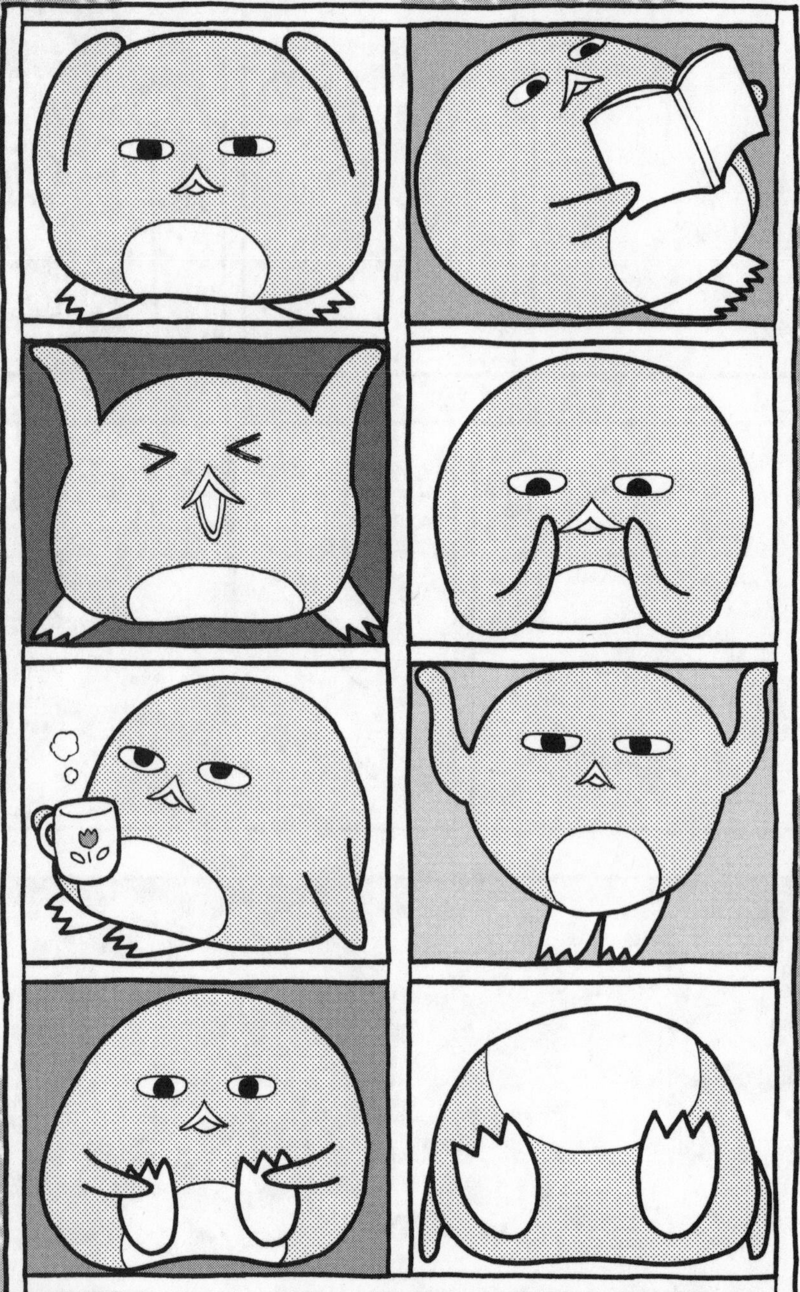

Pen 34 The Penguin Does Some DIY

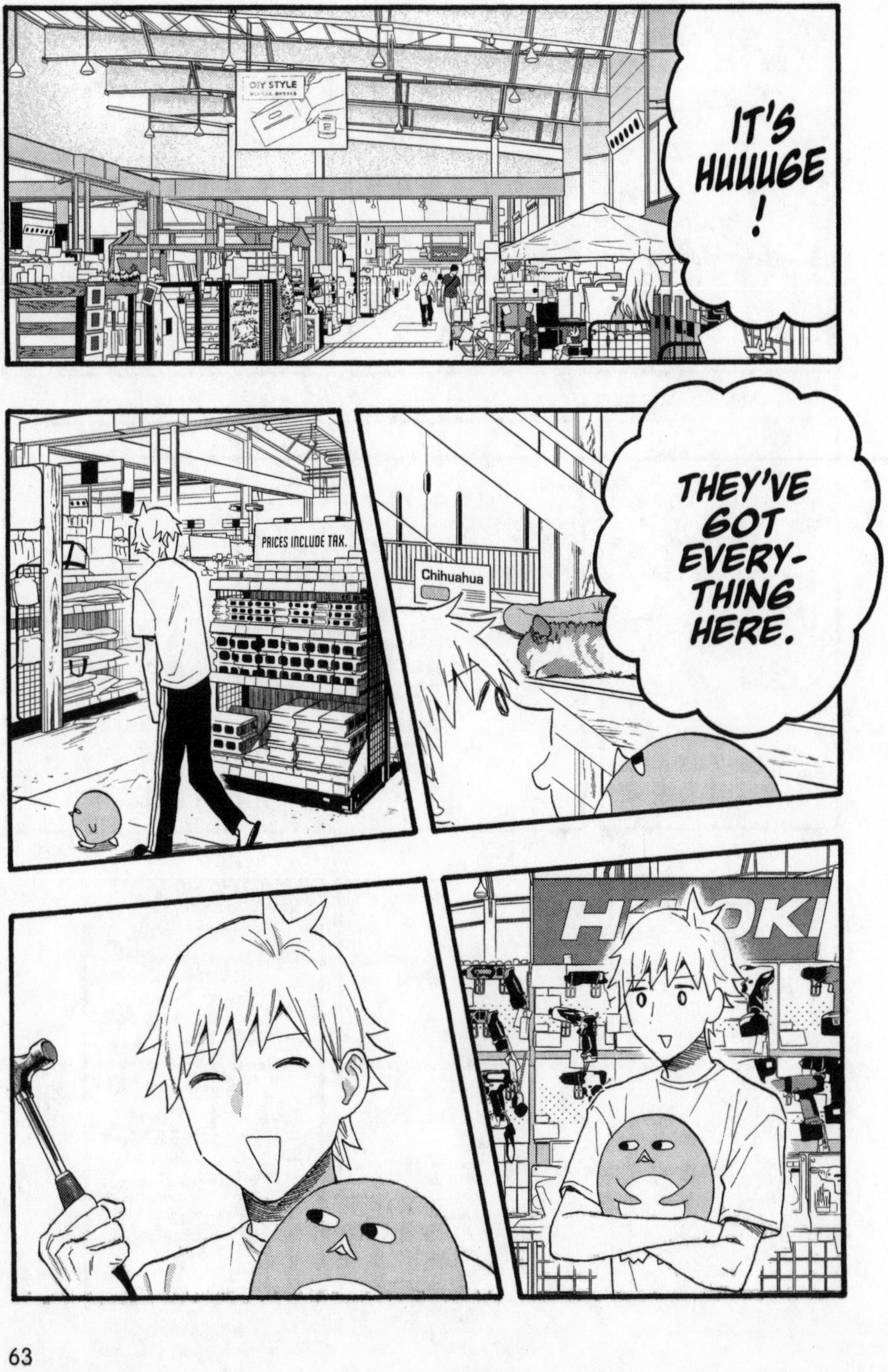
IT'S HUUUGE!
DIY STYLE
THEY'VE GOT EVERY-THING HERE.
Chihuahua
PRICES INCLUDE TAX.

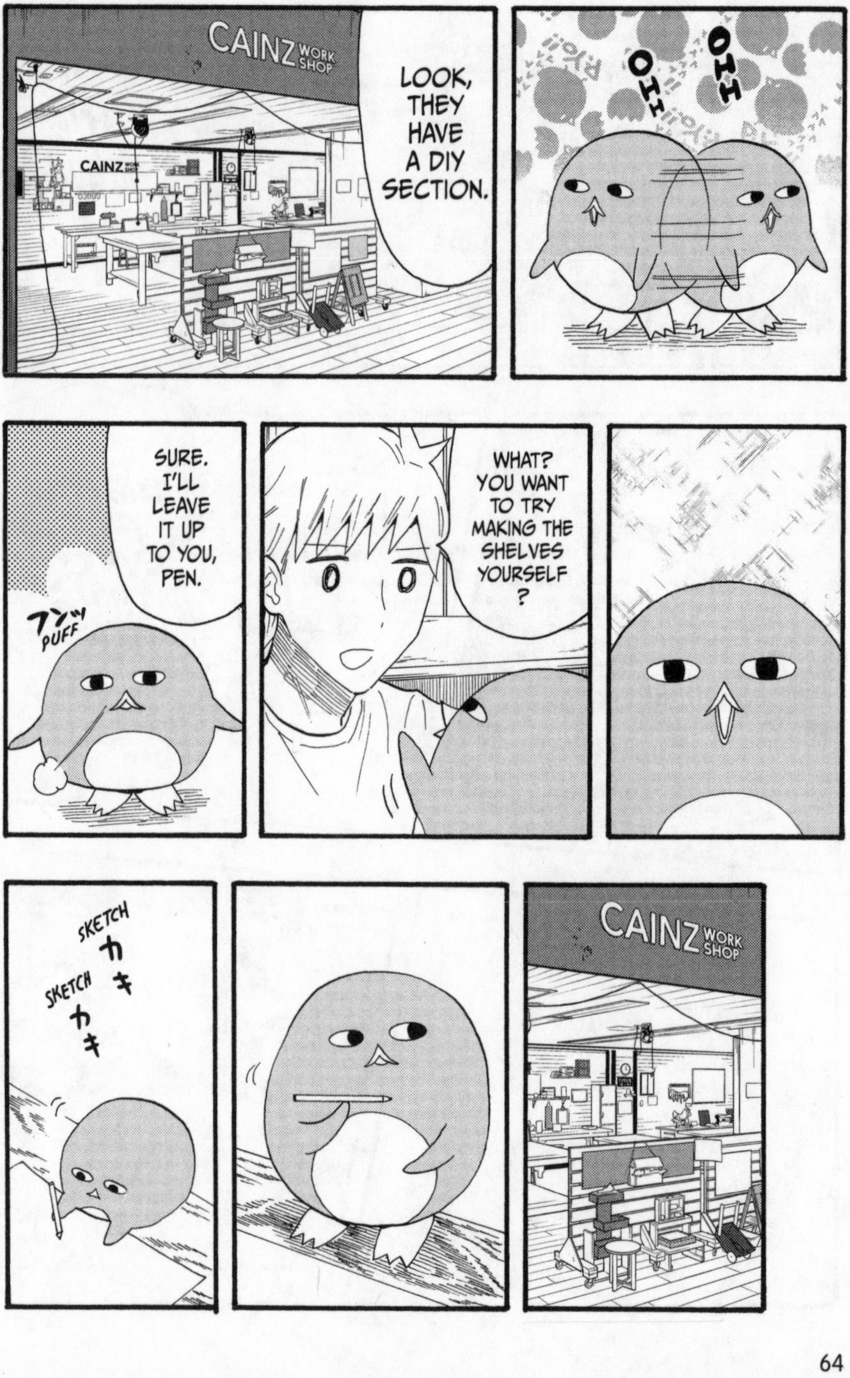
OHH
OHH
LOOK, THEY HAVE A DIY SECTION.
CAINZ WORK SHOP
CAINZ WORK SHOP
WHAT? YOU WANT TO TRY MAKING THE SHELVES YOURSELF?
SURE. I'LL LEAVE IT UP TO YOU, PEN.
フンッ PUFF
CAINZ WORK SHOP
SKETCH カキ
SKETCH カキ

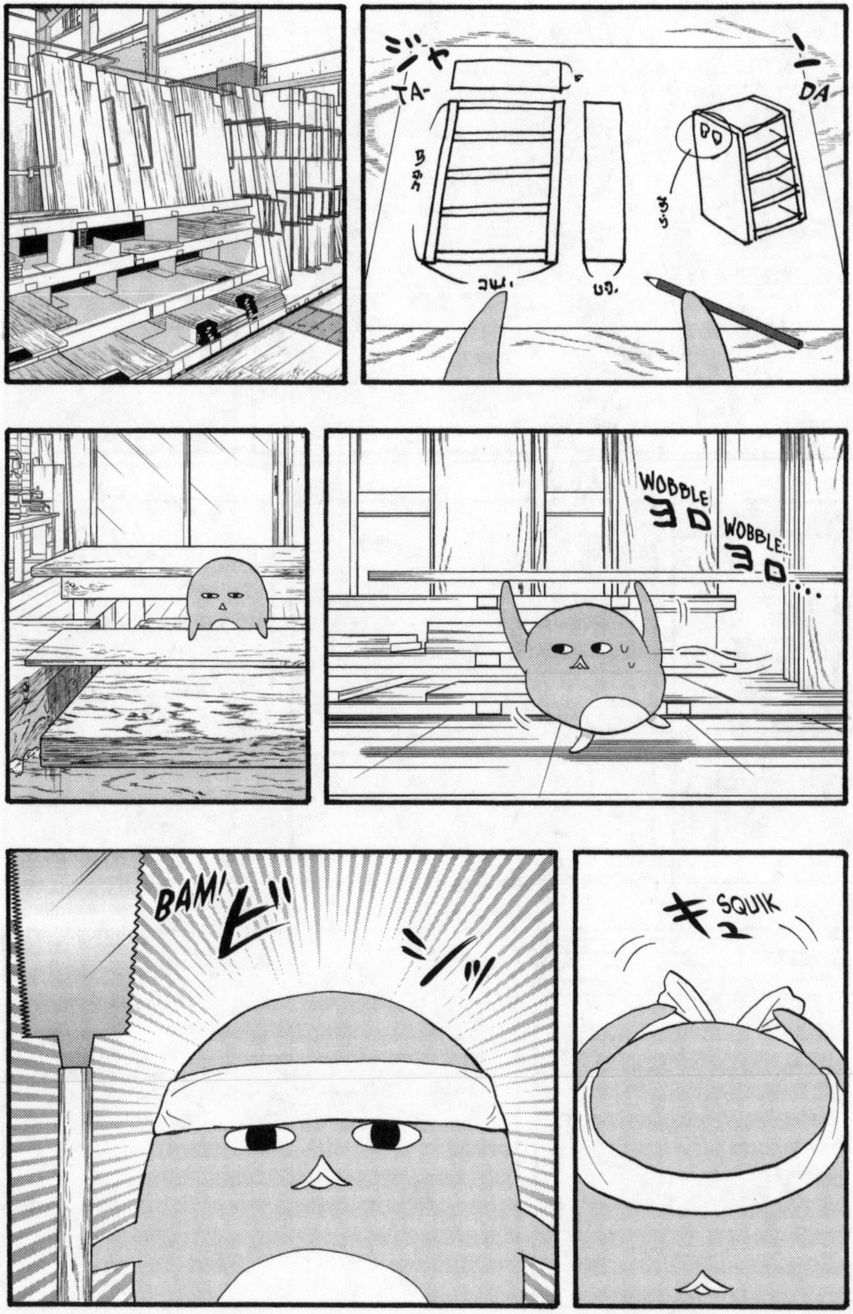
ジャ
TA-
ー
DA
WOBBLE
ヨロ
WOBBLE...
ヨロ...
キュ
SQUIK
BAM!
ビシッ

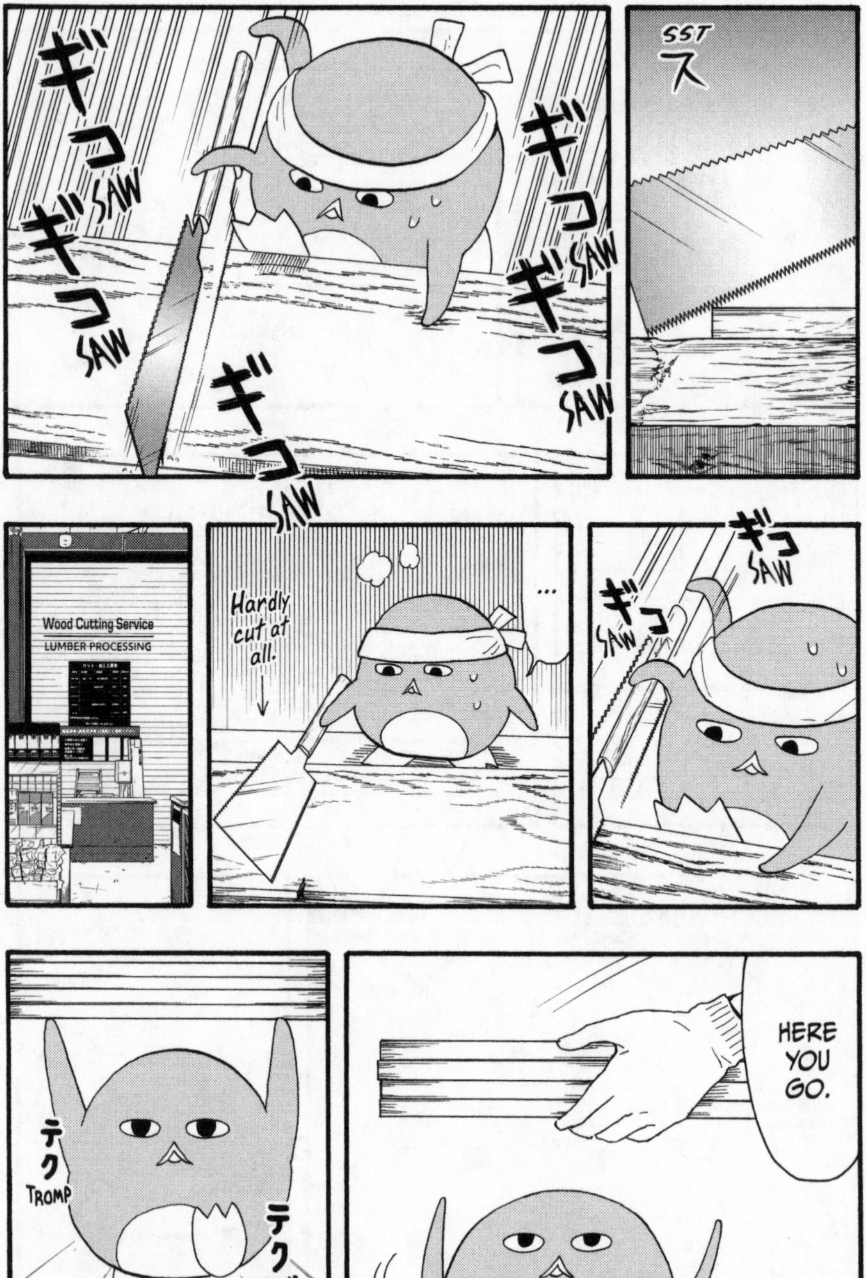

ス
SST
ギコ
SAW
ギコ
SAW
ギコ
SAW
ギコ
SAW
ギコ
SAW
ギコ
SAW
ギコ
SAW
...
Hardly cut at all.
Wood Cutting Service
LUMBER PROCESSING
HERE YOU GO.
テク
TROMP
テク
TROMP

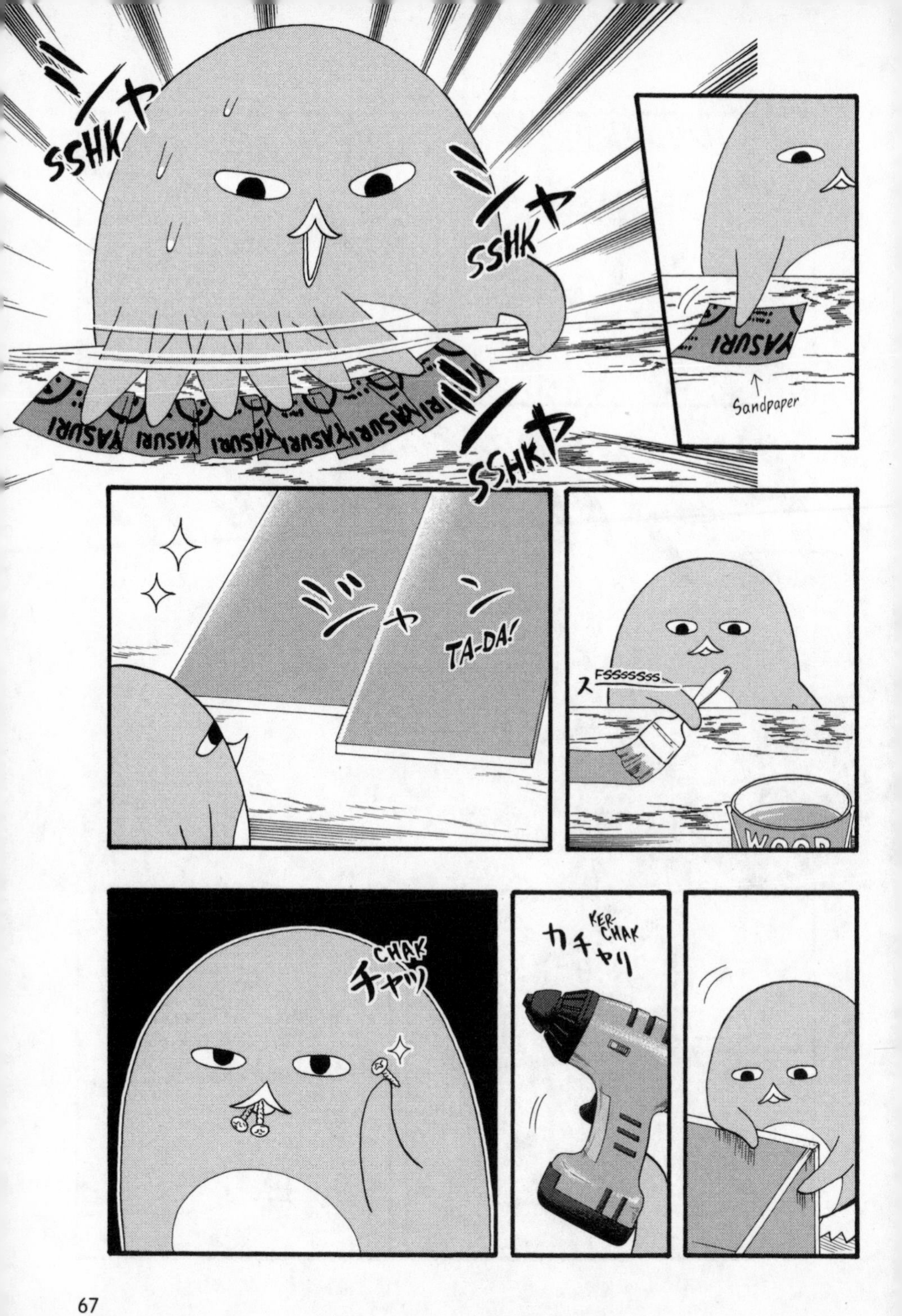
YASURI
Sandpaper
SSHK
SSHK
YASURI
YASURI
YASURI
YASURI
YASURI
SSHK
FSSSSSSS
WOOD
TA-DA!
KER-CHAK
CHAK

ドゥルルルルル
WHIRRRRR
ドゥルルルルル
WHIRRRRR
ドゥルルルルル
WHIRRRRRRRRRR
RUSTLE
カサ
RUSTLE
カサ
KRK
クリ
KRK
クリ

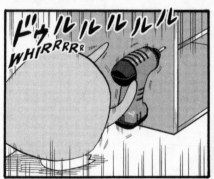

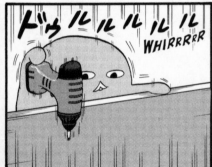

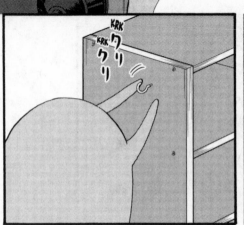

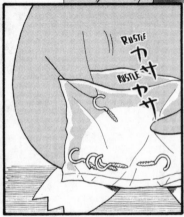

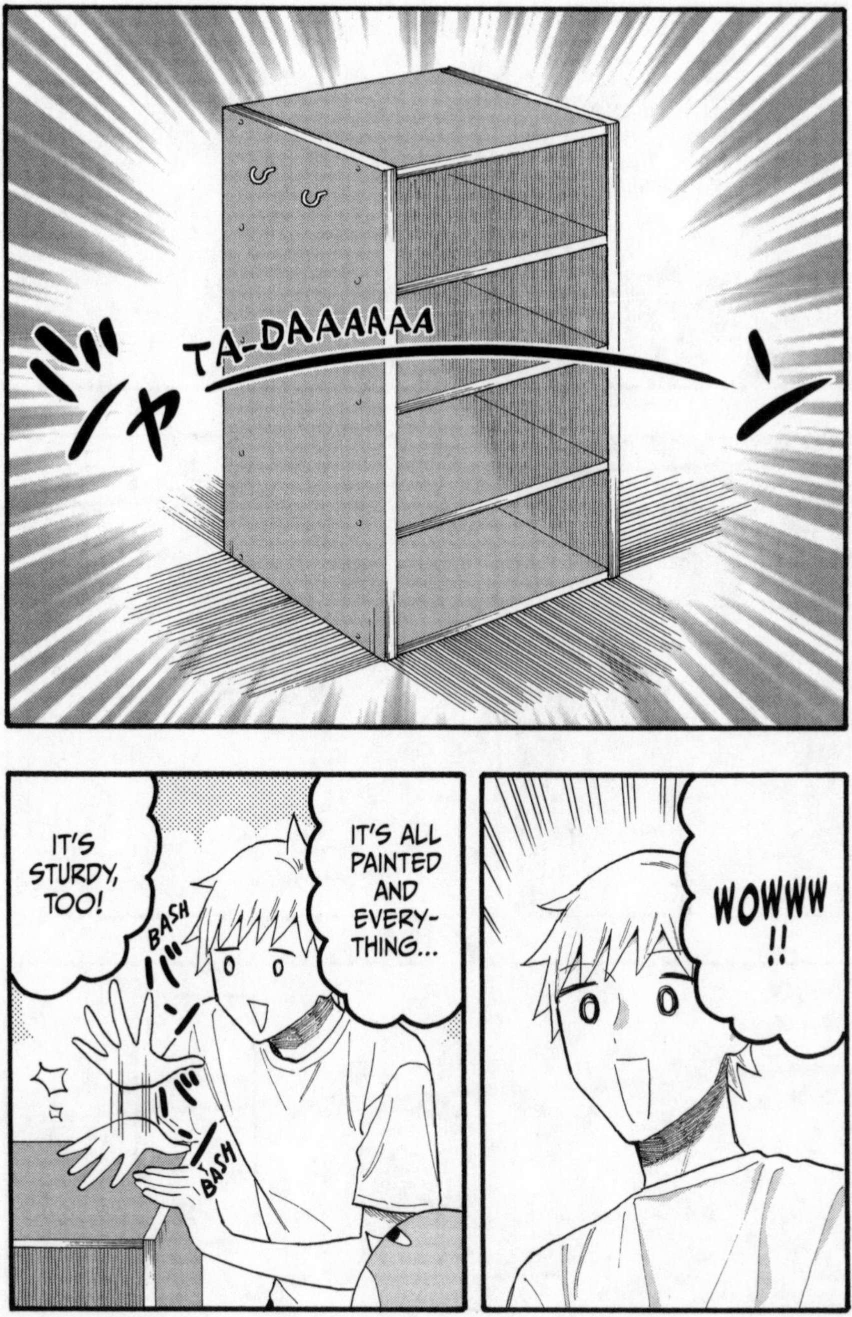
TA-DAAAAAA
WOWWW!!
IT'S ALL PAINTED AND EVERY-THING...
IT'S STURDY, TOO!
BASH
BASH

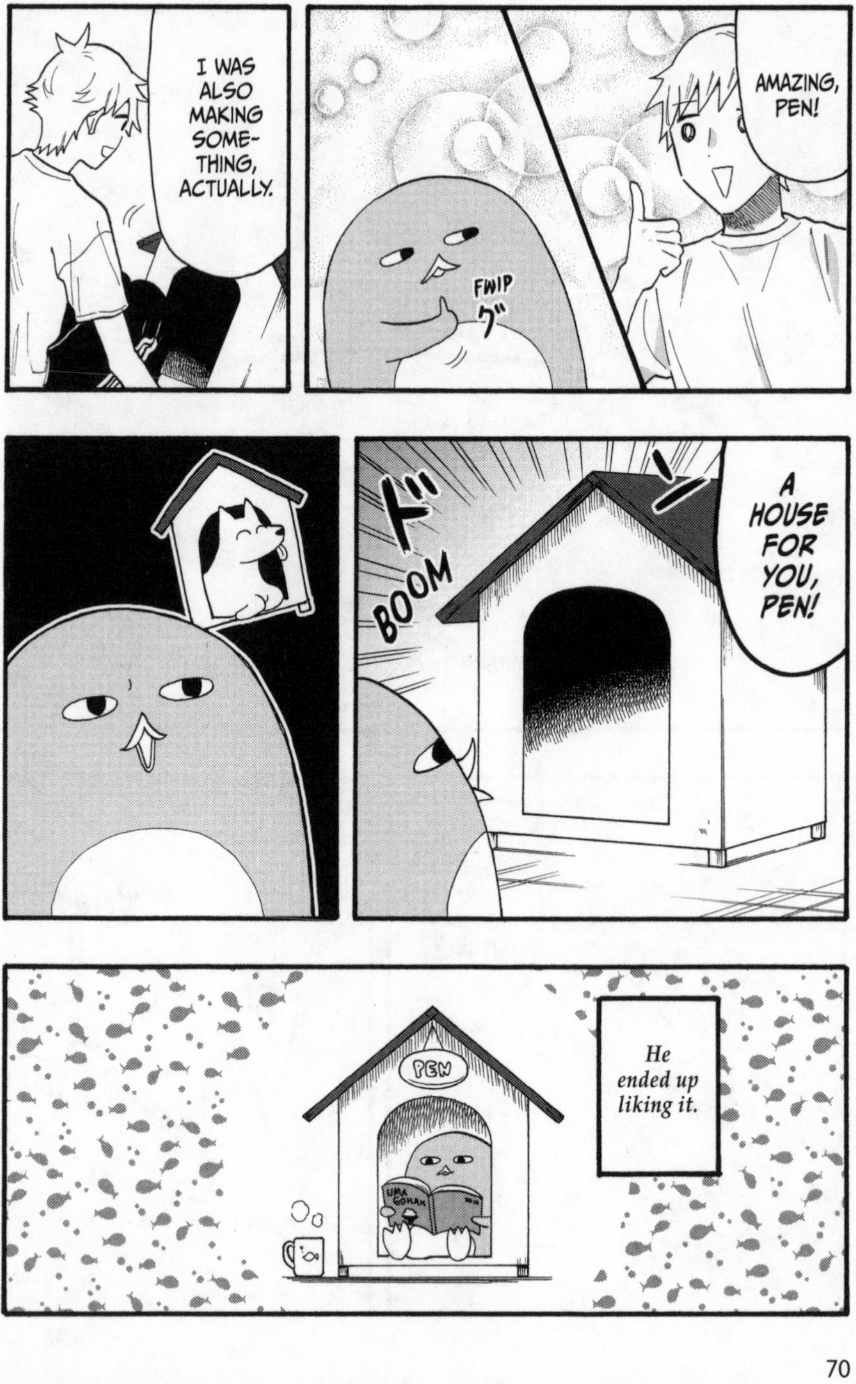
AMAZING, PEN!
FWIP
グ
I WAS ALSO MAKING SOME-THING, ACTUALLY.
A HOUSE FOR YOU, PEN!
ドン
BOOM
He ended up liking it.
PEN
UMA GOHAN

Pen 35 The Penguin and a Chick in Midsummer

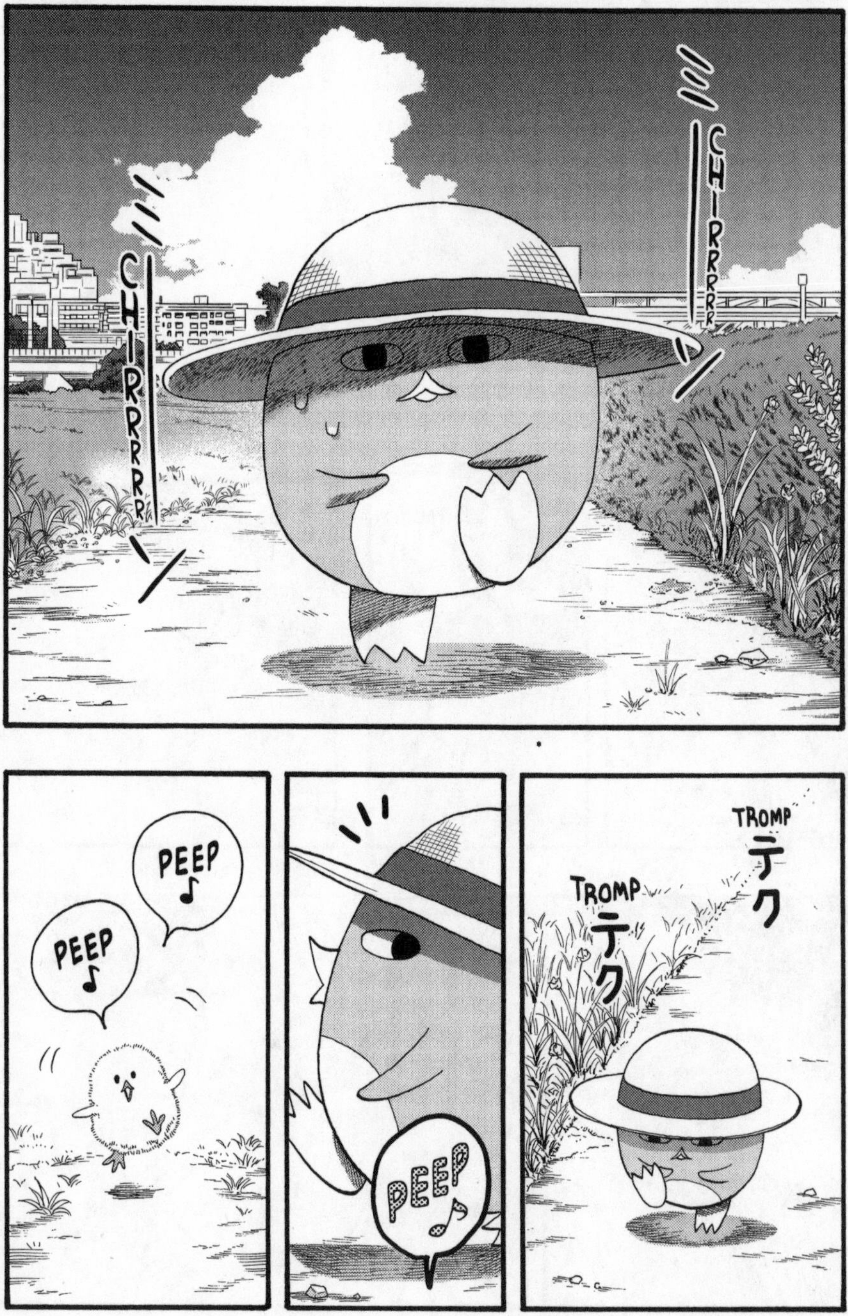

CHIRRRRR
CHIRRRRRR
TROMP
テク
TROMP
テク
PEEP
PEEP
PEEP

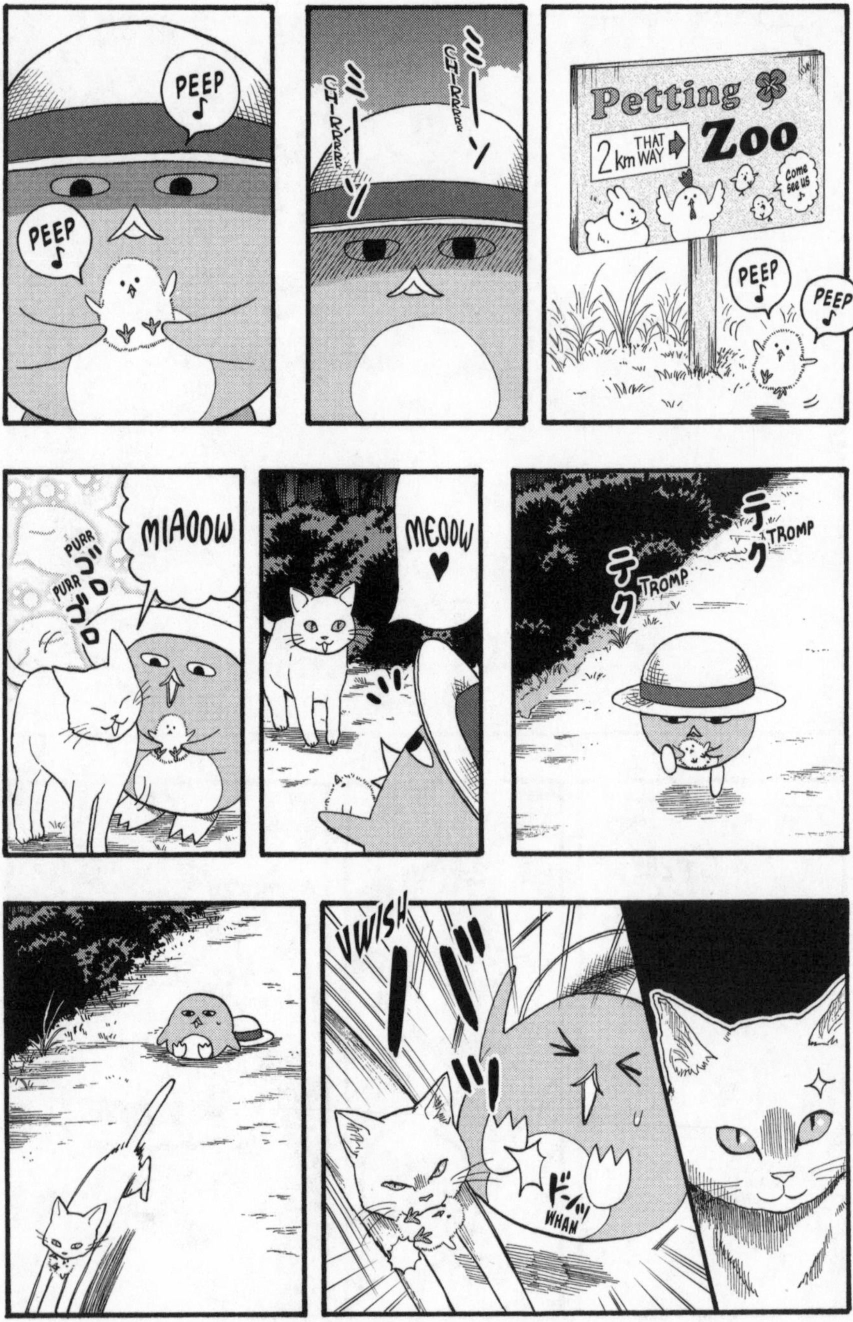

Petting Zoo
2 km THAT WAY
Come see us ♪
PEEP ♪
PEEP ♪
CHIRRRRR
CHIRRRRR
PEEP ♪
PEEP ♪
テク TROMP
テク TROMP
MEOOW ♥
MIAOOW
ゴロ PURR
ゴロ PURR
VWISH
ドーン WHAM

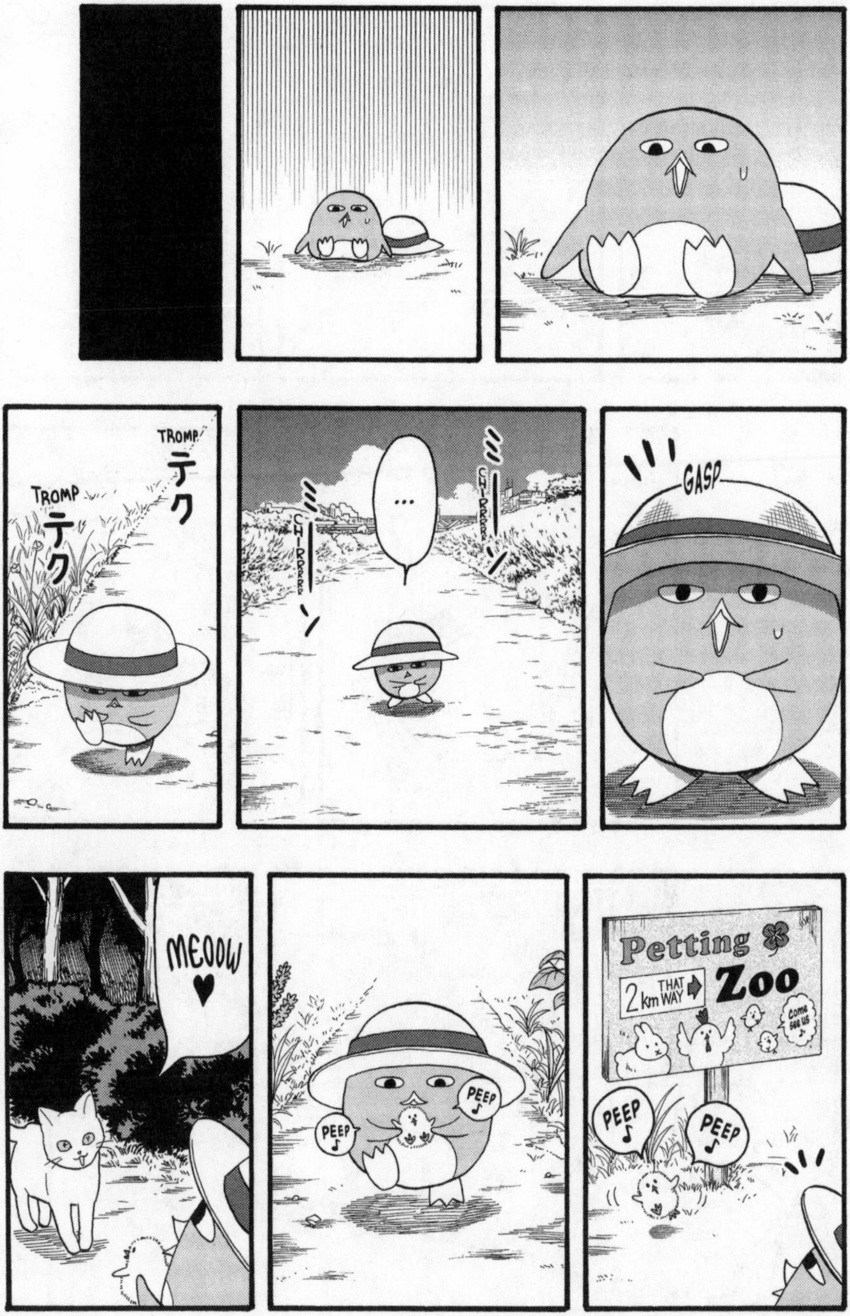
GASP
ミーン
CHIRRRR
…
ミーン
CHIRRRR
TROMP
テク
TROMP
テク
Petting
Zoo
2 km THAT WAY
Come see us ♪
PEEP ♪
PEEP ♪
PEEP ♪
PEEP ♪
MEOOW ♥

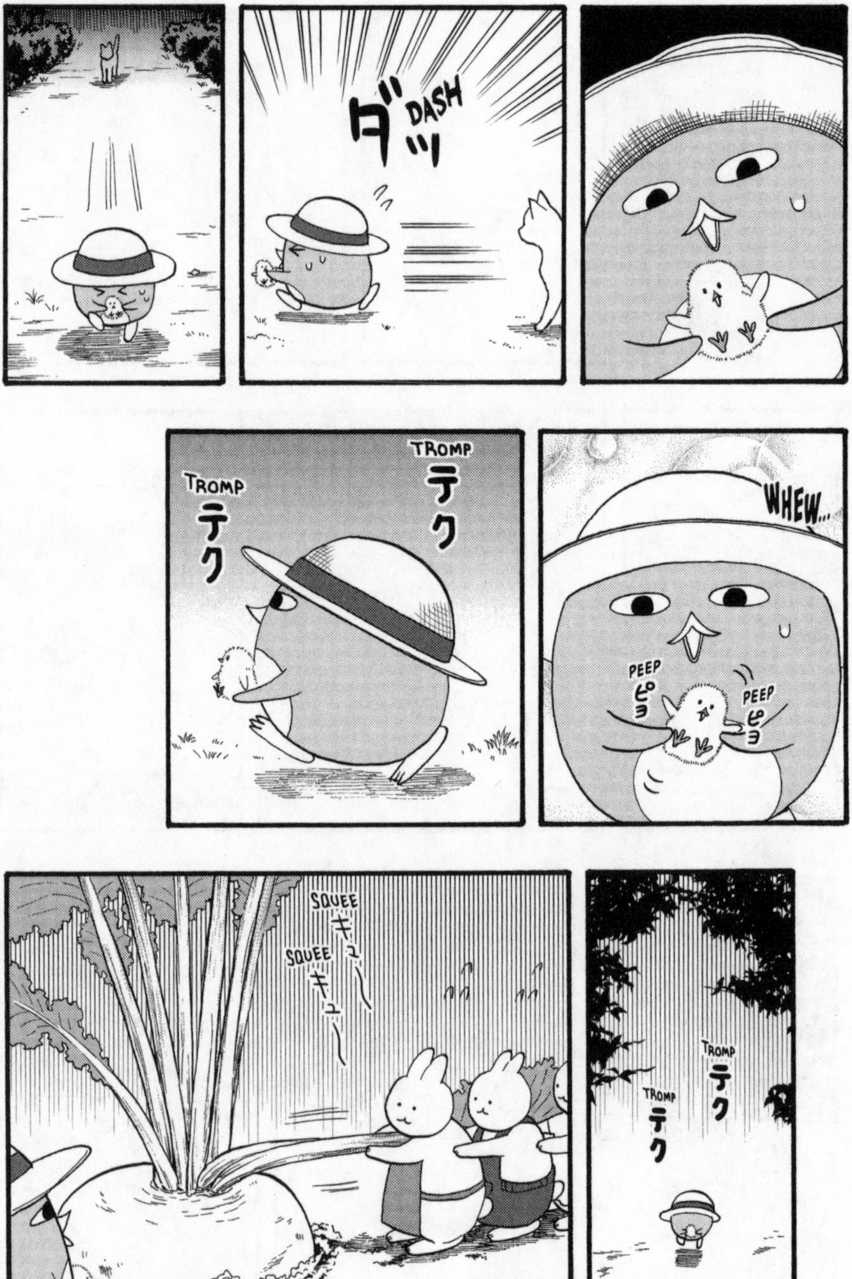
ダッ
DASH
WHEW...
PEEP
ピョ
PEEP
ピョ
TROMP
テク
TROMP
テク
TROMP
テク
TROMP
テク
SQUEE
キュ〜
SQUEE
キュ〜

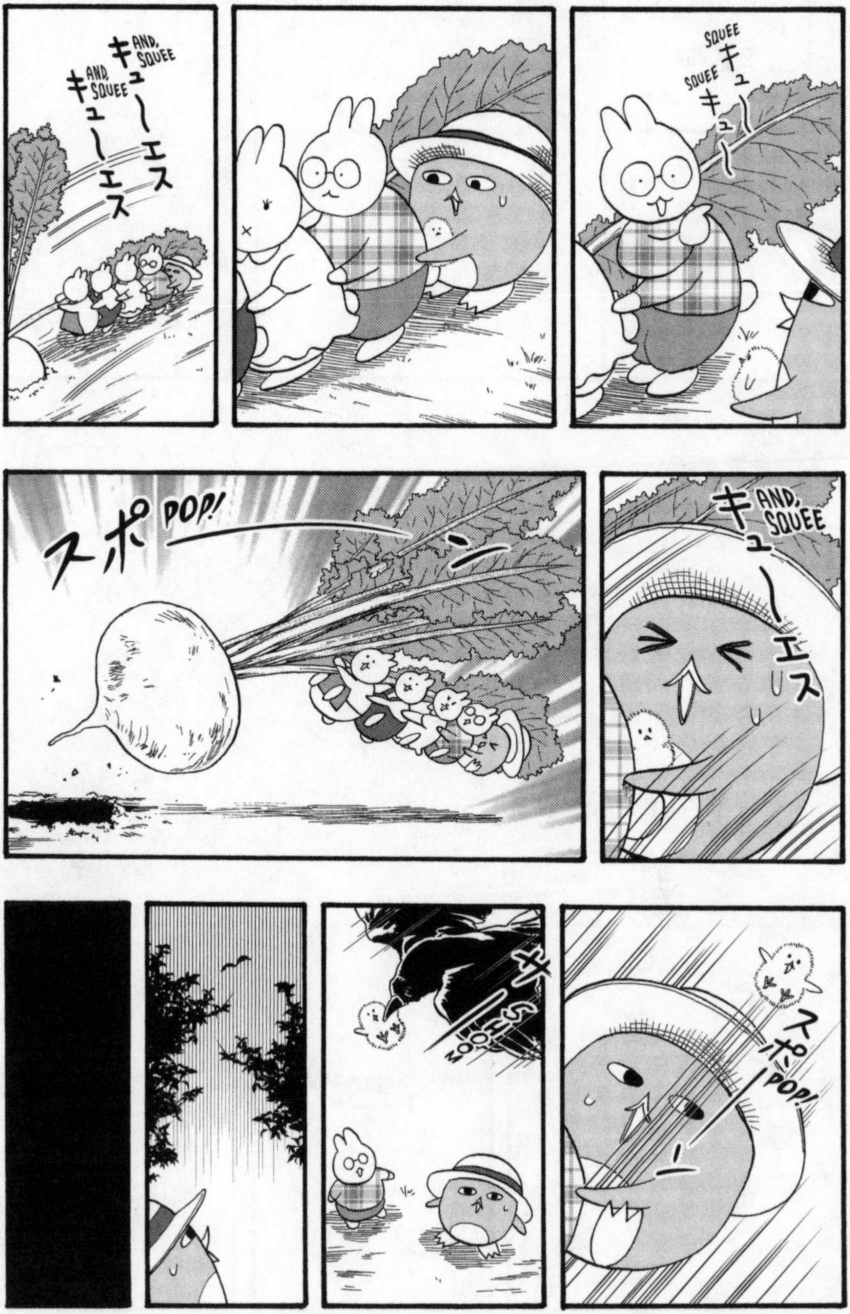
キュ―キュ―
SQUEE
SQUEE
キュ―エス
AND, SQUEE
キュ―エス
AND, SQUEE
キュ―エス
AND, SQUEE
スポ
POP!
ン
スポン
POP!
サー
SHOOM

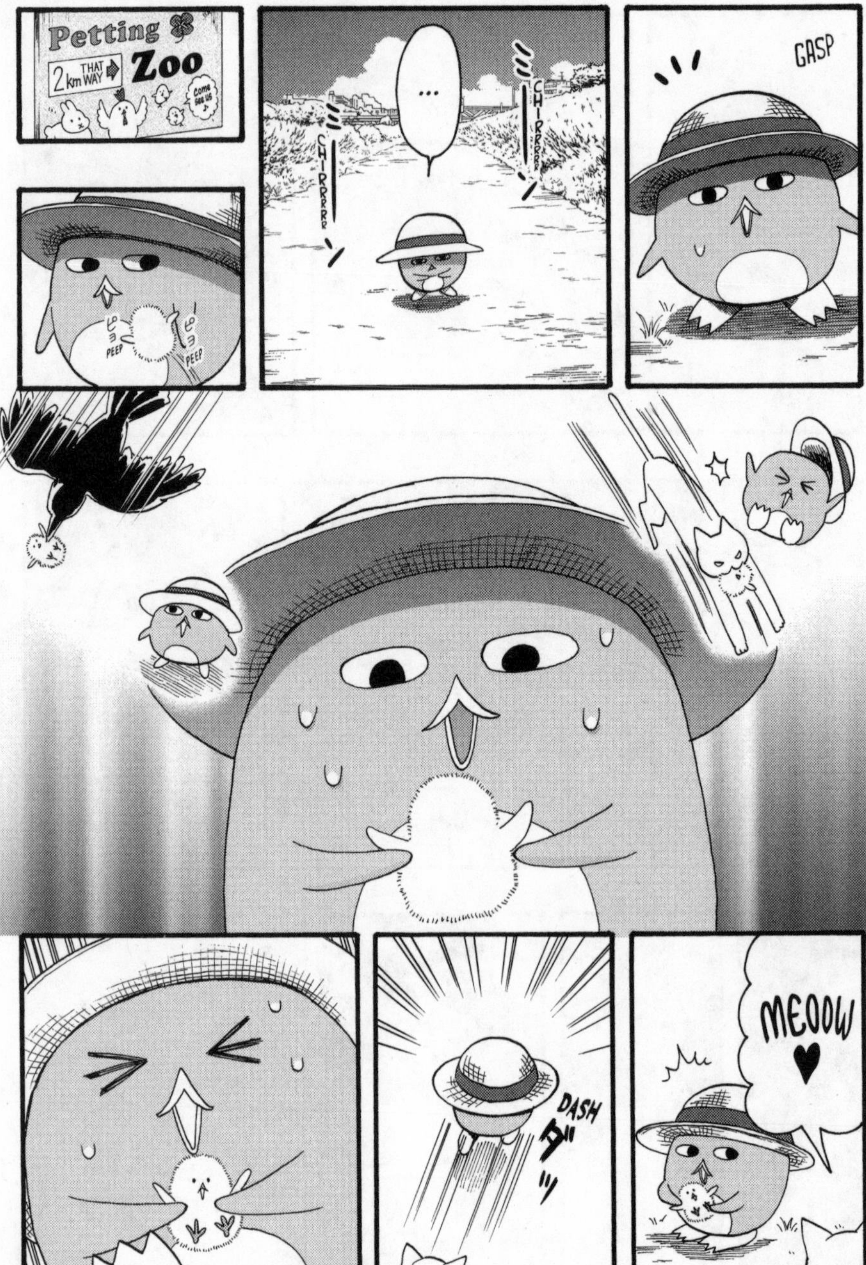
GASP
...
CHIRRRR
CHIRRRR
Petting
Zoo
2km THAT WAY
Come see us ♪
ピョ
PEEP
ピョ
PEEP
MEOOW ♥
DASH
ダッ

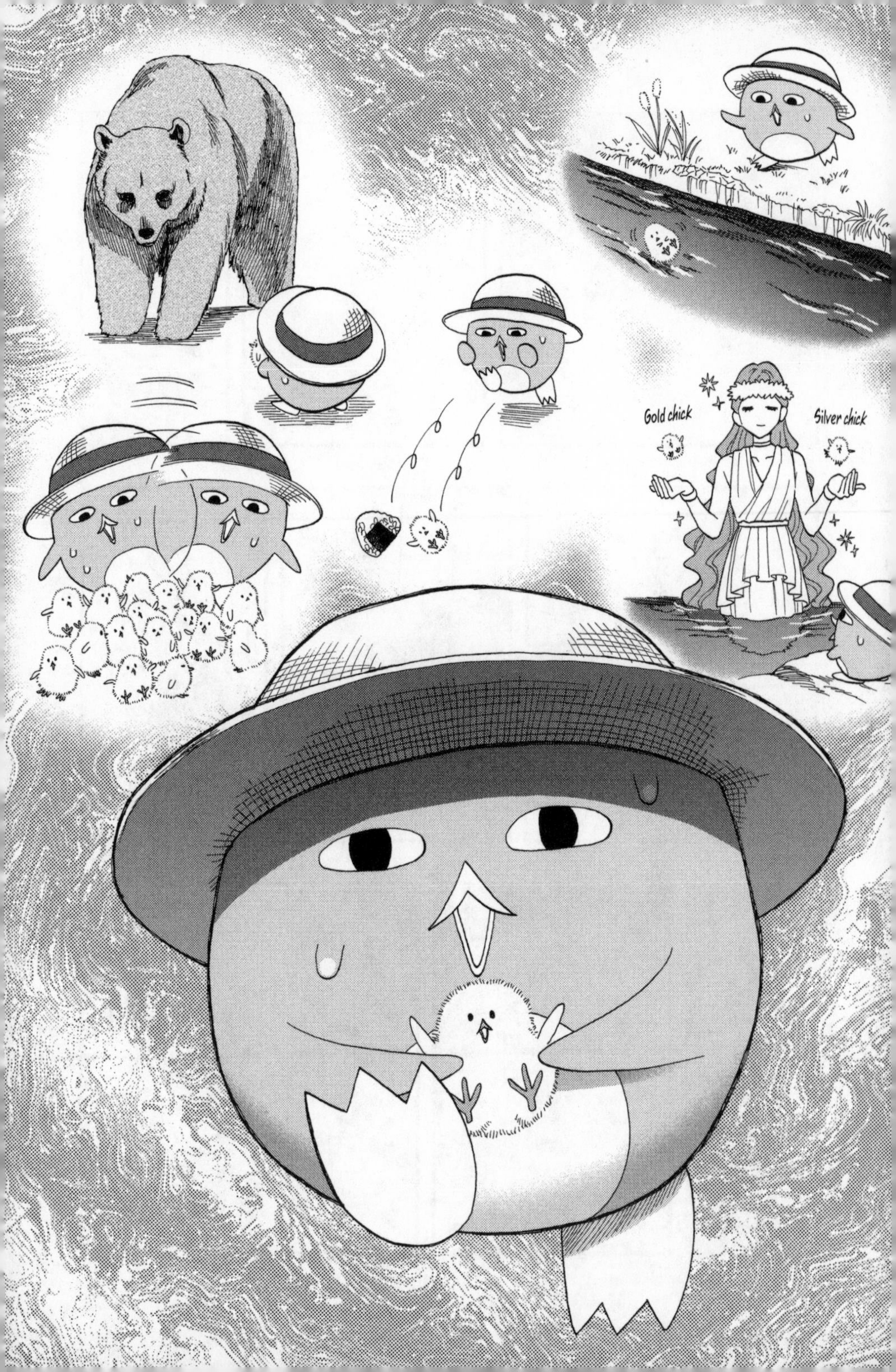
Gold chick
Silver chick

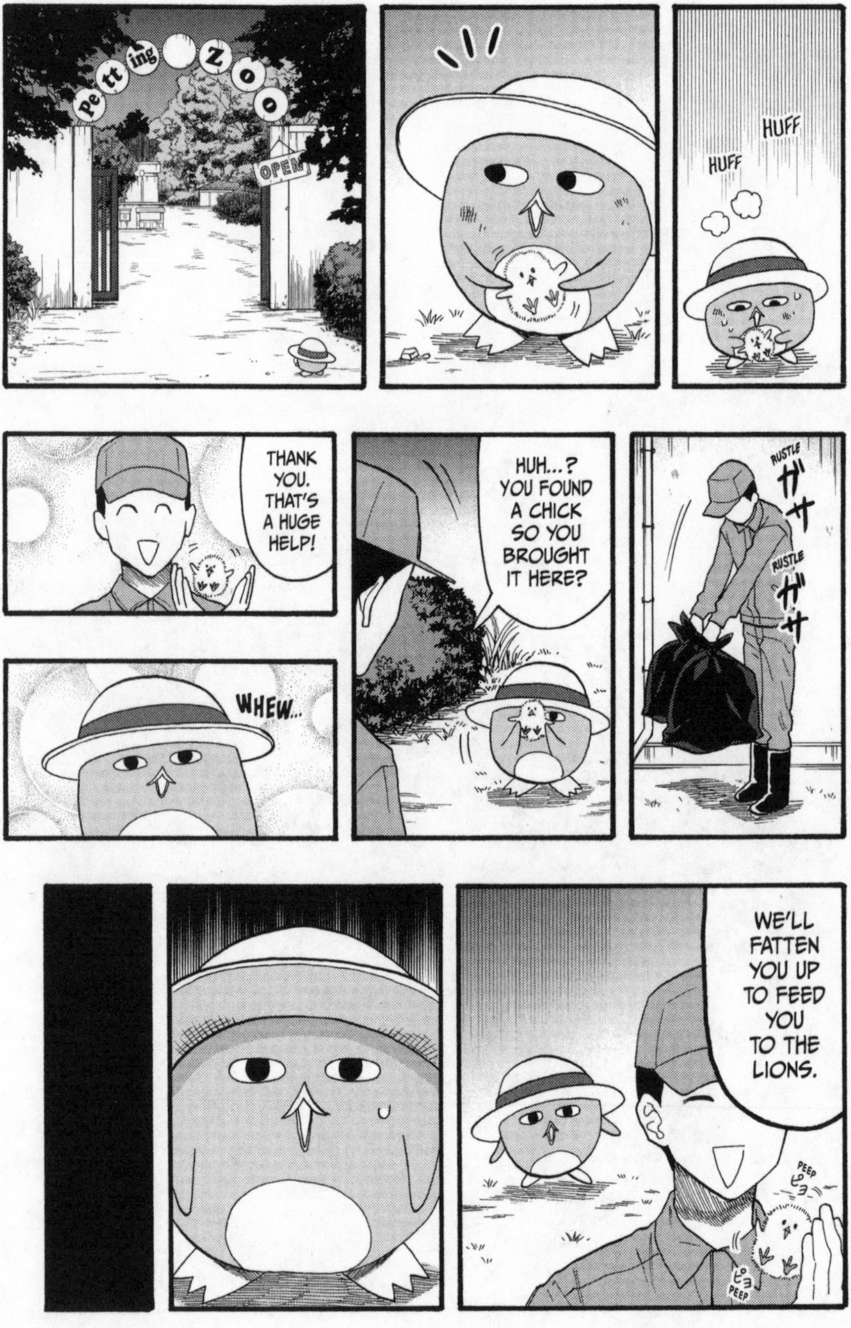
HUFF
HUFF
Petting Zoo
OPEN
RUSTLE
ガサ
RUSTLE
ガサ
HUH...? YOU FOUND A CHICK SO YOU BROUGHT IT HERE?
THANK YOU. THAT'S A HUGE HELP!
WHEW...
WE'LL FATTEN YOU UP TO FEED YOU TO THE LIONS.
PEEP
ピヨ
ピヨ
PEEP

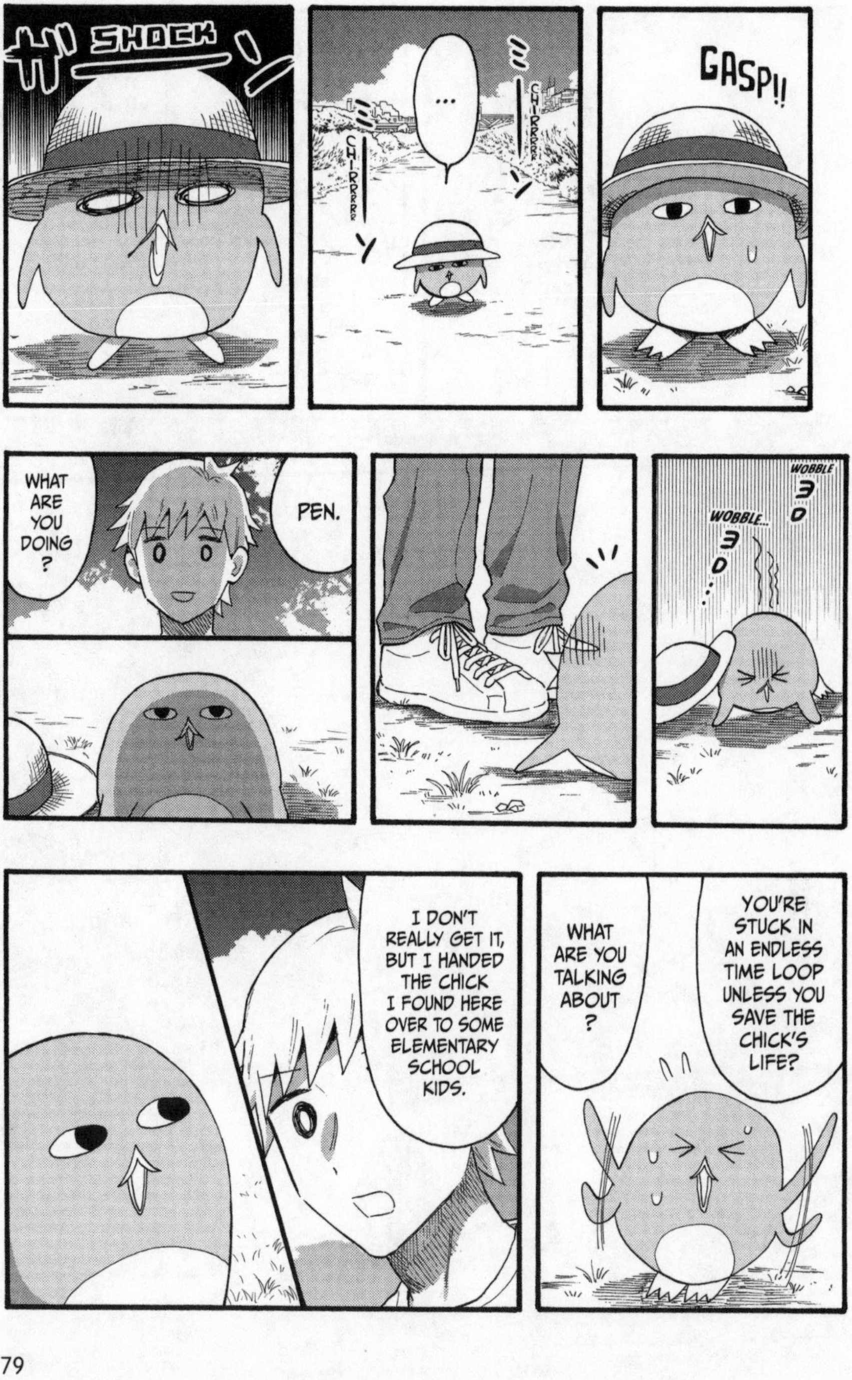
GASP!!
...
CHIRRRRR
CHIRRRRR
SHOCK
WOBBLE
WOBBLE...
PEN.
WHAT ARE YOU DOING?
YOU'RE STUCK IN AN ENDLESS TIME LOOP UNLESS YOU SAVE THE CHICK'S LIFE?
WHAT ARE YOU TALKING ABOUT?
I DON'T REALLY GET IT, BUT I HANDED THE CHICK I FOUND HERE OVER TO SOME ELEMENTARY SCHOOL KIDS.

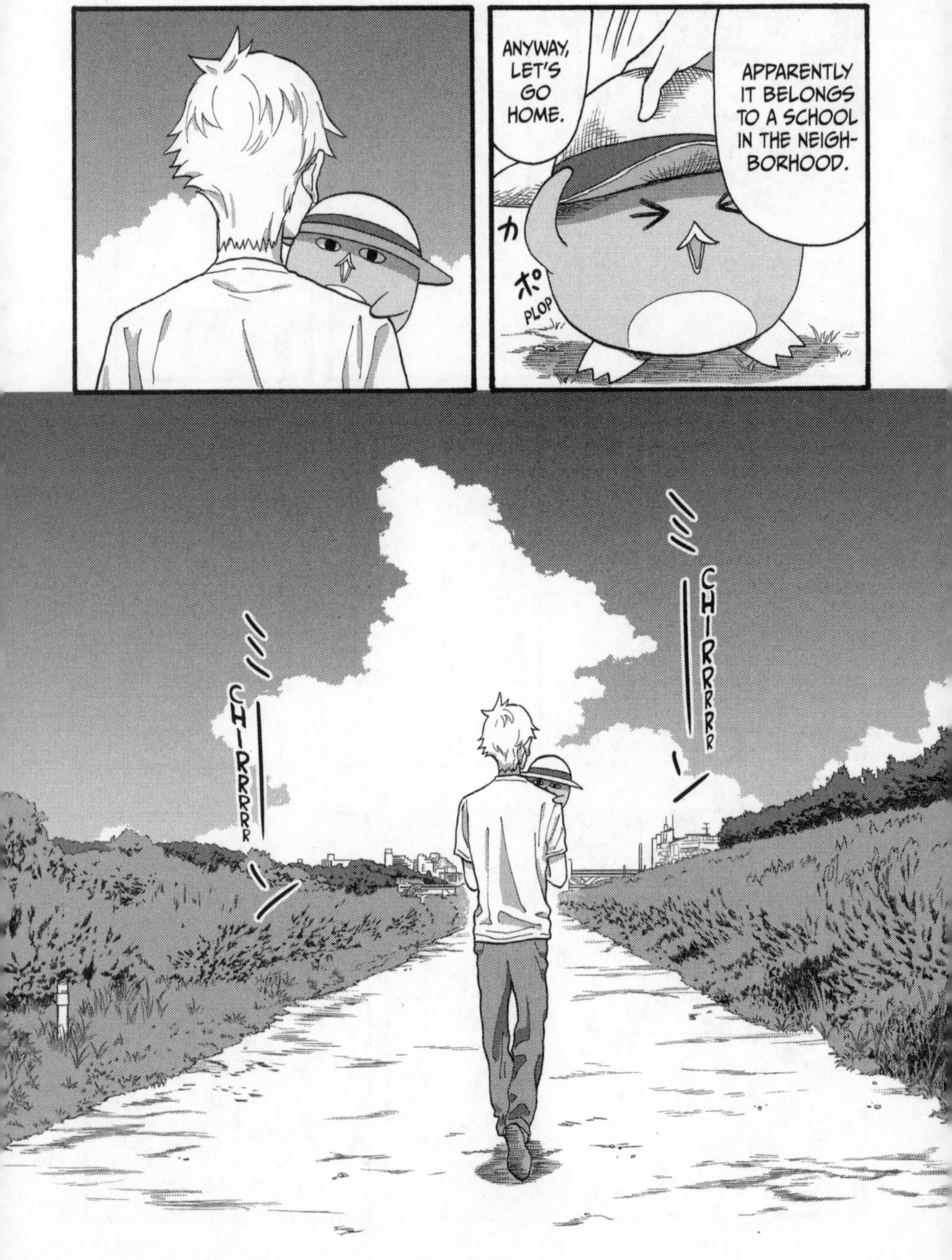
APPARENTLY IT BELONGS TO A SCHOOL IN THE NEIGH-BORHOOD.
ANYWAY, LET'S GO HOME.
カ
ポ
PLOP
CHIRRRRR
CHIRRRRR

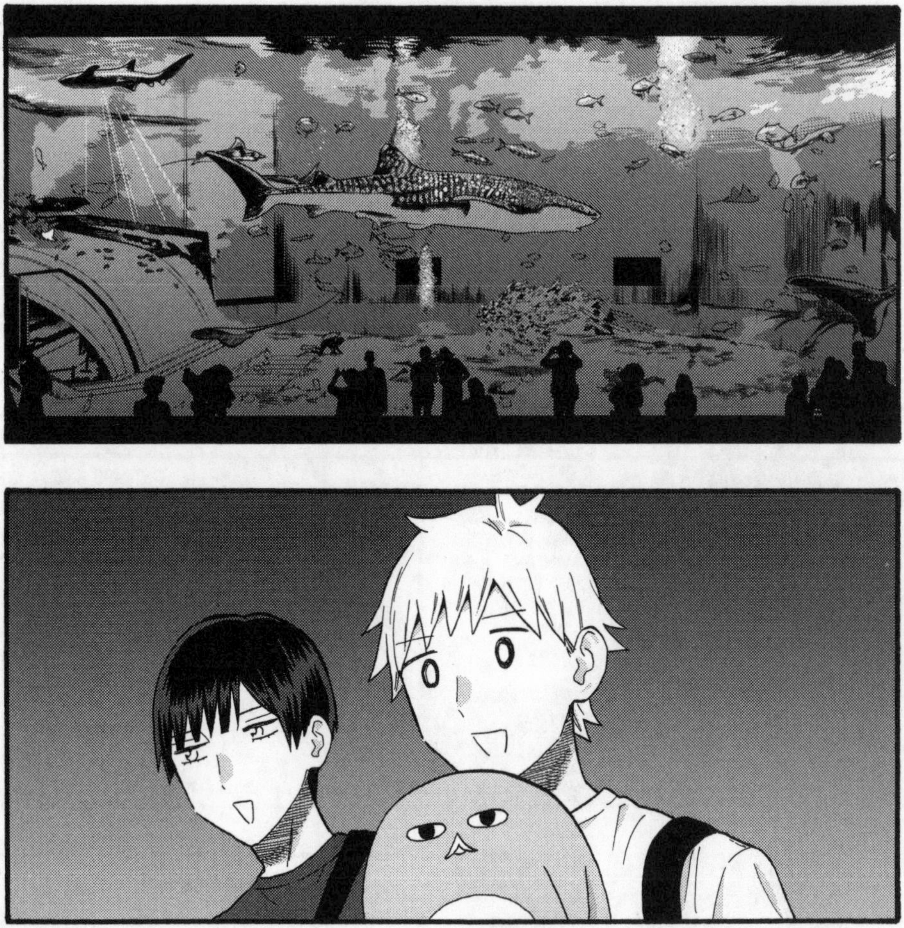

Pen 36 The Penguin Goes to an Aquarium With His Owner and Friend

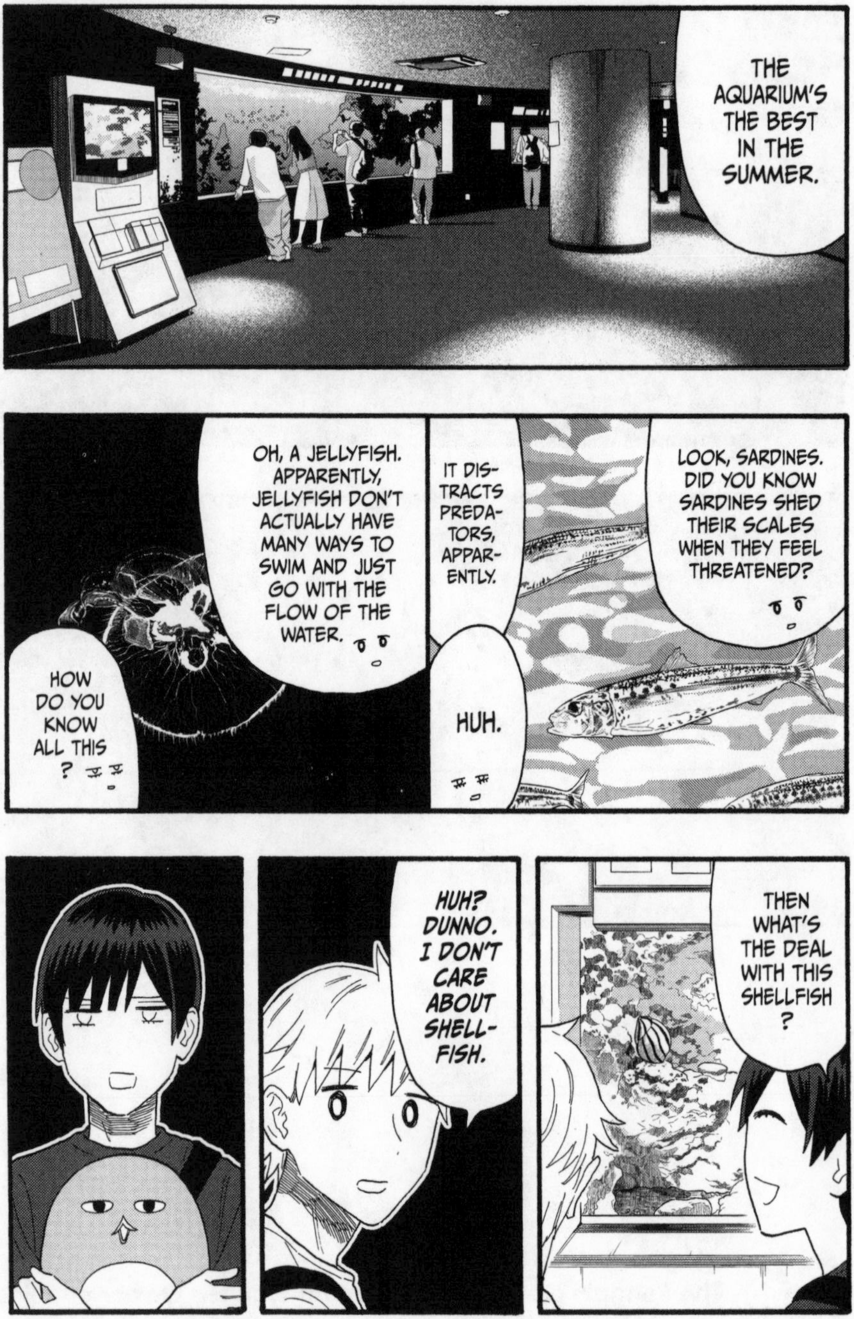
THE AQUARIUM'S THE BEST IN THE SUMMER.
LOOK, SARDINES. DID YOU KNOW SARDINES SHED THEIR SCALES WHEN THEY FEEL THREATENED?
IT DISTRACTS PREDATORS, APPARENTLY.
HUH.
OH, A JELLYFISH. APPARENTLY, JELLYFISH DON'T ACTUALLY HAVE MANY WAYS TO SWIM AND JUST GO WITH THE FLOW OF THE WATER.
HOW DO YOU KNOW ALL THIS?
THEN WHAT'S THE DEAL WITH THIS SHELLFISH?
HUH? DUNNO. I DON'T CARE ABOUT SHELLFISH.

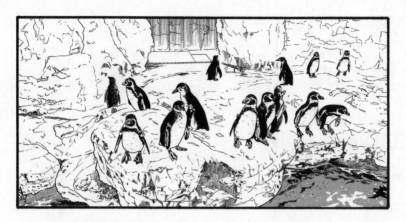

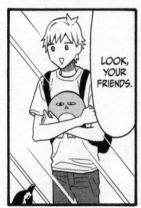

OOH, WE'RE FINALLY AT THE PENGUIN AREA.
LOOK, YOUR FRIENDS.

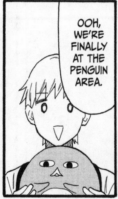

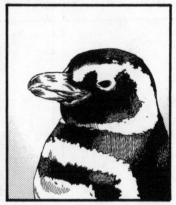

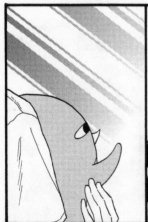

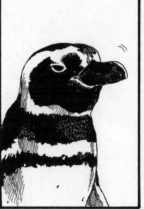

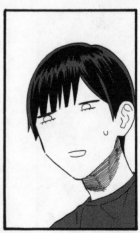

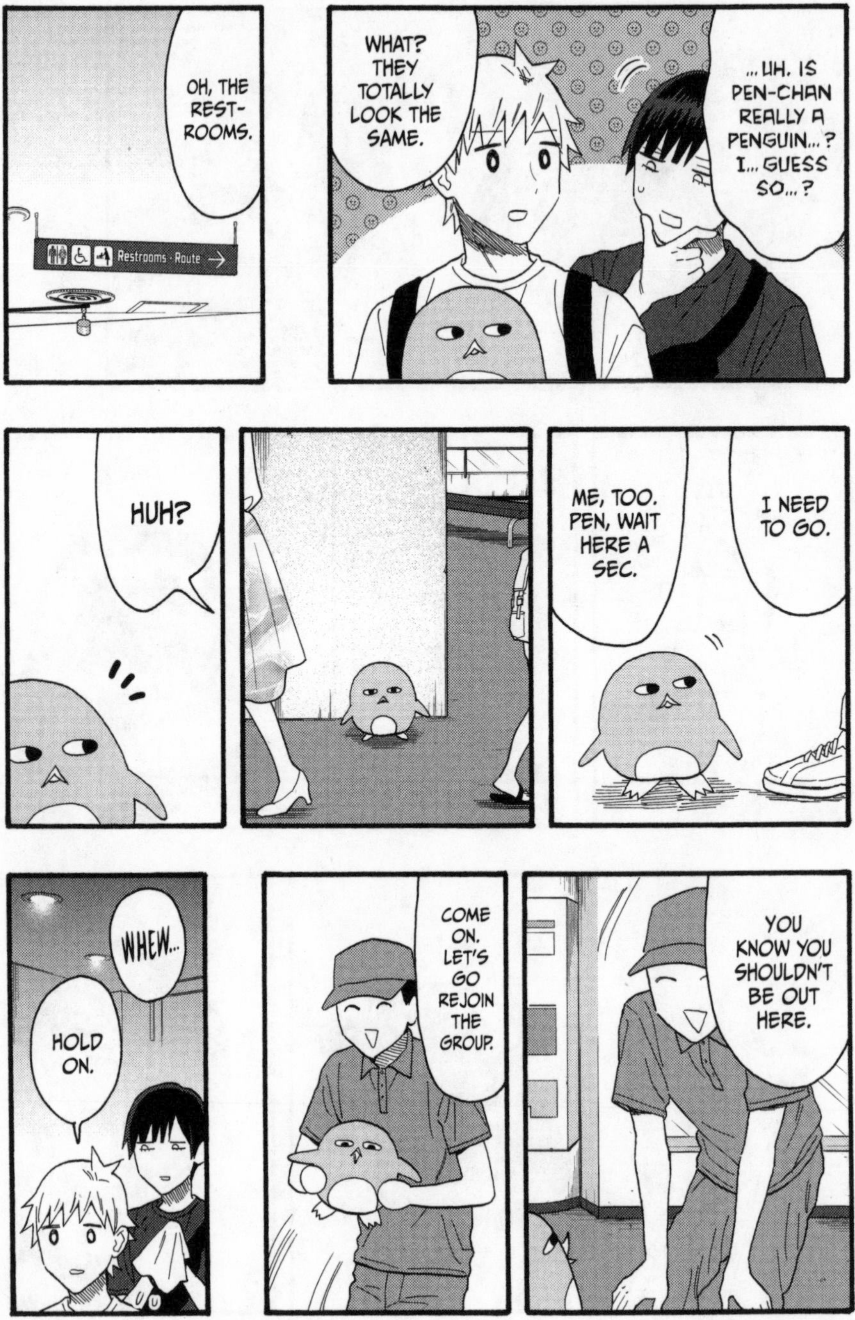
...UH. IS PEN-CHAN REALLY A PENGUIN...? I... GUESS SO...?
WHAT? THEY TOTALLY LOOK THE SAME.
OH, THE REST-ROOMS.
Restrooms · Route
I NEED TO GO.
ME, TOO. PEN, WAIT HERE A SEC.
HUH?
YOU KNOW YOU SHOULDN'T BE OUT HERE.
COME ON. LET'S GO REJOIN THE GROUP.
WHEW...
HOLD ON.

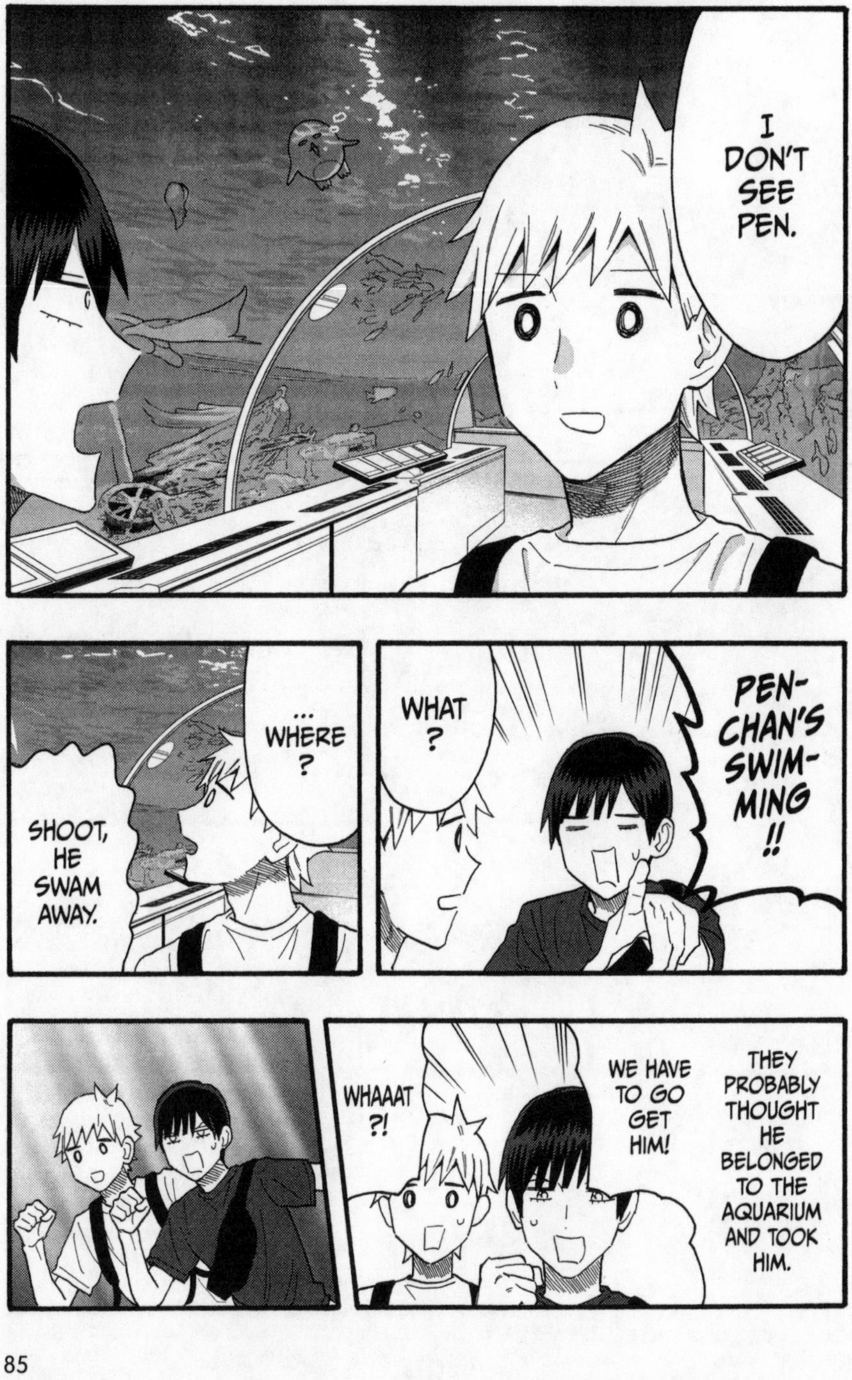
I DON'T SEE PEN.
PEN-CHAN'S SWIMMING!!
WHAT?
...WHERE?
SHOOT, HE SWAM AWAY.
THEY PROBABLY THOUGHT HE BELONGED TO THE AQUARIUM AND TOOK HIM.
WE HAVE TO GO GET HIM!
WHAAAT?!

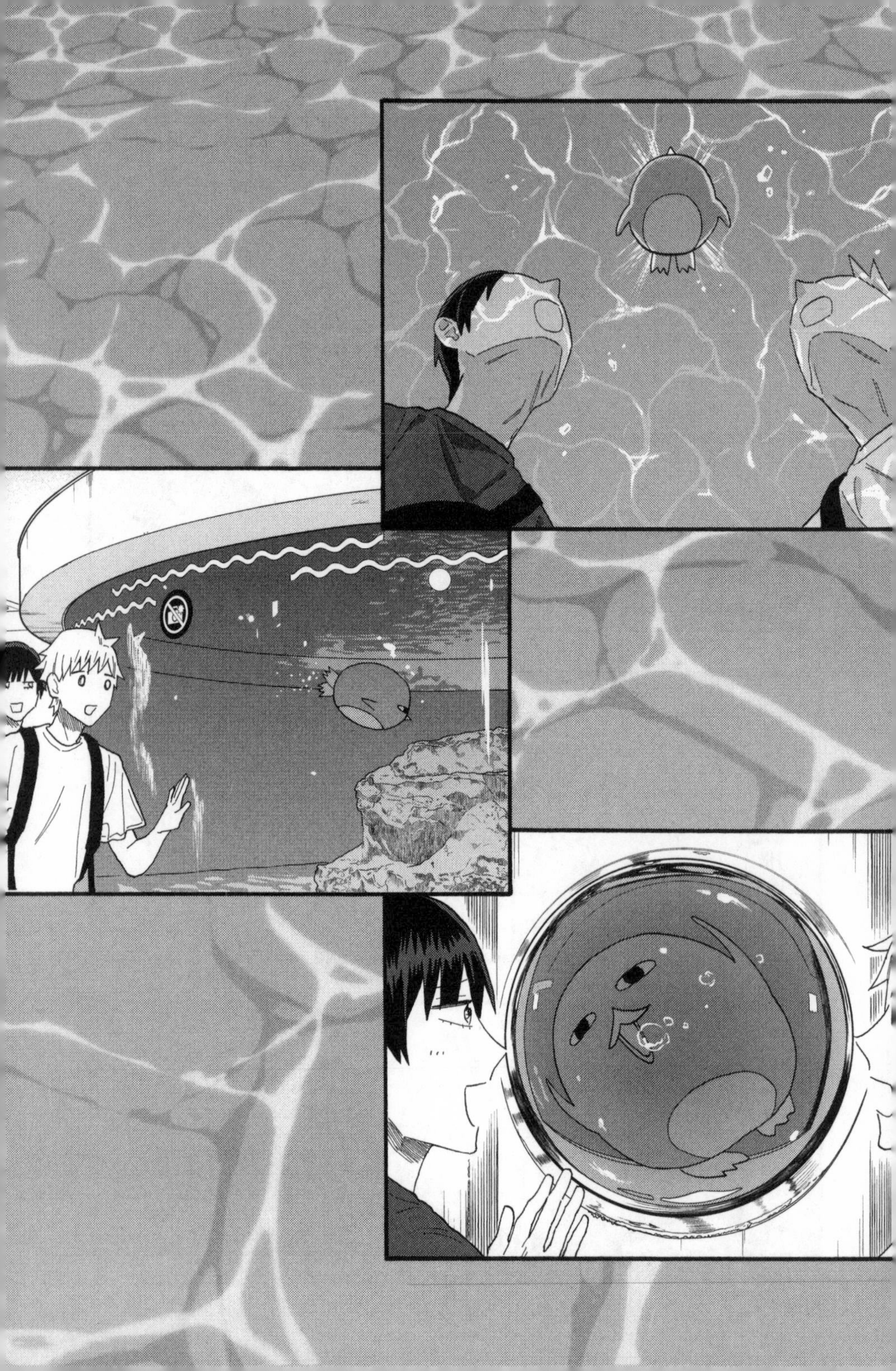

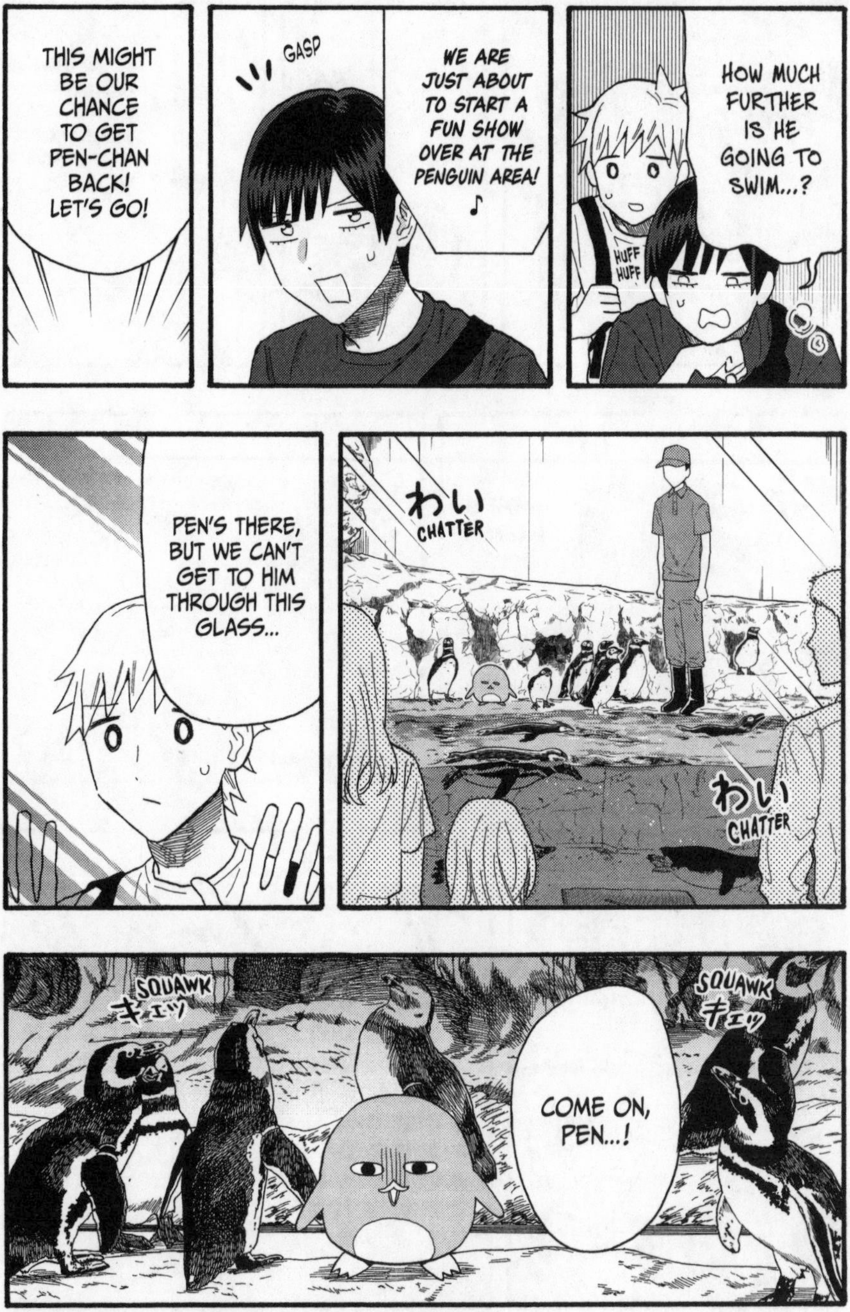
HOW MUCH FURTHER IS HE GOING TO SWIM...?
HUFF HUFF
WE ARE JUST ABOUT TO START A FUN SHOW OVER AT THE PENGUIN AREA! ♪
GASP
THIS MIGHT BE OUR CHANCE TO GET PEN-CHAN BACK! LET'S GO!
わい CHATTER
わい CHATTER
PEN'S THERE, BUT WE CAN'T GET TO HIM THROUGH THIS GLASS...
SQUAWK キェッ
COME ON, PEN...!
SQUAWK キェッ

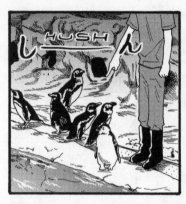

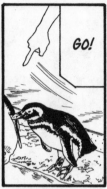

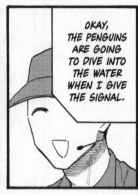

OKAY, THE PENGUINS ARE GOING TO DIVE INTO THE WATER WHEN I GIVE THE SIGNAL.
GO!
HUSH
NO GOOD. I GUESS THEY'RE NOT TRAINED VERY WELL, AND IT'S KIND OF A MESS.
NONE OF THEM LOOK EVEN CLOSE TO DIVING...
HMM, WHAT'S WRONG, GUYS?
...
LET'S TRY THAT AGAIN!
GO!
SPLOSH
PEN!!
HE DIDN'T HAVE THE HEART TO IGNORE THE GUY!
PEN-CHAN, YOU'RE TOO NICE!

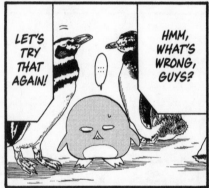

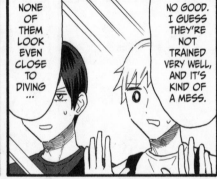

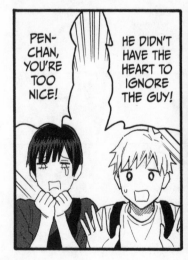

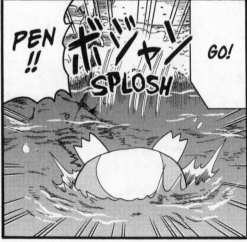

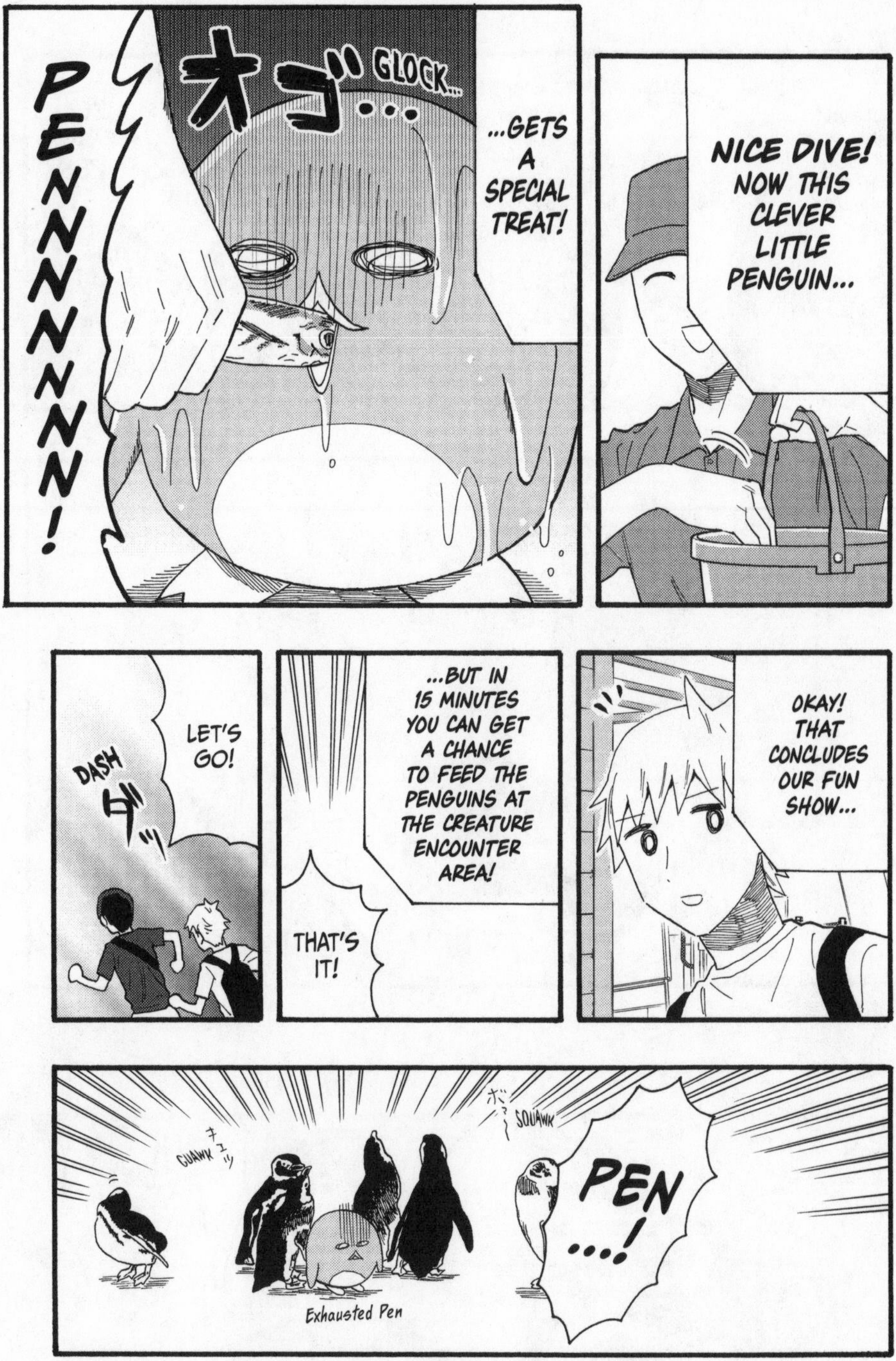
NICE DIVE! NOW THIS CLEVER LITTLE PENGUIN...
...GETS A SPECIAL TREAT!
オゴ...
GLOCK...
PENNNNNNN!
OKAY! THAT CONCLUDES OUR FUN SHOW...
...BUT IN 15 MINUTES YOU CAN GET A CHANCE TO FEED THE PENGUINS AT THE CREATURE ENCOUNTER AREA!
THAT'S IT!
LET'S GO!
ダッ
DASH
PEN ...!
SQUAWK
GUAWK
Exhausted Pen

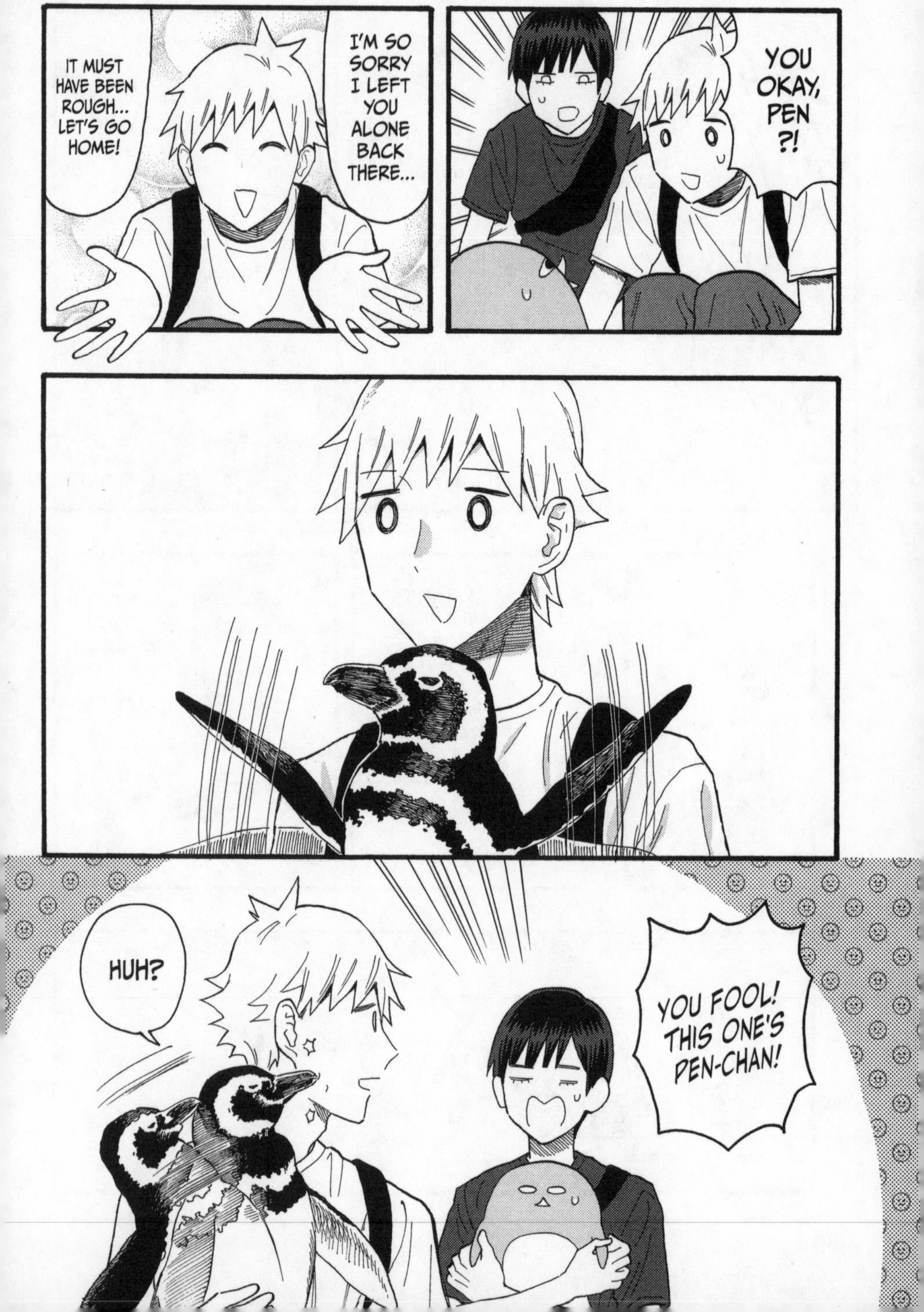
YOU OKAY, PEN?!
I'M SO SORRY I LEFT YOU ALONE BACK THERE...
IT MUST HAVE BEEN ROUGH... LET'S GO HOME!
YOU FOOL! THIS ONE'S PEN-CHAN!
HUH?

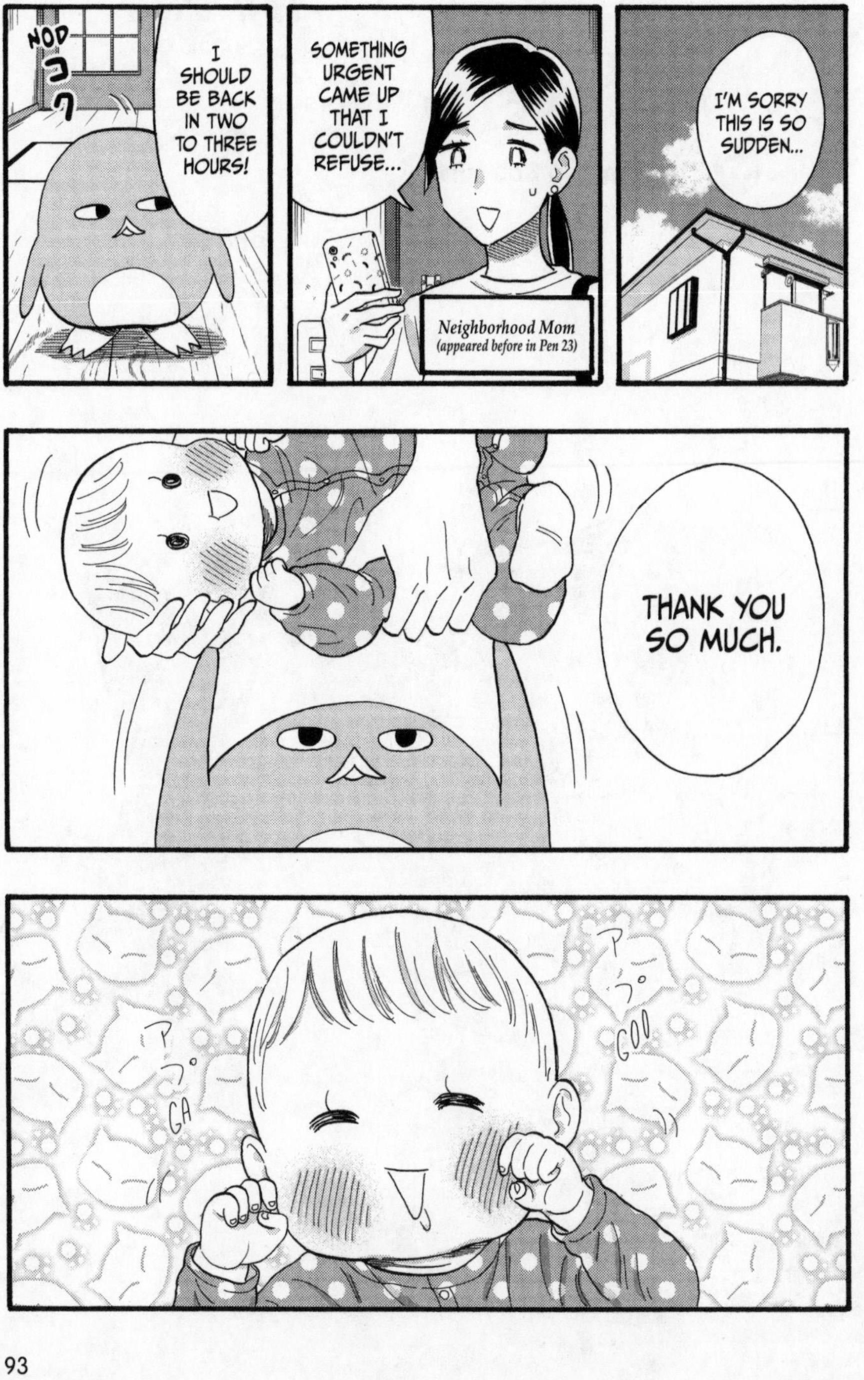
I'M SORRY THIS IS SO SUDDEN...
SOMETHING URGENT CAME UP THAT I COULDN'T REFUSE...
Neighborhood Mom
(appeared before in Pen 23)
I SHOULD BE BACK IN TWO TO THREE HOURS!
NOD
コク
THANK YOU SO MUCH.
アプ
GOO
アプ
GA

Pen 37 The Penguin Babysits

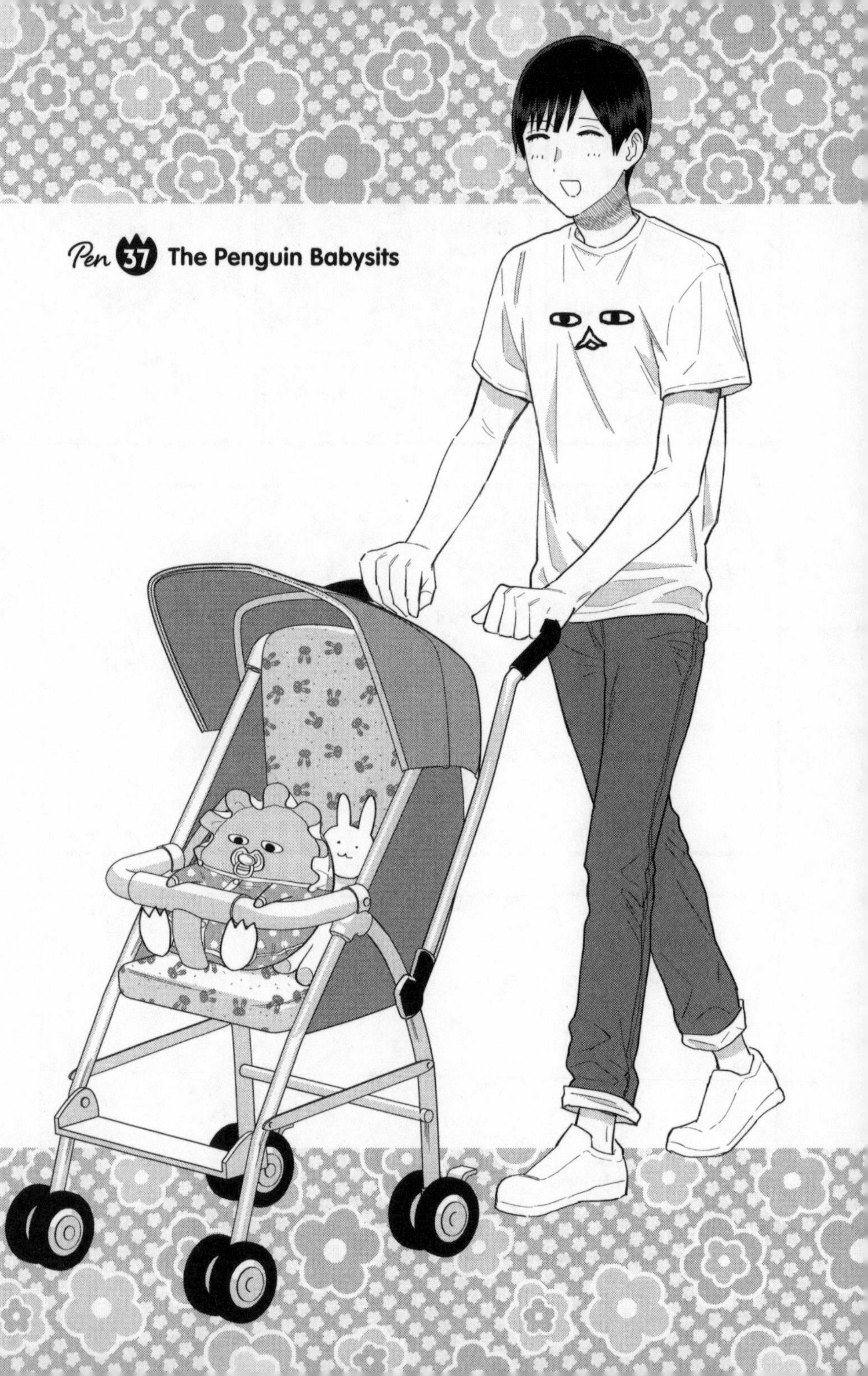

SCRUNCH

COO

GAA

Tasty Breakfast

RECIPE

RRIP

EASY YUMMY CIPES

NNH...

SNATCH

TUMP
TUMP
TUMP

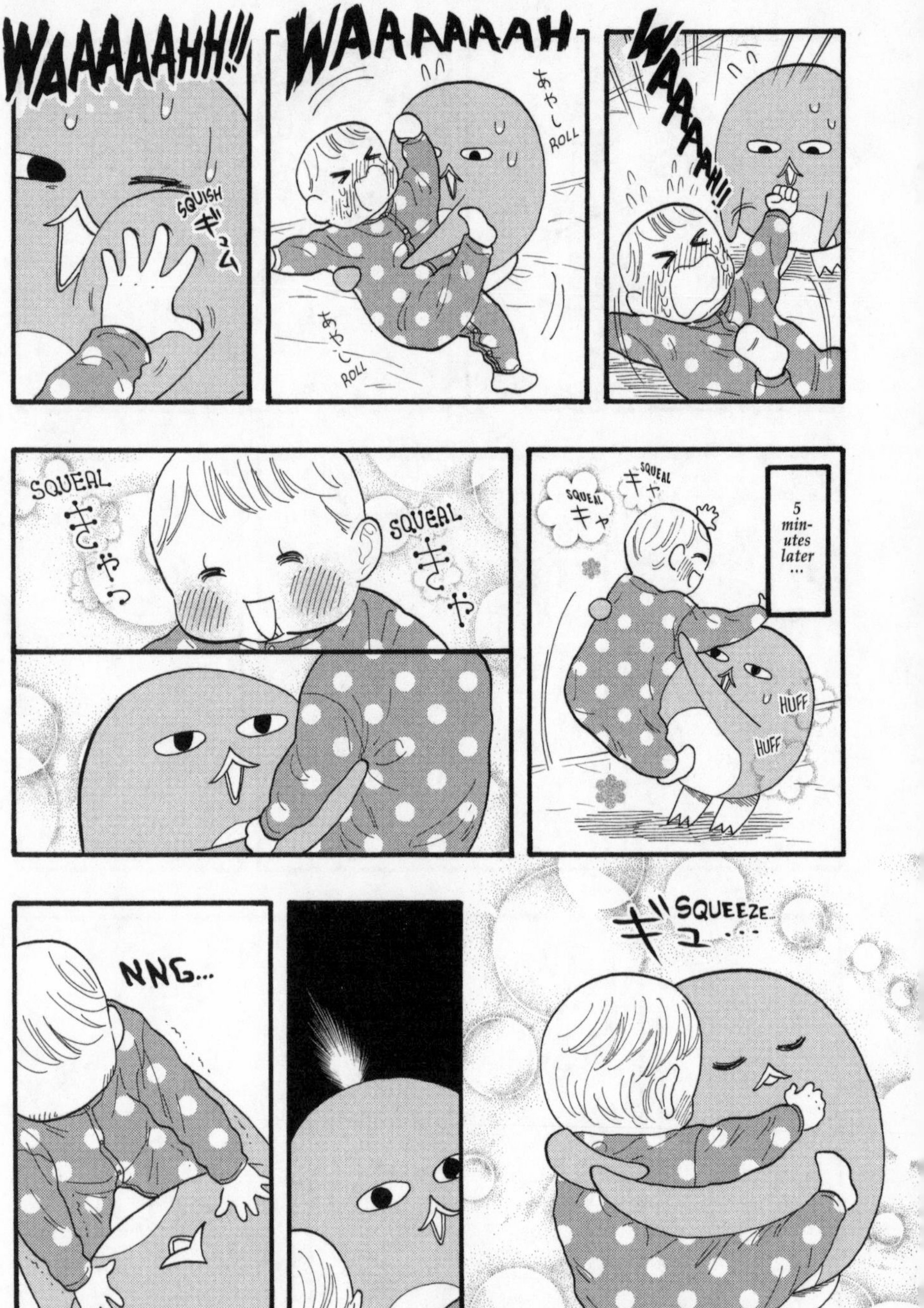
WAAAAAAH!!
WAAAAAAAH
あやし
ROLL
あやし
ROLL
WAAAAAHH!!
SQUISH
ギュム
5 minutes later...
SQUEAL
キャ
SQUEAL
キャ
HUFF
HUFF
SQUEAL
きゃっ
SQUEAL
きゃ
ギュ
SQUEEZE...
NNG...

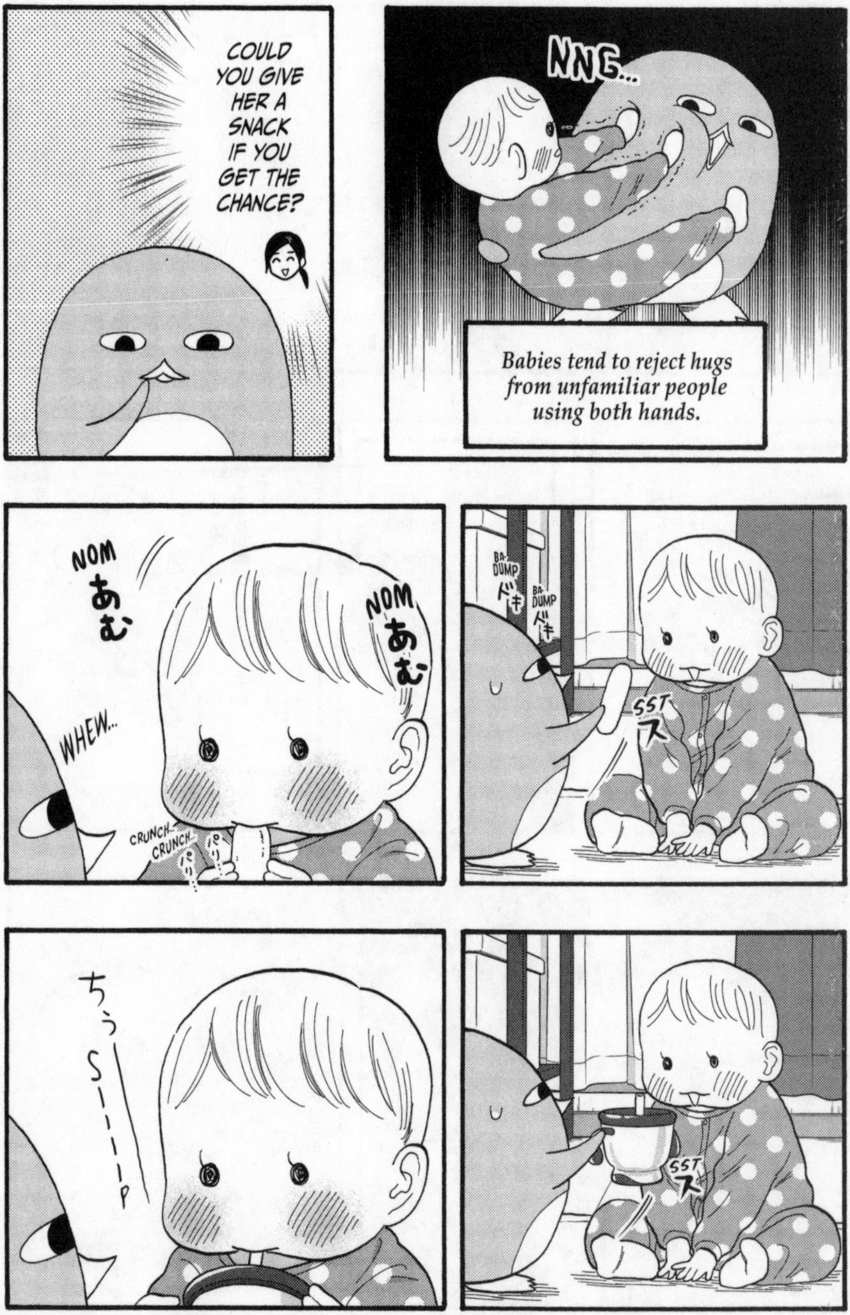
NNG...
Babies tend to reject hugs from unfamiliar people using both hands.
COULD YOU GIVE HER A SNACK IF YOU GET THE CHANCE?
BA-DUMP ドキ
BA-DUMP ドキ
SST ス
NOM あむ
NOM あむ
WHEW...
CRUNCH... CRUNCH... パリ... パリ...
SST ス
ちぅ
S----IP

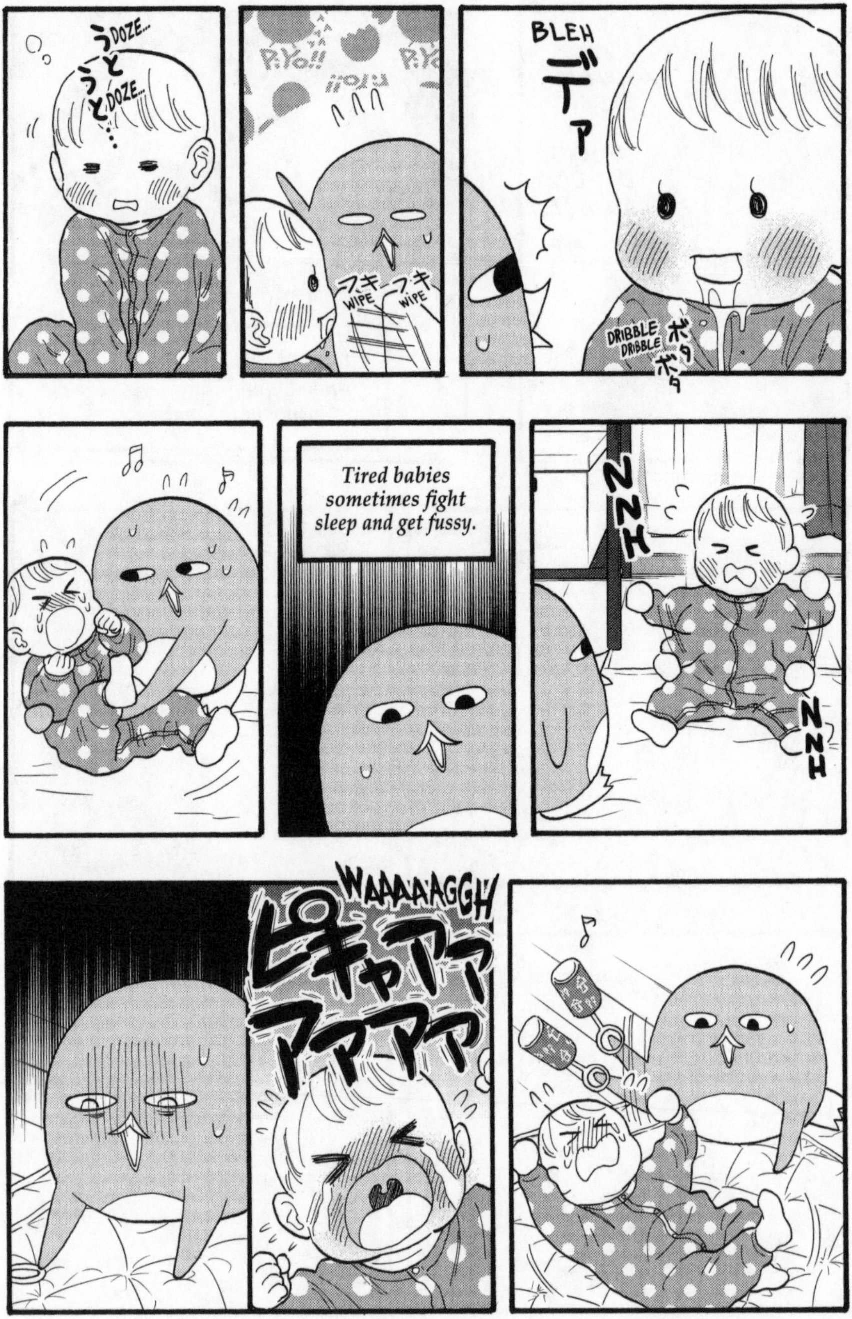
BLEH
デア
DRIBBLE DRIBBLE
ボタボタ
PiYo!!
PiYo!!
フキ WIPE
フキ WIPE
うとうと
DOZE...
DOZE...
NNH
NNH
Tired babies sometimes fight sleep and get fussy.
WAAAAAGGH
ピキャアアアアア

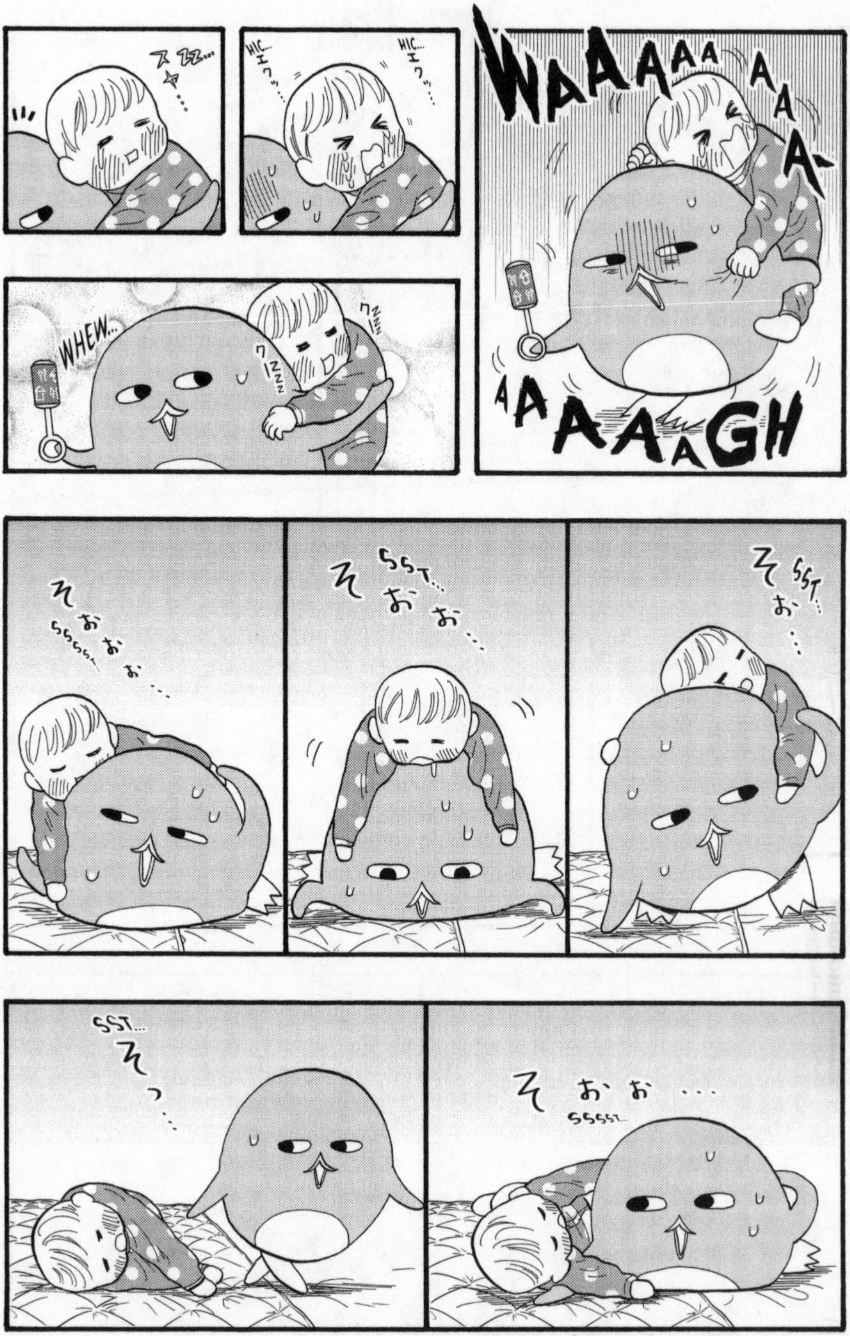

WAAAAAAAAA-
AAAAAGH
HIC... エクッ…
HIC... エクッ…
ZZZ... スヤ…
WHEW...
SST... そお…
SSST... そおお…
そおおお…
SSSST... そおお…
SST... そっ…

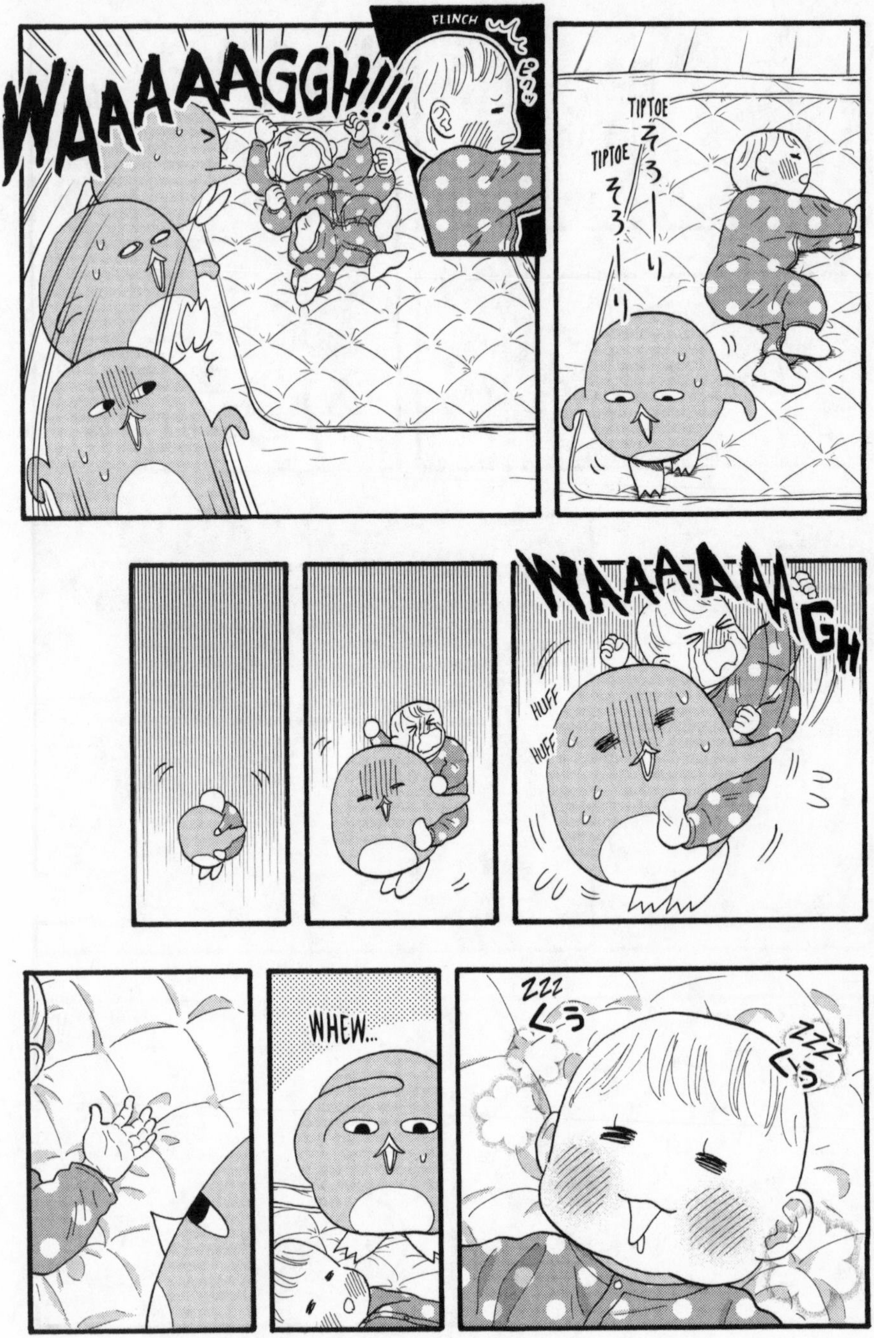
TIPTOE
そろーり
TIPTOE
そろーり
FLINCH
ビクッ
WAAAAAGGH!!!
WAAAAAAGH
HUFF
HUFF
ZZZ
くう
ZZZ
くぅ
WHEW...

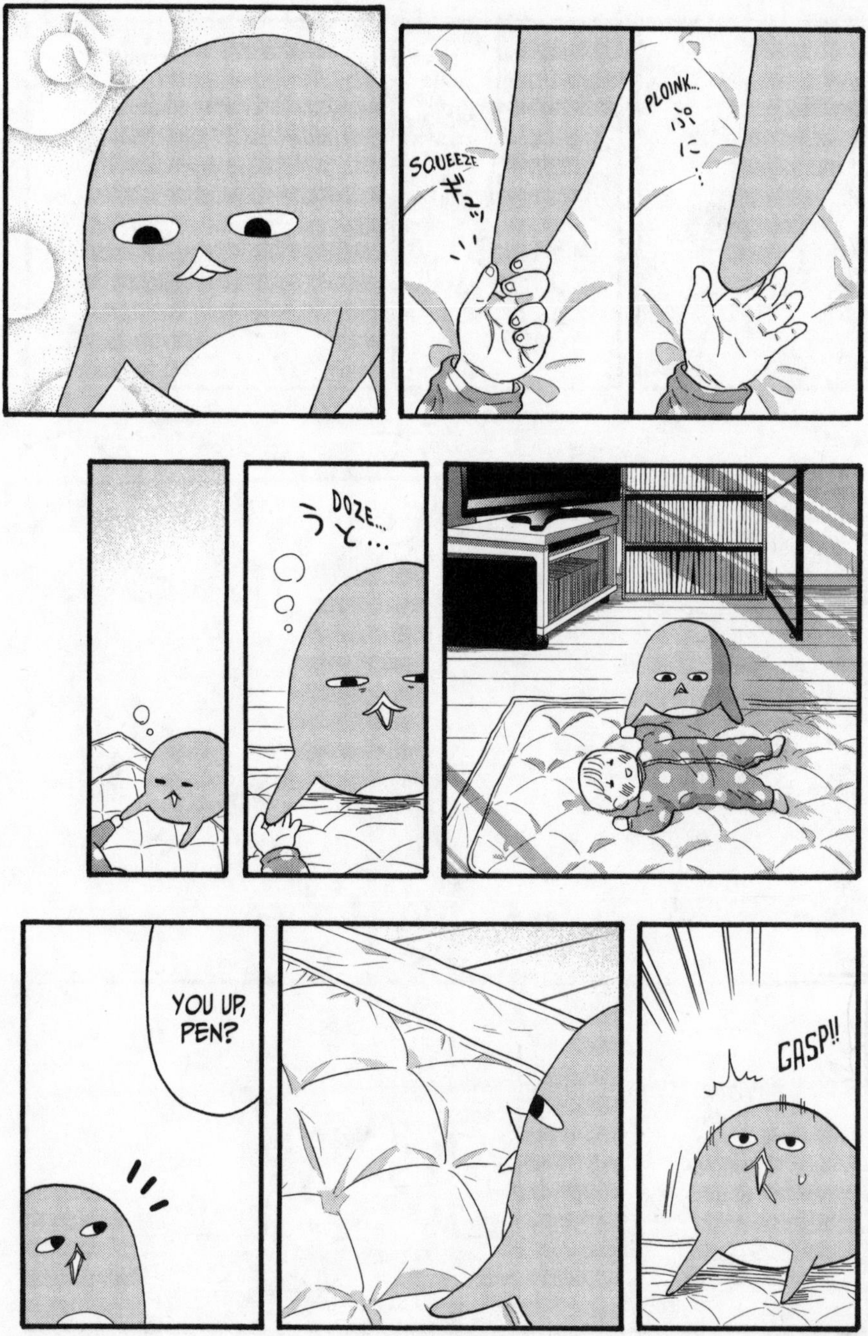
PLOINK...
ぷに...
SQUEEZE
ギュッ
DOZE...
うと...
GASP!!
YOU UP, PEN?

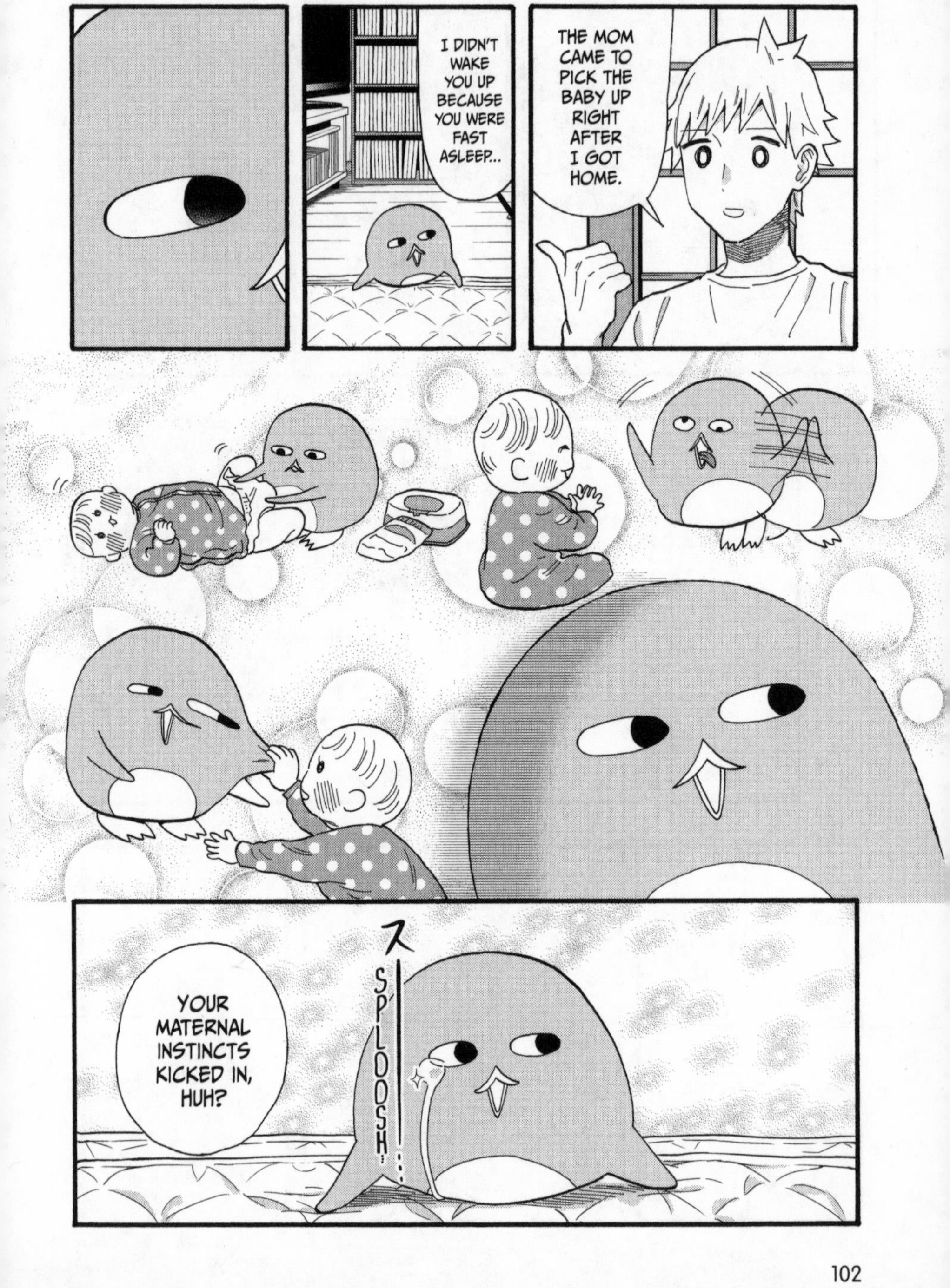
THE MOM CAME TO PICK THE BABY UP RIGHT AFTER I GOT HOME.
I DIDN'T WAKE YOU UP BECAUSE YOU WERE FAST ASLEEP...
ス SPLOOSH...
YOUR MATERNAL INSTINCTS KICKED IN, HUH?

This always happens with babies:
They never eat the baby food that
took the most time to make.

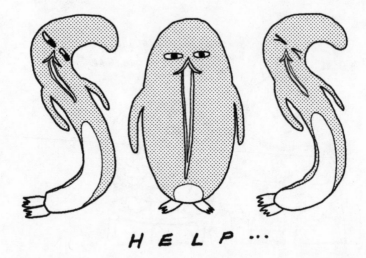

H E L P ...

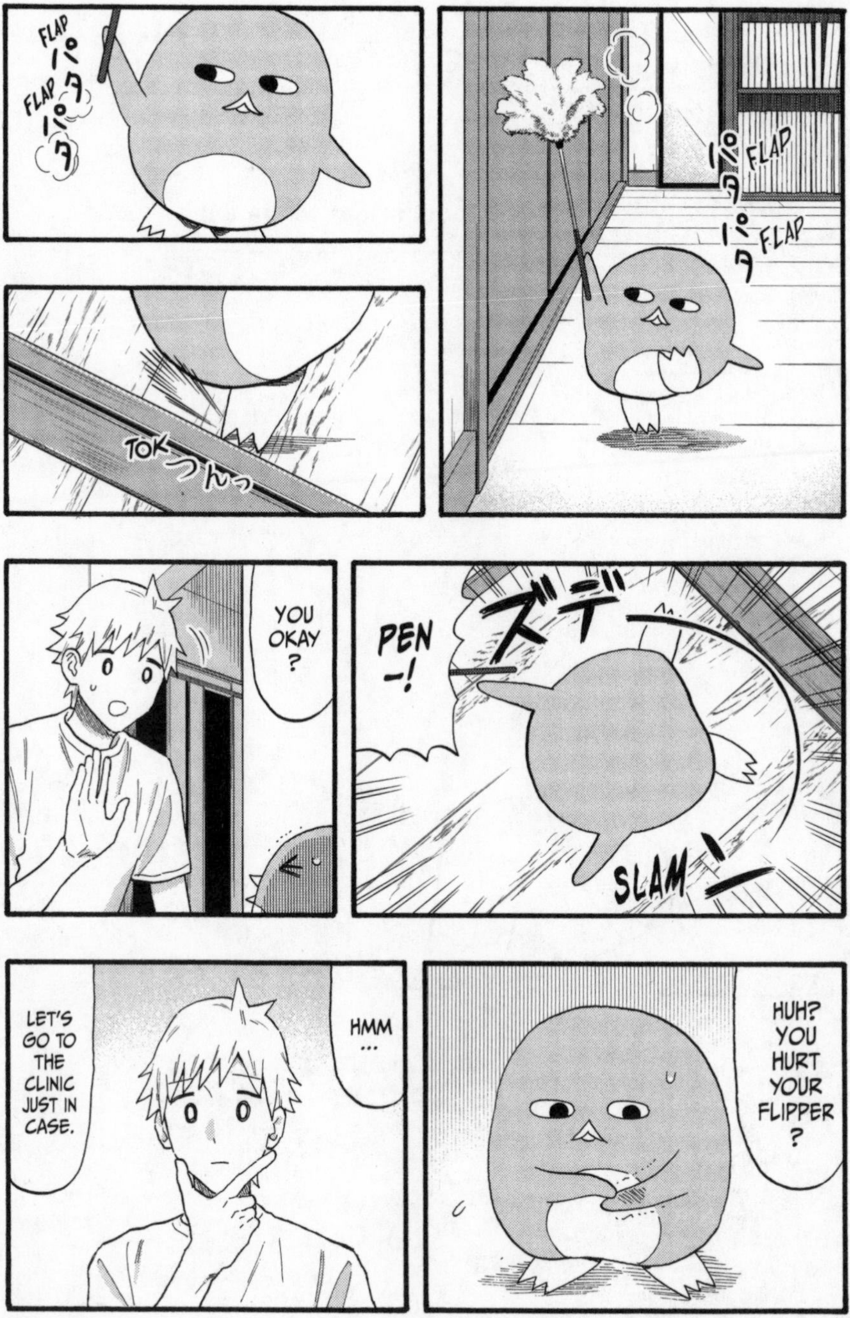

パタ FLAP
パタ FLAP
FLAP パタ
FLAP パタ
TOK つんっ
ズデー
PEN—!
SLAM
YOU OKAY?
HUH? YOU HURT YOUR FLIPPER?
HMM...
LET'S GO TO THE CLINIC JUST IN CASE.

Pen 38 The Penguin Goes to the Vet

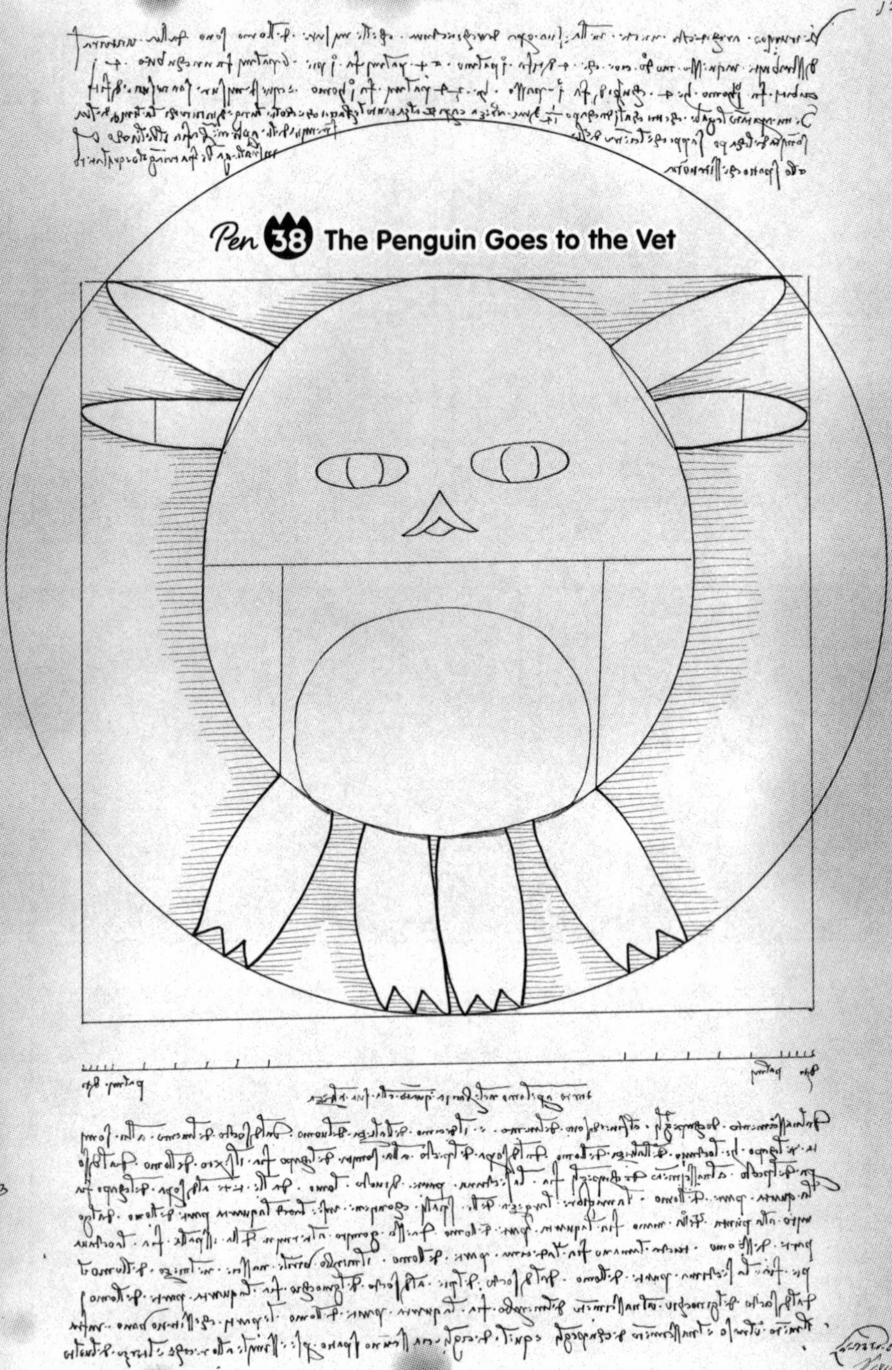

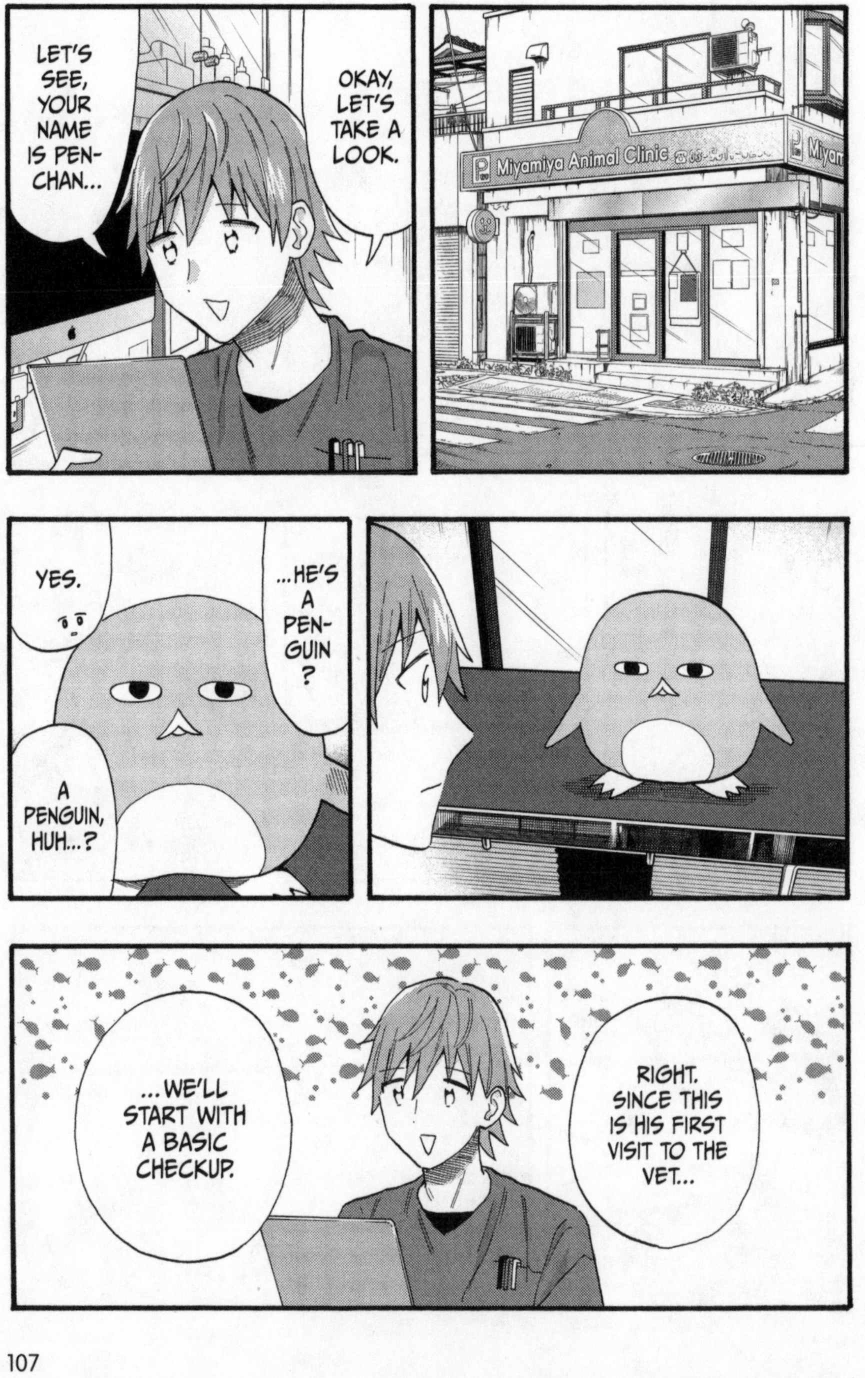
Miyamiya Animal Clinic
OKAY, LET'S TAKE A LOOK.
LET'S SEE, YOUR NAME IS PEN-CHAN...
...HE'S A PENGUIN?
YES.
A PENGUIN, HUH...?
RIGHT. SINCE THIS IS HIS FIRST VISIT TO THE VET...
...WE'LL START WITH A BASIC CHECKUP.

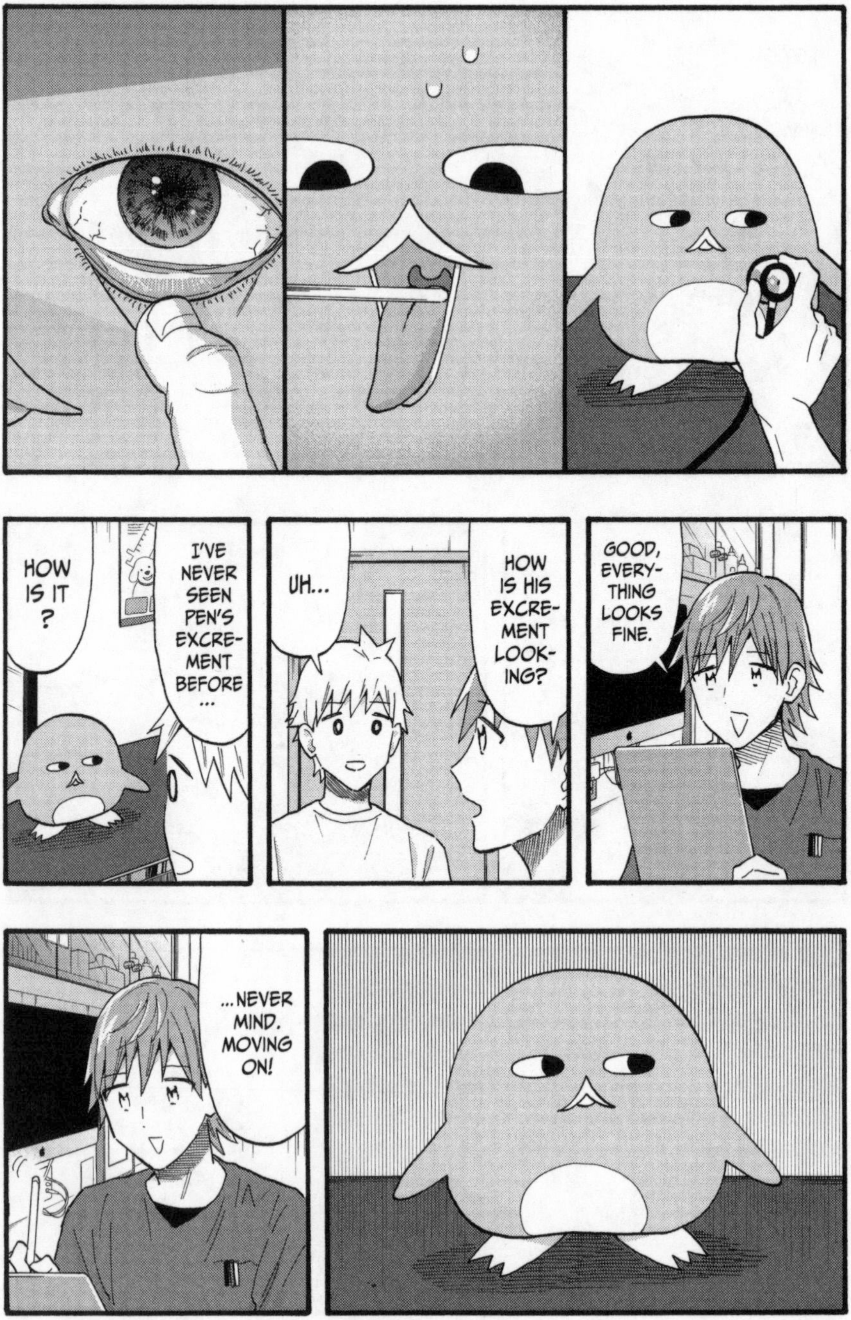
GOOD, EVERYTHING LOOKS FINE.
HOW IS HIS EXCREMENT LOOKING?
UH...
I'VE NEVER SEEN PEN'S EXCREMENT BEFORE ...
HOW IS IT ?
...NEVER MIND. MOVING ON!

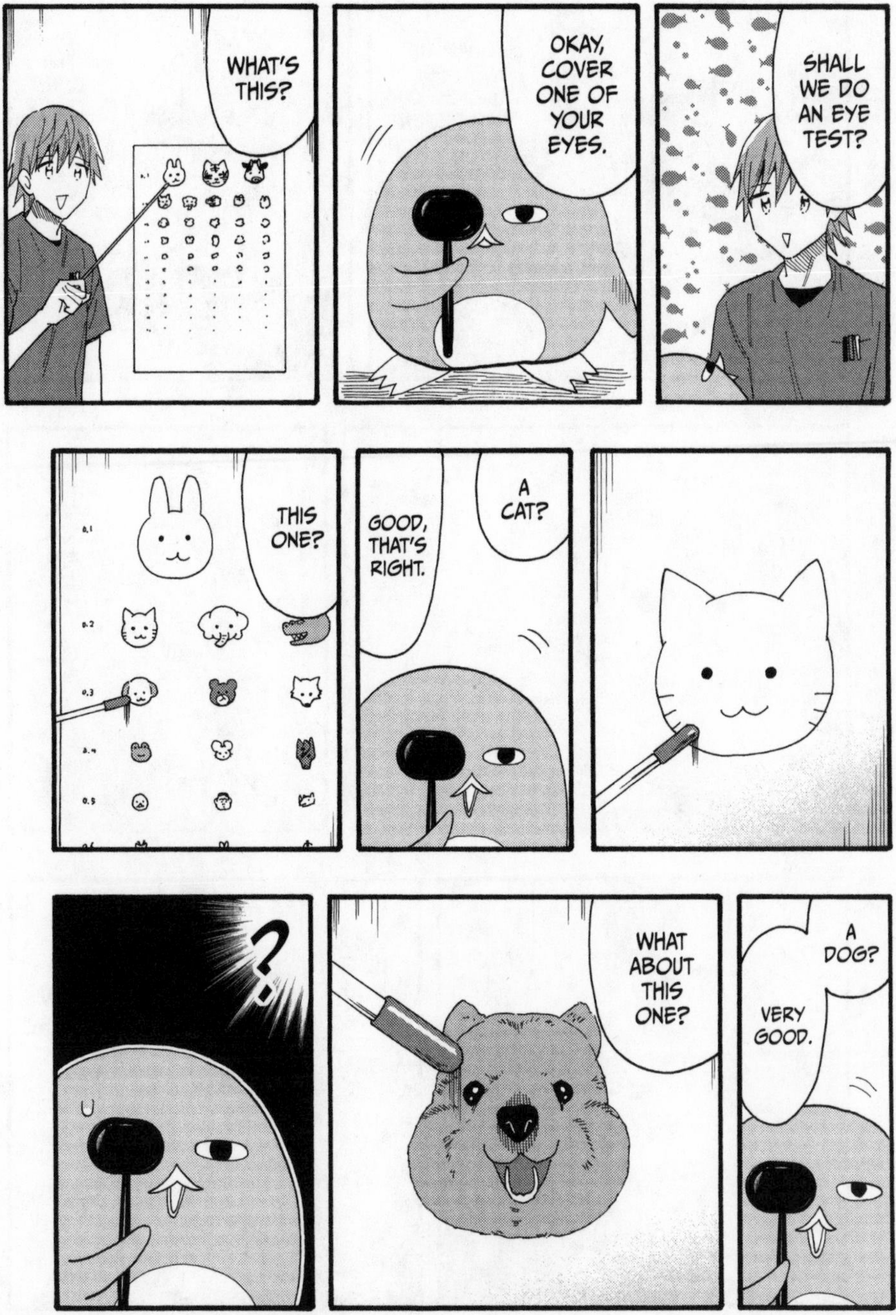
SHALL WE DO AN EYE TEST?
OKAY, COVER ONE OF YOUR EYES.
WHAT'S THIS?
A CAT?
GOOD, THAT'S RIGHT.
THIS ONE?
A DOG?
VERY GOOD.
WHAT ABOUT THIS ONE?
?

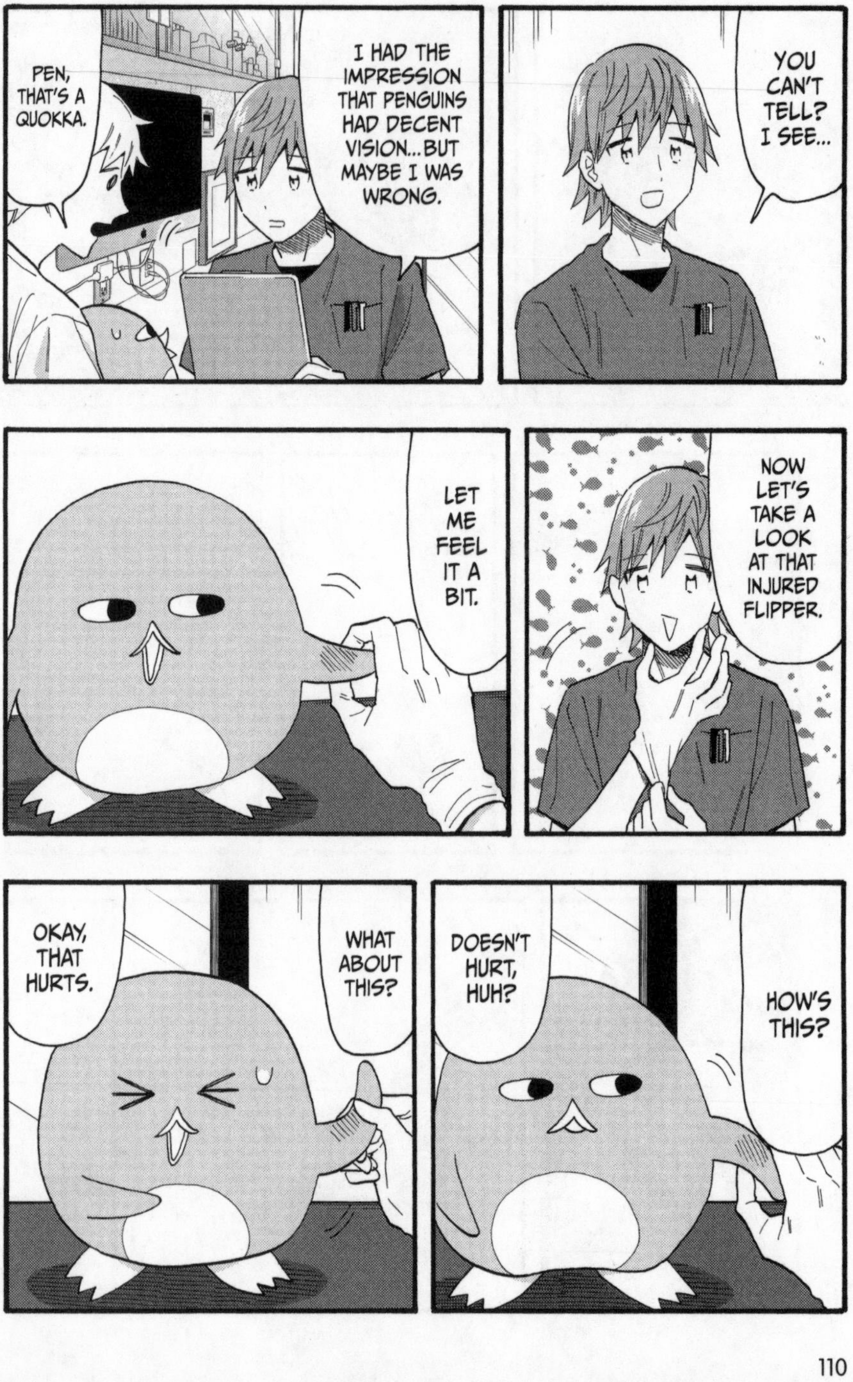
YOU CAN'T TELL? I SEE...
I HAD THE IMPRESSION THAT PENGUINS HAD DECENT VISION...BUT MAYBE I WAS WRONG.
PEN, THAT'S A QUOKKA.
NOW LET'S TAKE A LOOK AT THAT INJURED FLIPPER.
LET ME FEEL IT A BIT.
HOW'S THIS?
DOESN'T HURT, HUH?
WHAT ABOUT THIS?
OKAY, THAT HURTS.

ザッ
FWIP
THEN HOW'S THIS?
ザッ
FWIP
AND THIS?
ザッ
FWIP
...
OKAY, I SEE.
I DON'T THINK IT'S SERIOUS BUT SHALL WE TAKE AN X-RAY JUST IN CASE?
ウィ WHIRRRRRRRRRRRRRRRRR ン
LET'S SEE...

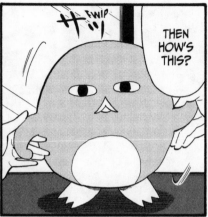

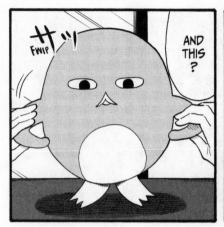

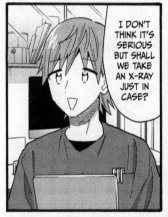

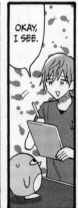

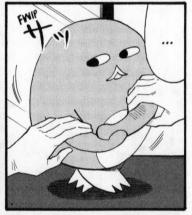

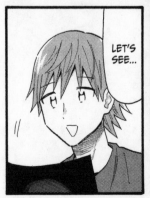

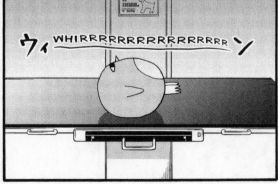

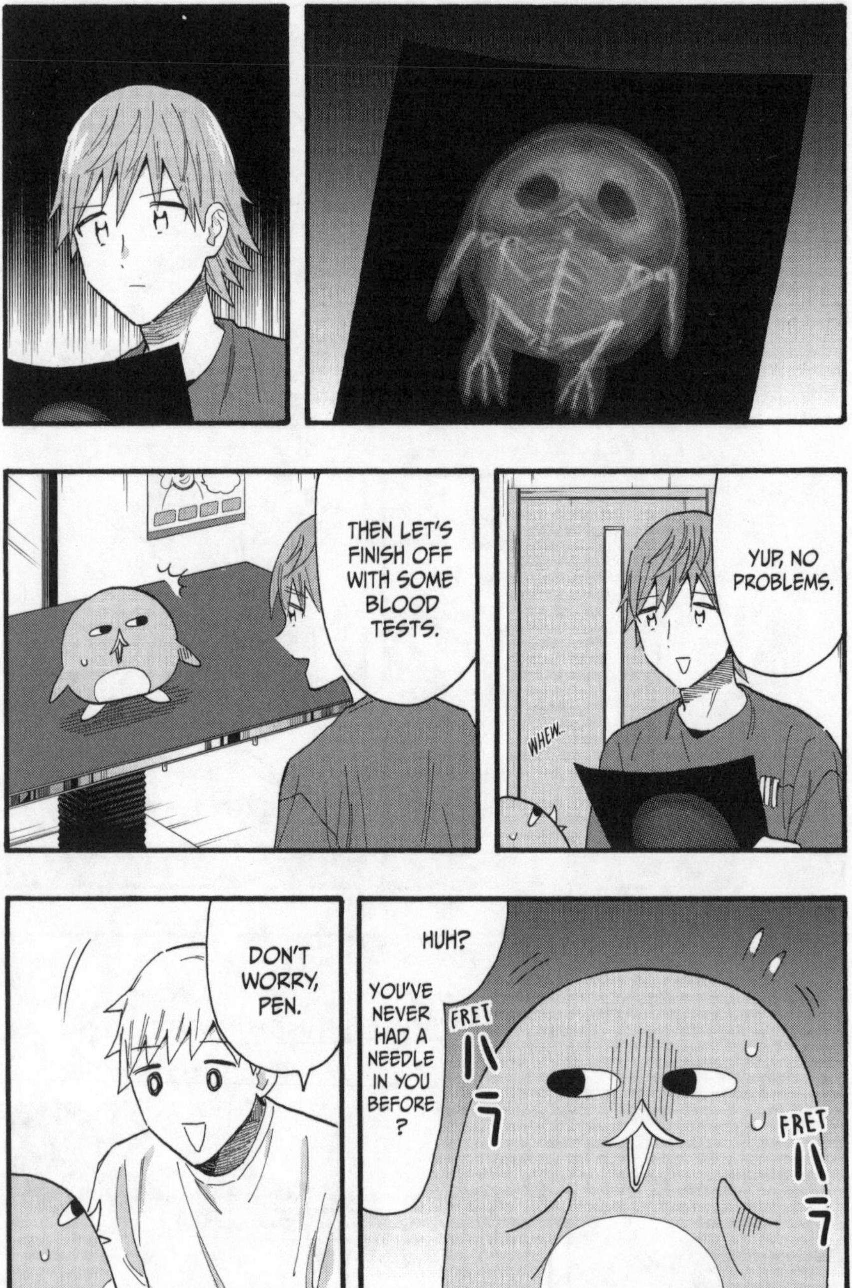
YUP, NO PROBLEMS.
WHEW...
THEN LET'S FINISH OFF WITH SOME BLOOD TESTS.
HUH?
YOU'VE NEVER HAD A NEEDLE IN YOU BEFORE?
FRET
ハラ
FRET
ハラ
DON'T WORRY, PEN.

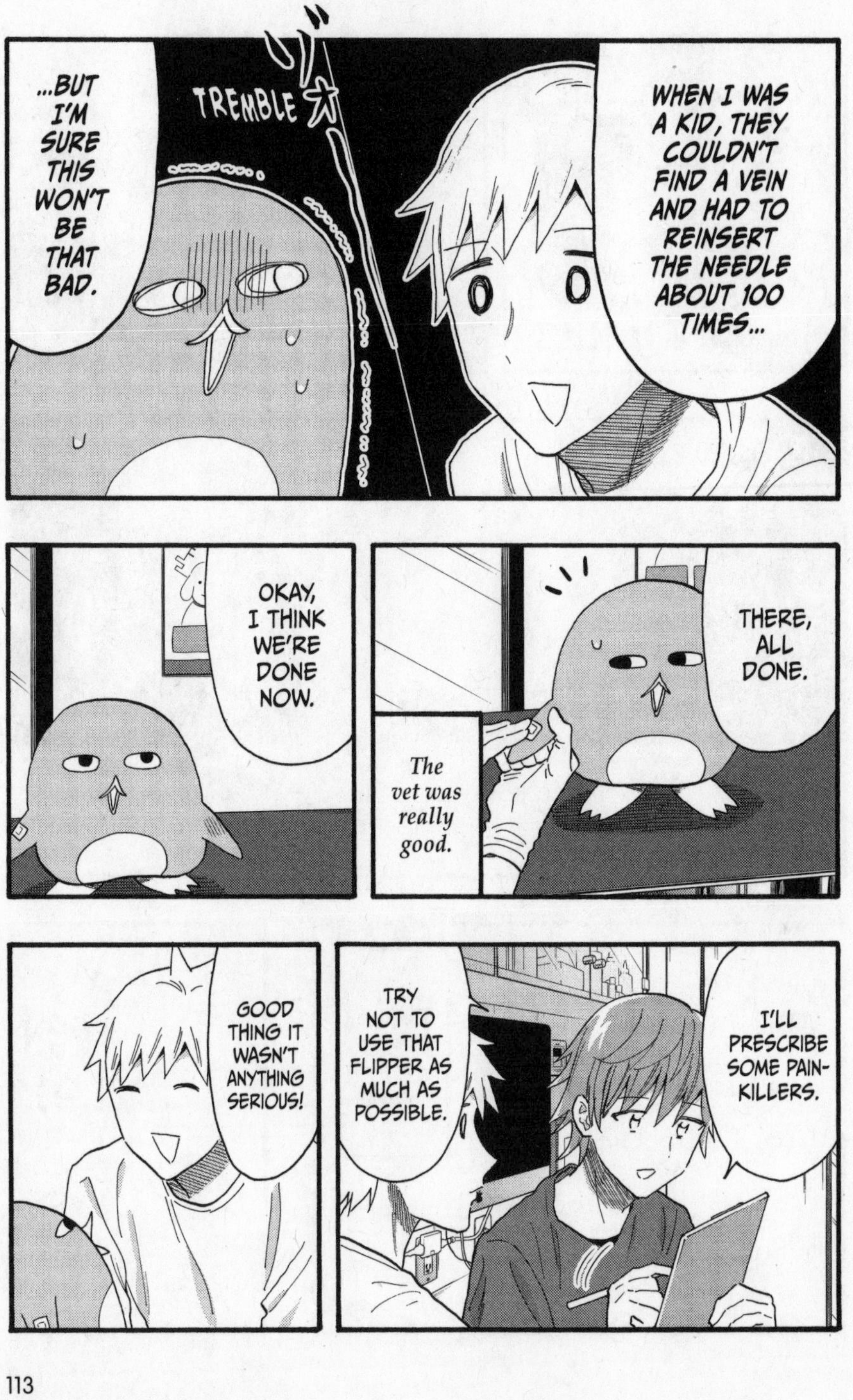
WHEN I WAS A KID, THEY COULDN'T FIND A VEIN AND HAD TO REINSERT THE NEEDLE ABOUT 100 TIMES...
TREMBLE
...BUT I'M SURE THIS WON'T BE THAT BAD.
THERE, ALL DONE.
The vet was really good.
OKAY, I THINK WE'RE DONE NOW.
I'LL PRESCRIBE SOME PAIN-KILLERS.
TRY NOT TO USE THAT FLIPPER AS MUCH AS POSSIBLE.
GOOD THING IT WASN'T ANYTHING SERIOUS!

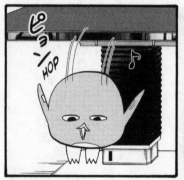

YOU DID A GOOD JOB TODAY, PEN.
LET'S GO EAT SOME SUSHI ON THE WAY HOME!
ピョ
HOP
GRK
PEN —!
He had to stay put for a while.
TIME TO EAT.

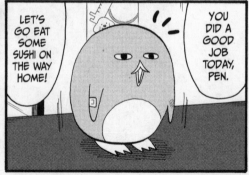

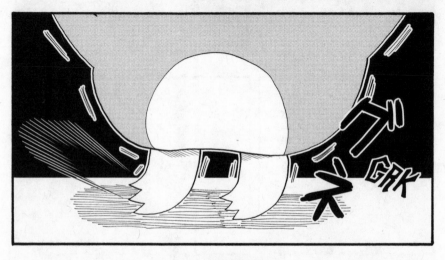

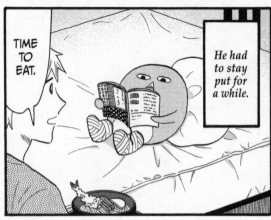

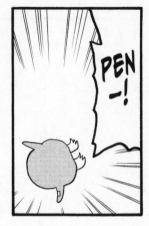

Pen 39 Run, Penguin!

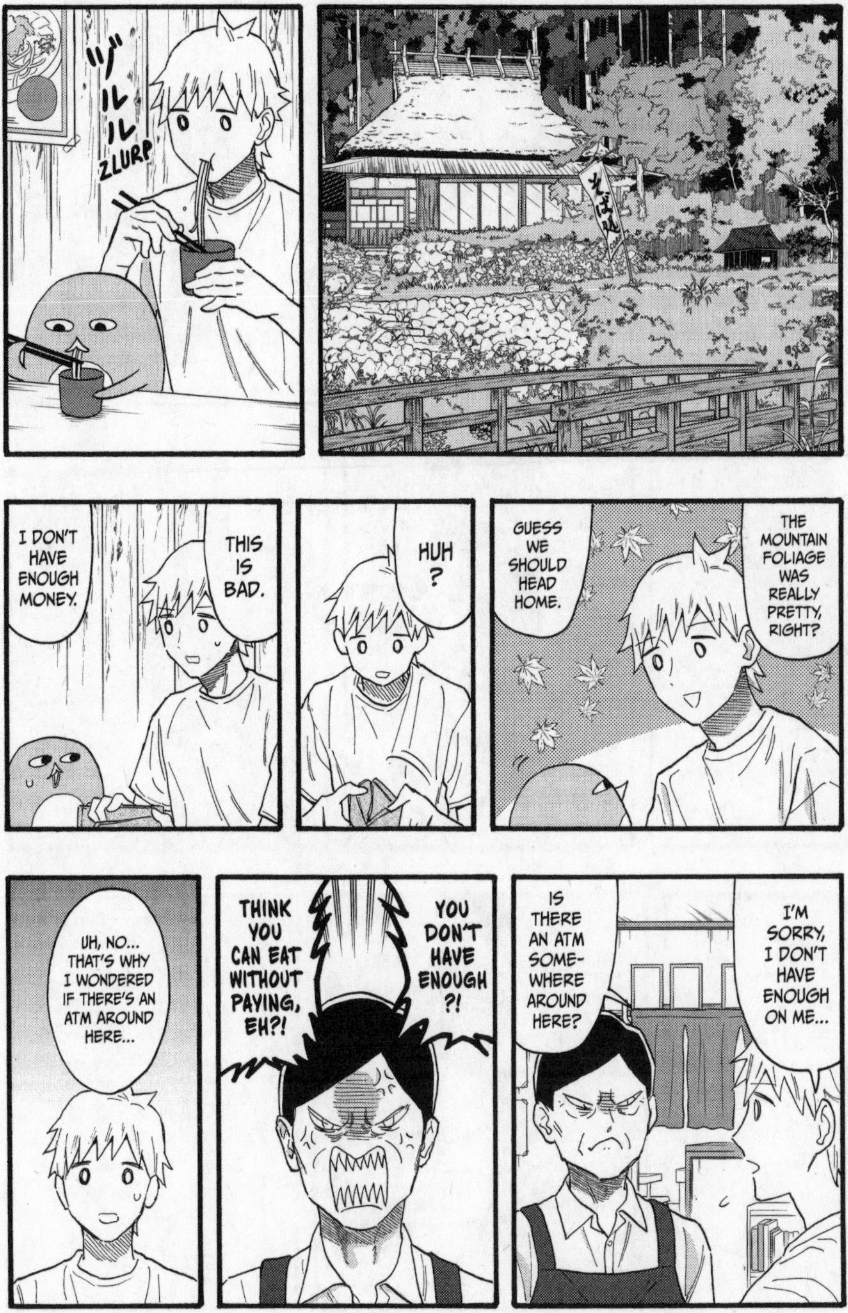
ZLURP
THE MOUNTAIN FOLIAGE WAS REALLY PRETTY, RIGHT?
GUESS WE SHOULD HEAD HOME.
HUH?
THIS IS BAD.
I DON'T HAVE ENOUGH MONEY.
I'M SORRY, I DON'T HAVE ENOUGH ON ME...
IS THERE AN ATM SOME-WHERE AROUND HERE?
YOU DON'T HAVE ENOUGH?!
THINK YOU CAN EAT WITHOUT PAYING, EH?!
UH, NO... THAT'S WHY I WONDERED IF THERE'S AN ATM AROUND HERE...

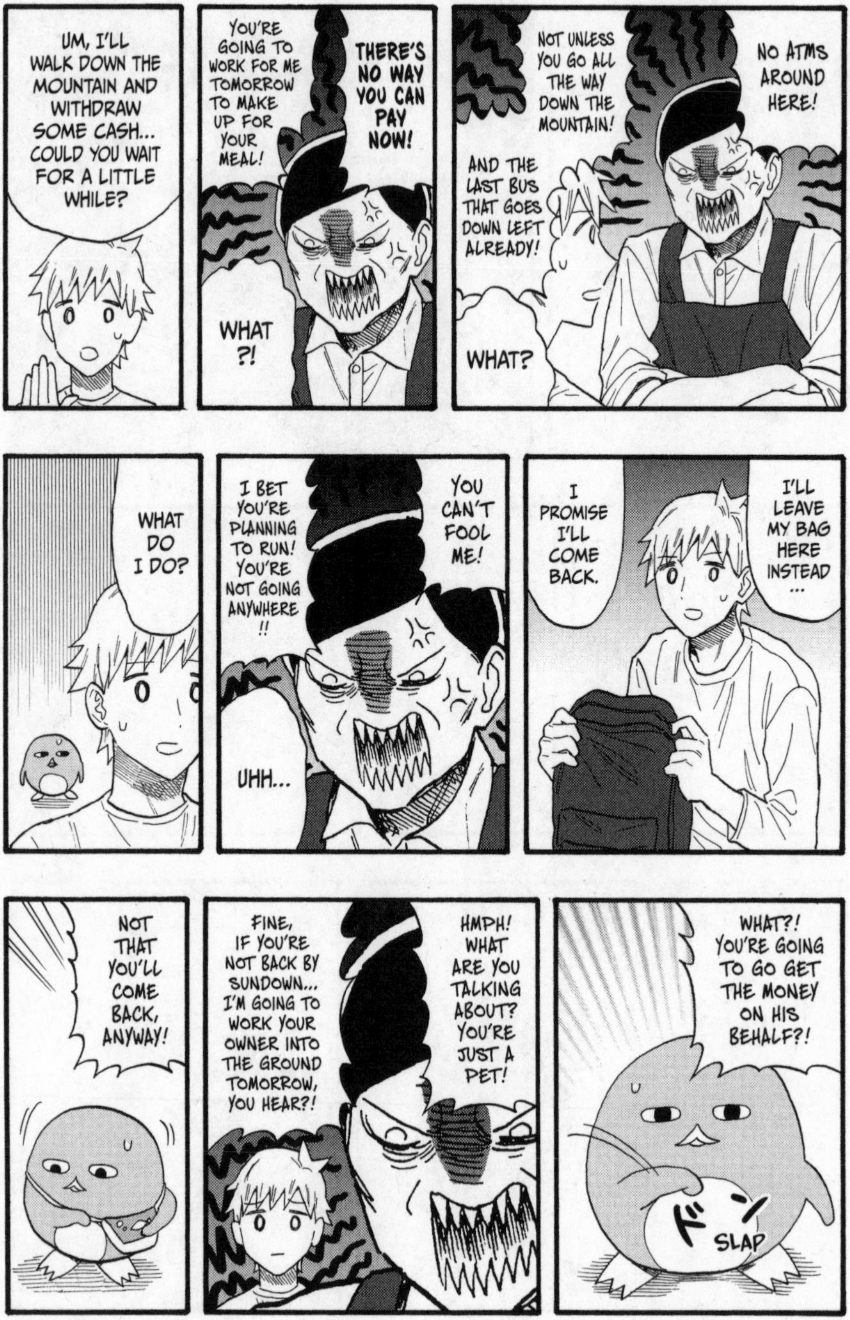
NO ATMS AROUND HERE!
NOT UNLESS YOU GO ALL THE WAY DOWN THE MOUNTAIN!
AND THE LAST BUS THAT GOES DOWN LEFT ALREADY!
WHAT?
THERE'S NO WAY YOU CAN PAY NOW!
YOU'RE GOING TO WORK FOR ME TOMORROW TO MAKE UP FOR YOUR MEAL!
WHAT ?!
UM, I'LL WALK DOWN THE MOUNTAIN AND WITHDRAW SOME CASH... COULD YOU WAIT FOR A LITTLE WHILE?
I'LL LEAVE MY BAG HERE INSTEAD ...
I PROMISE I'LL COME BACK.
YOU CAN'T FOOL ME!
I BET YOU'RE PLANNING TO RUN! YOU'RE NOT GOING ANYWHERE !!
UHH...
WHAT DO I DO?
WHAT?! YOU'RE GOING TO GO GET THE MONEY ON HIS BEHALF?!
SLAP
HMPH! WHAT ARE YOU TALKING ABOUT? YOU'RE JUST A PET!
FINE, IF YOU'RE NOT BACK BY SUNDOWN... I'M GOING TO WORK YOUR OWNER INTO THE GROUND TOMORROW, YOU HEAR?!
NOT THAT YOU'LL COME BACK, ANYWAY!

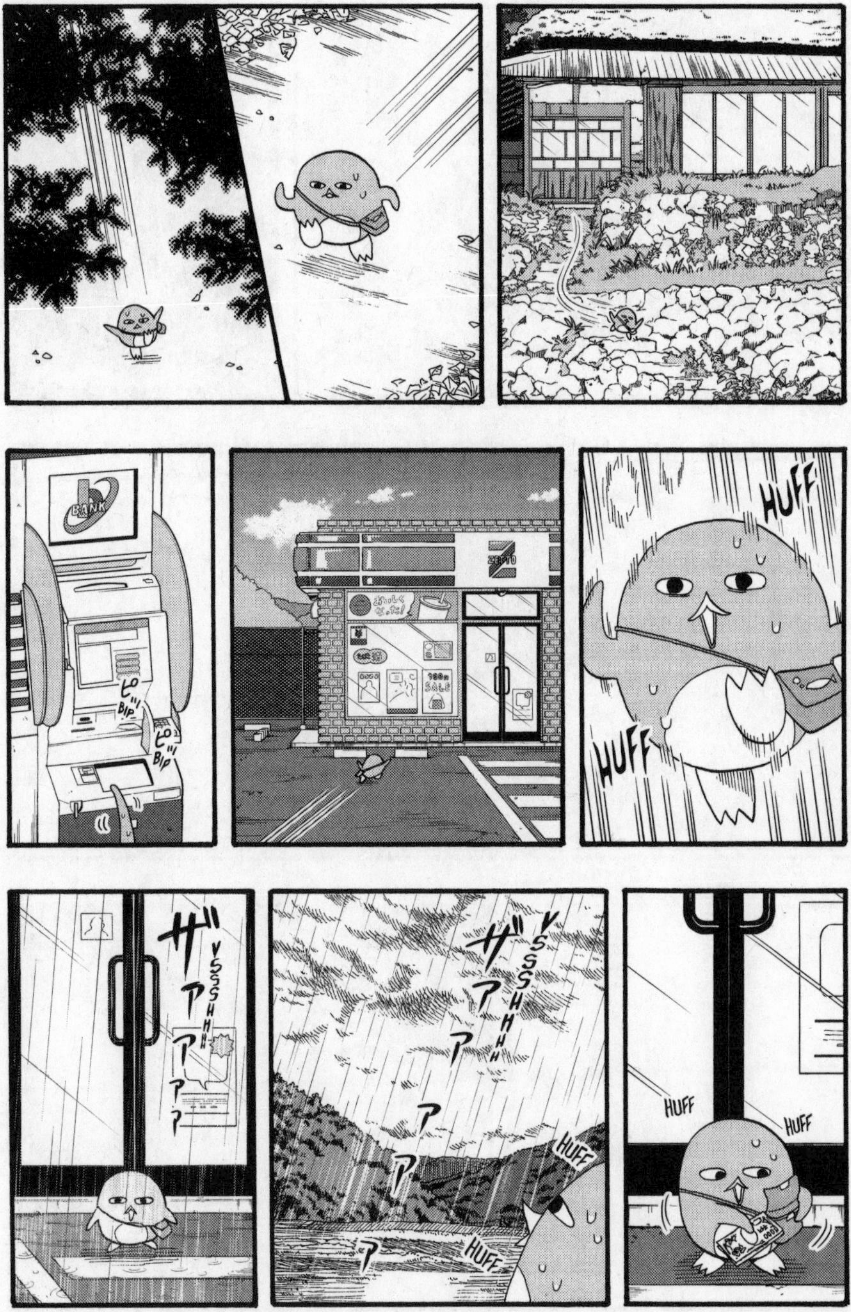
HUFF
HUFF
BANK
ピッ BIP
ピッ BIP
HUFF
HUFF
ザァァァァ
VSSHHHH
HUFF
HUFF
ザァァァ
VSSHHH

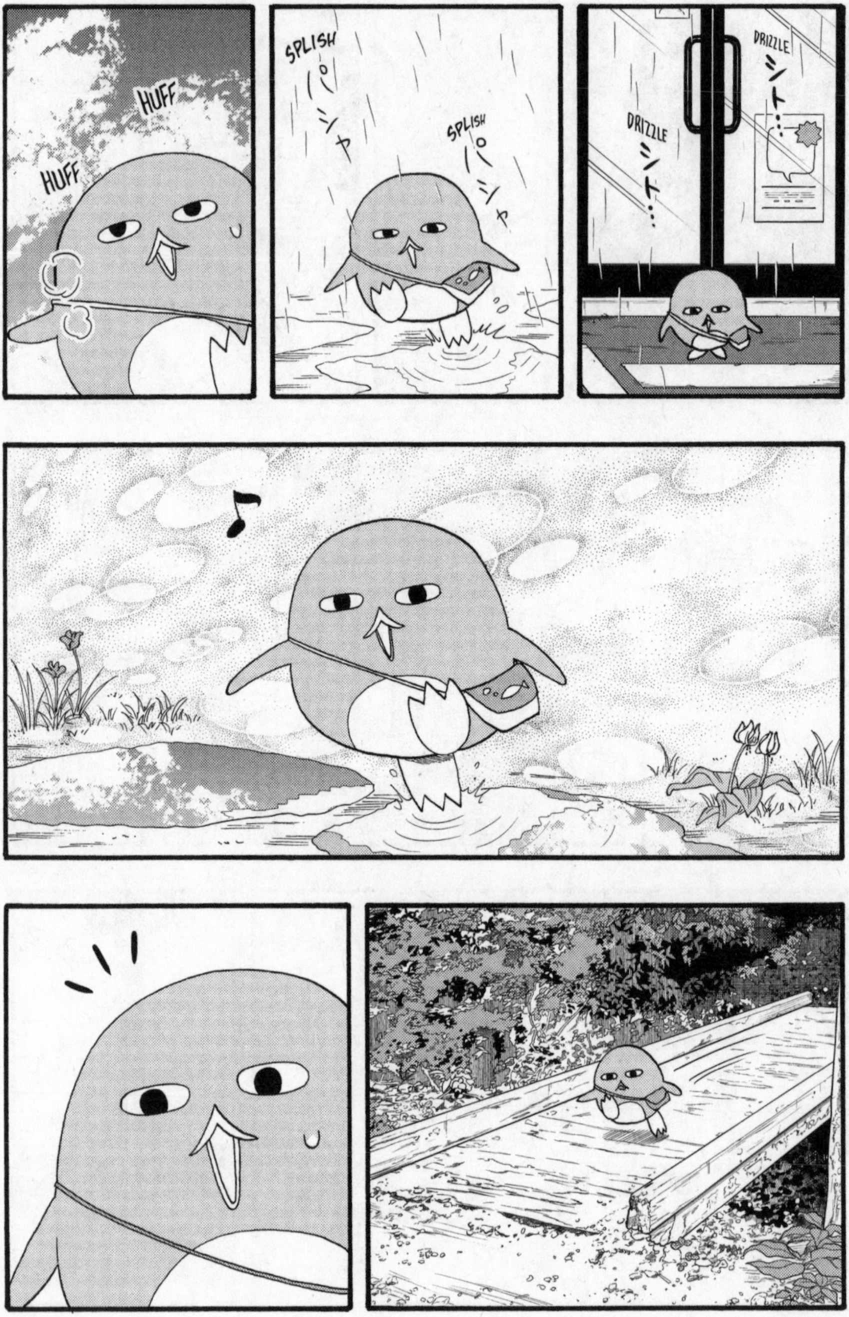
DRIZZLE
シト…
DRIZZLE
シト…
SPLISH
パシャ
SPLISH
パシャ
HUFF
HUFF

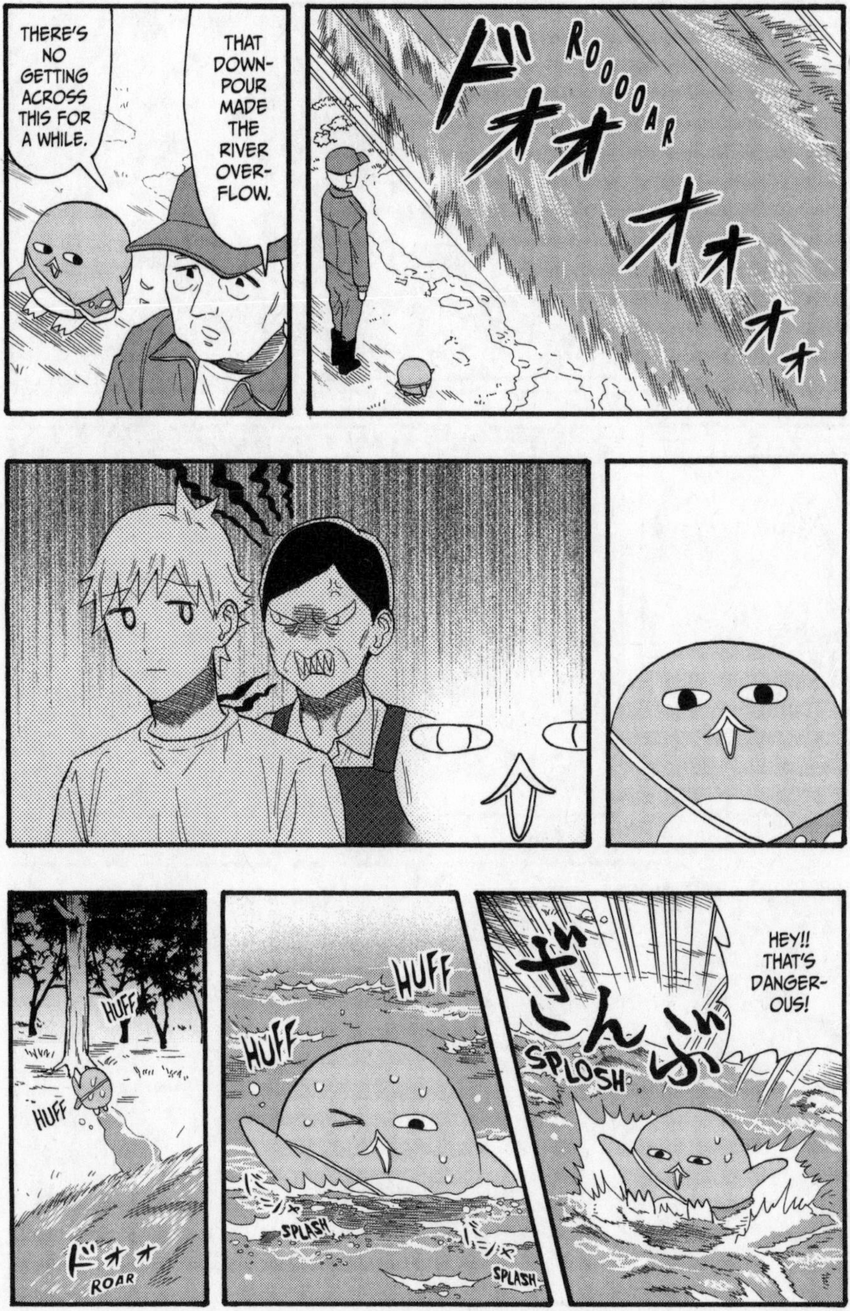
ドオオオオオオ
ROOOOAR
THAT DOWN-POUR MADE THE RIVER OVER-FLOW.
THERE'S NO GETTING ACROSS THIS FOR A WHILE.
ざんぶ
SPLOSH
HEY!! THAT'S DANGER-OUS!
HUFF
HUFF
バシャ
SPLASH
バシャ
SPLASH
HUFF
HUFF
ドオオ
ROAR

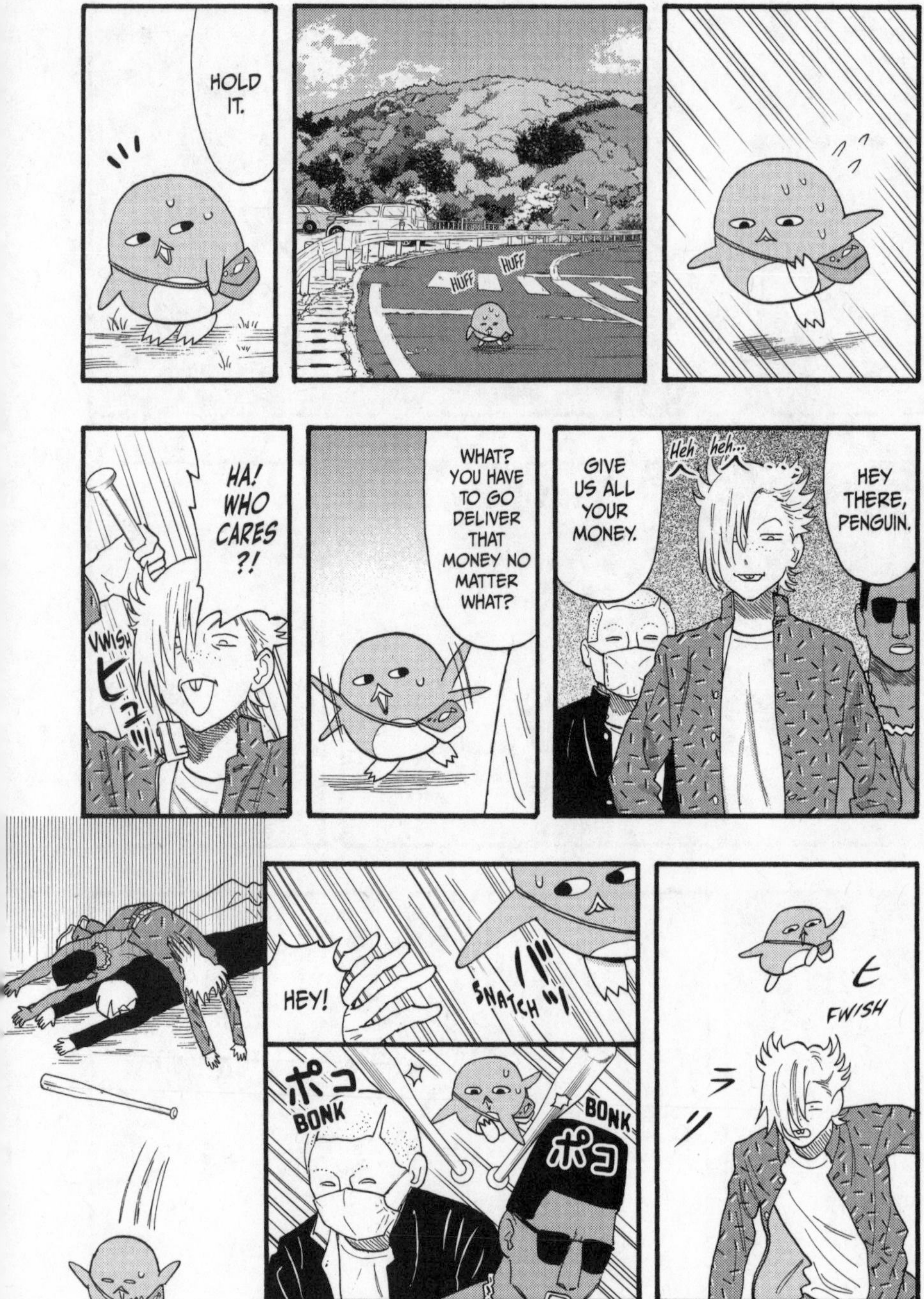
HUFF
HUFF
HOLD IT.
HEY THERE, PENGUIN.
Heh heh...
GIVE US ALL YOUR MONEY.
WHAT? YOU HAVE TO GO DELIVER THAT MONEY NO MATTER WHAT?
HA! WHO CARES?!
VWISH
ビュッ
ヒ
FWISH
ラッ
HEY!
バッ
SNATCH
ポコ
BONK
BONK
ポコ

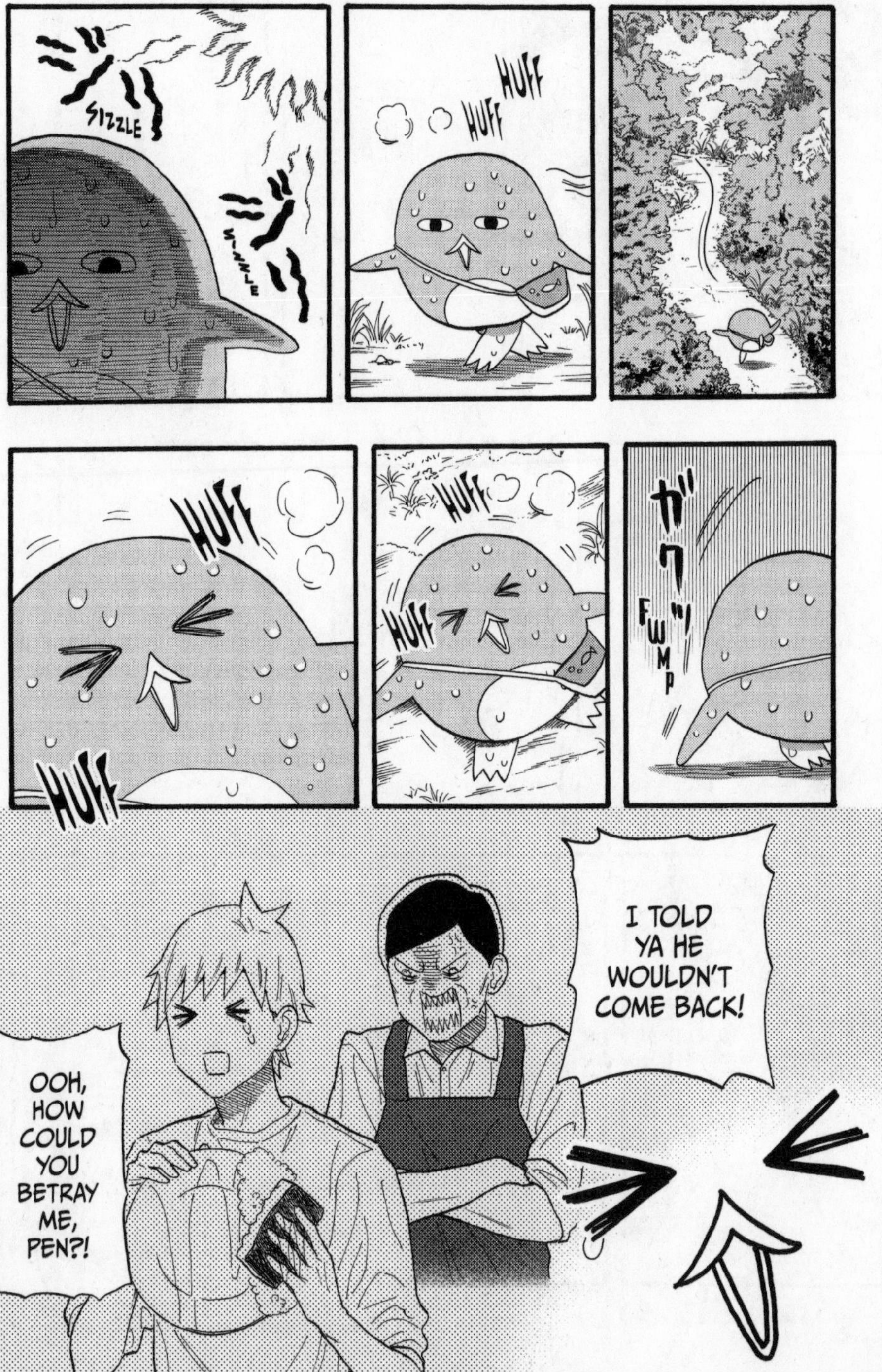
HUFF
HUFF
SIZZLE
SIZZLE
FWMP
HUFF
HUFF
HUFF
HUFF
I TOLD YA HE WOULDN'T COME BACK!
OOH, HOW COULD YOU BETRAY ME, PEN?!

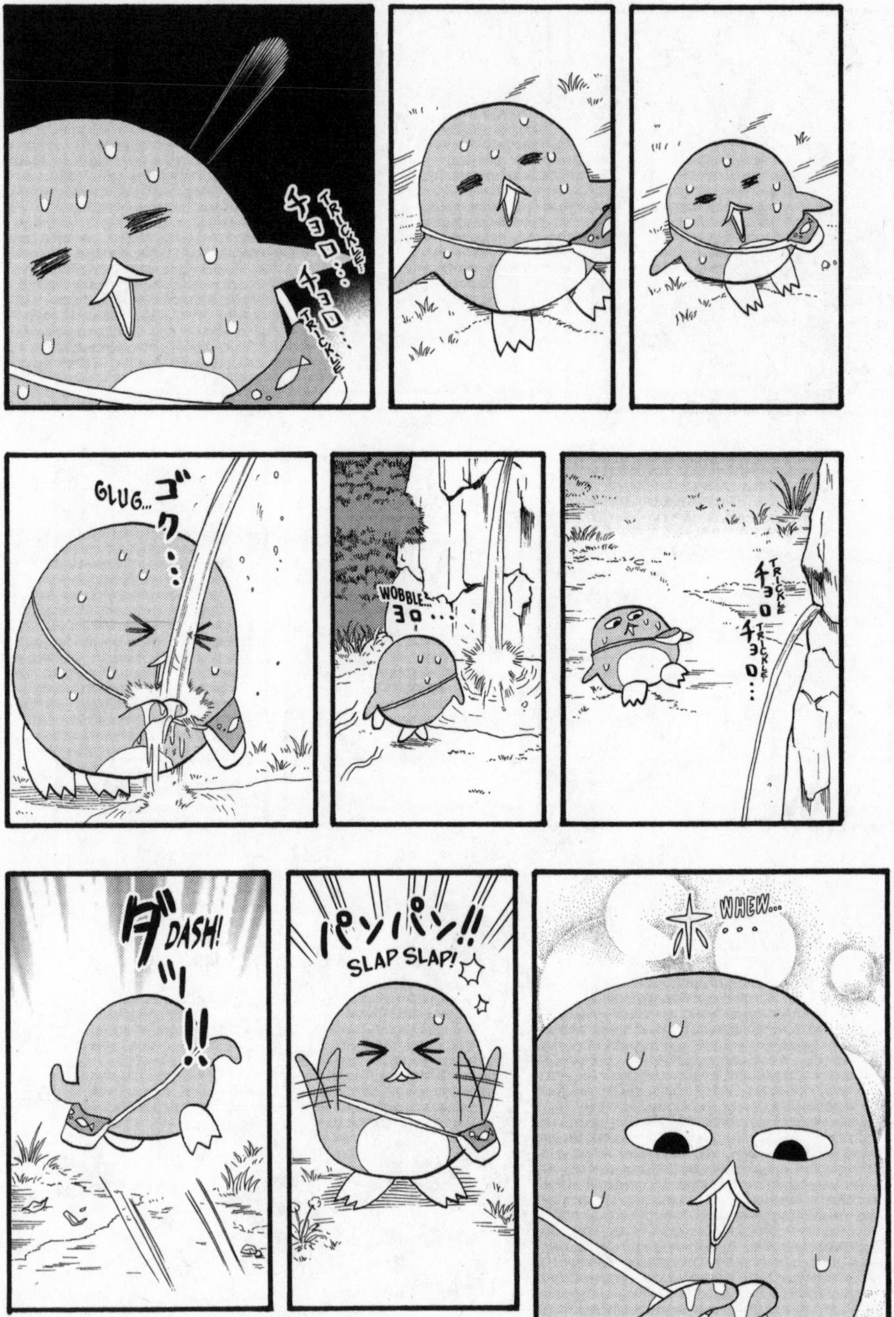
TRICKLE
チョロ...
チョロ...
TRICKLE
チョロ
TRICKLE
チョロ...
TRICKLE
WOBBLE...
ヨロ...
GLUG...
ゴク...
WHEW...
ホ...
パンパン!!
SLAP SLAP!
ダッ!!
DASH!

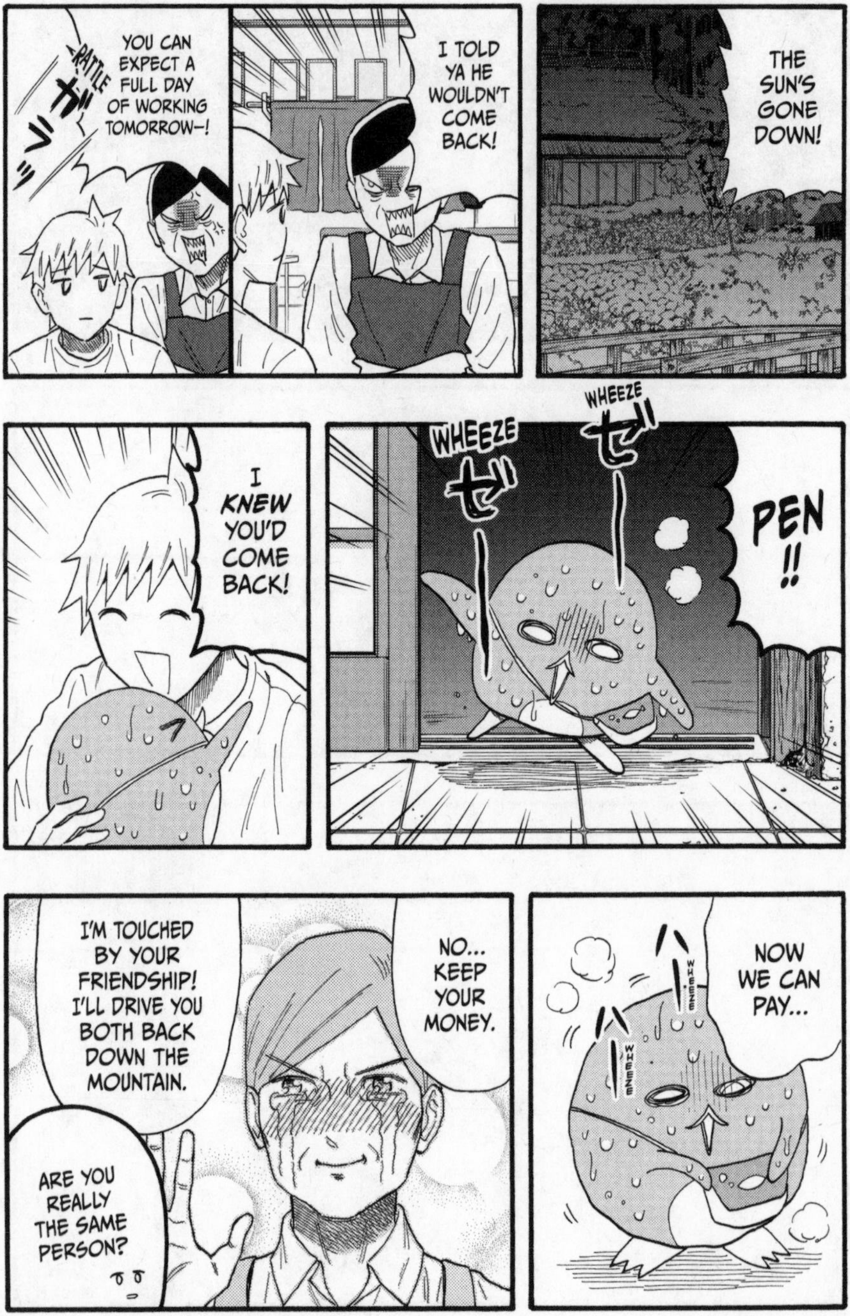
THE SUN'S GONE DOWN!
I TOLD YA HE WOULDN'T COME BACK!
RATTLE
YOU CAN EXPECT A FULL DAY OF WORKING TOMORROW—!
WHEEZE
WHEEZE
PEN!!
I *KNEW* YOU'D COME BACK!
NOW WE CAN PAY...
WHEEZE
WHEEZE
NO... KEEP YOUR MONEY.
I'M TOUCHED BY YOUR FRIENDSHIP! I'LL DRIVE YOU BOTH BACK DOWN THE MOUNTAIN.
ARE YOU REALLY THE SAME PERSON?

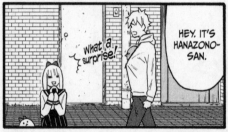

TROMP
テク
TROMP
テク
HEY. IT'S HANAZONO-SAN.
What a surprise!
WHAT ARE YOU DOING?
BLUUSH
OH, UH... I FORGOT TO EAT AGAIN... SO I'M EATING A RICE BALL...
OH, OKAY.
SEE YOU, THEN ...
OH...
UM...!
I ACTUALLY... LIVE CLOSE BY.
I STILL OWE YOU FOR HELPING ME OUT BEFORE... CAN I INVITE YOU OVER FOR A BIT?
SQUEAK
SQUEE

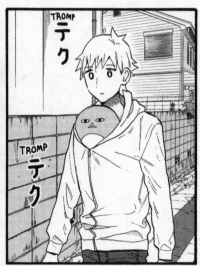

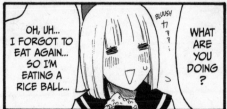

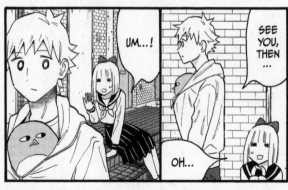

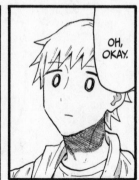

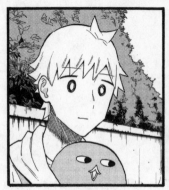

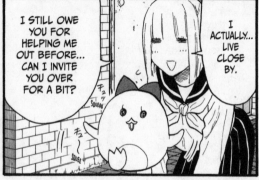

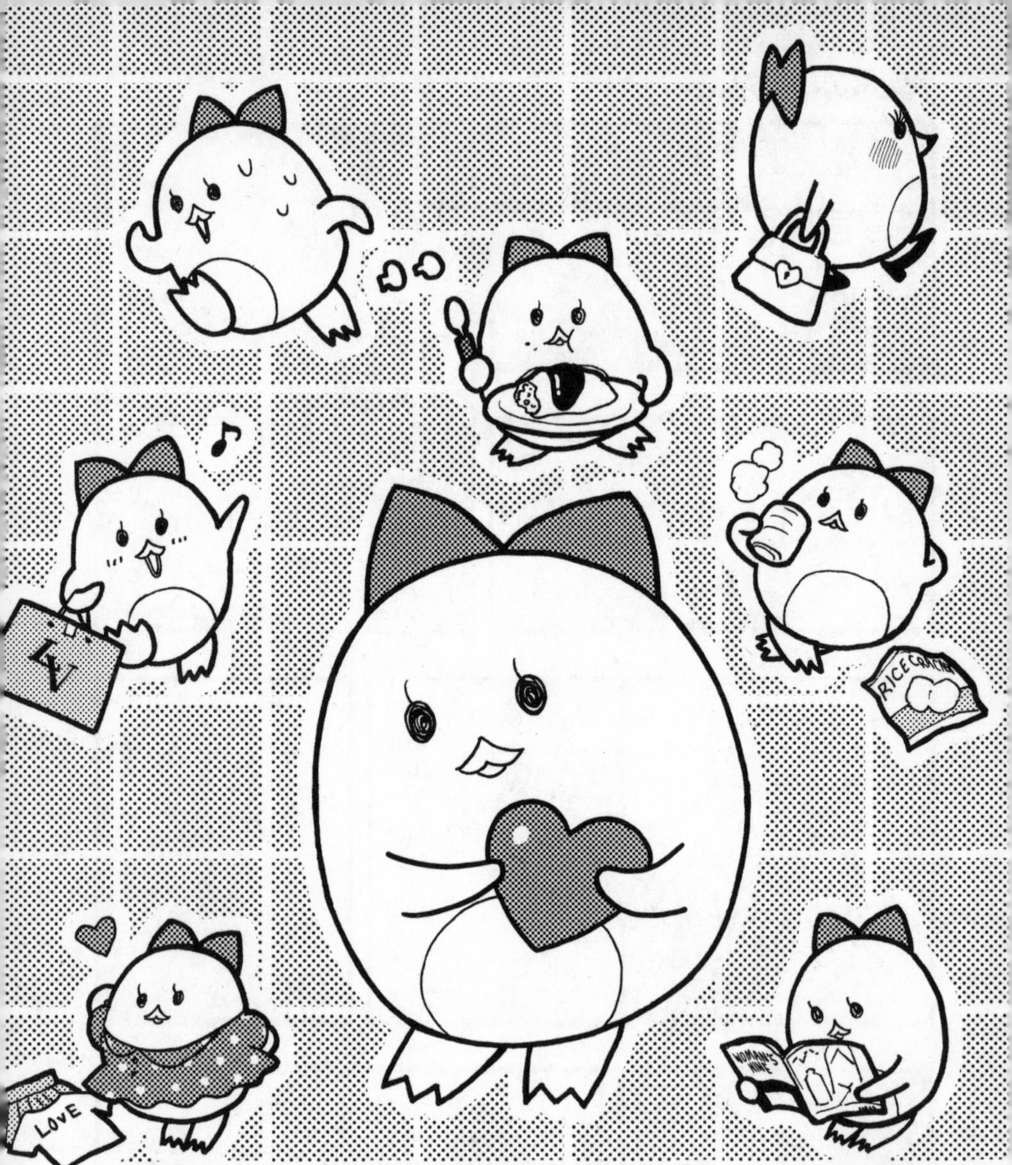
LOVE
BUGS BEGONE

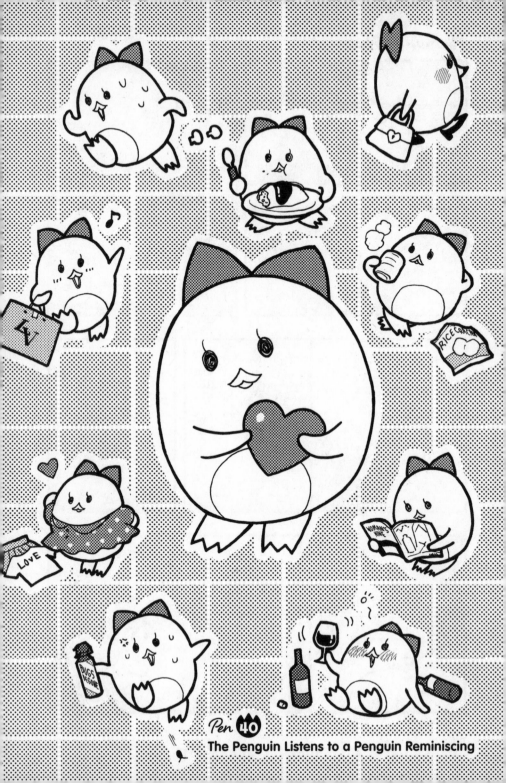

Pen 40
The Penguin Listens to a Penguin Reminiscing

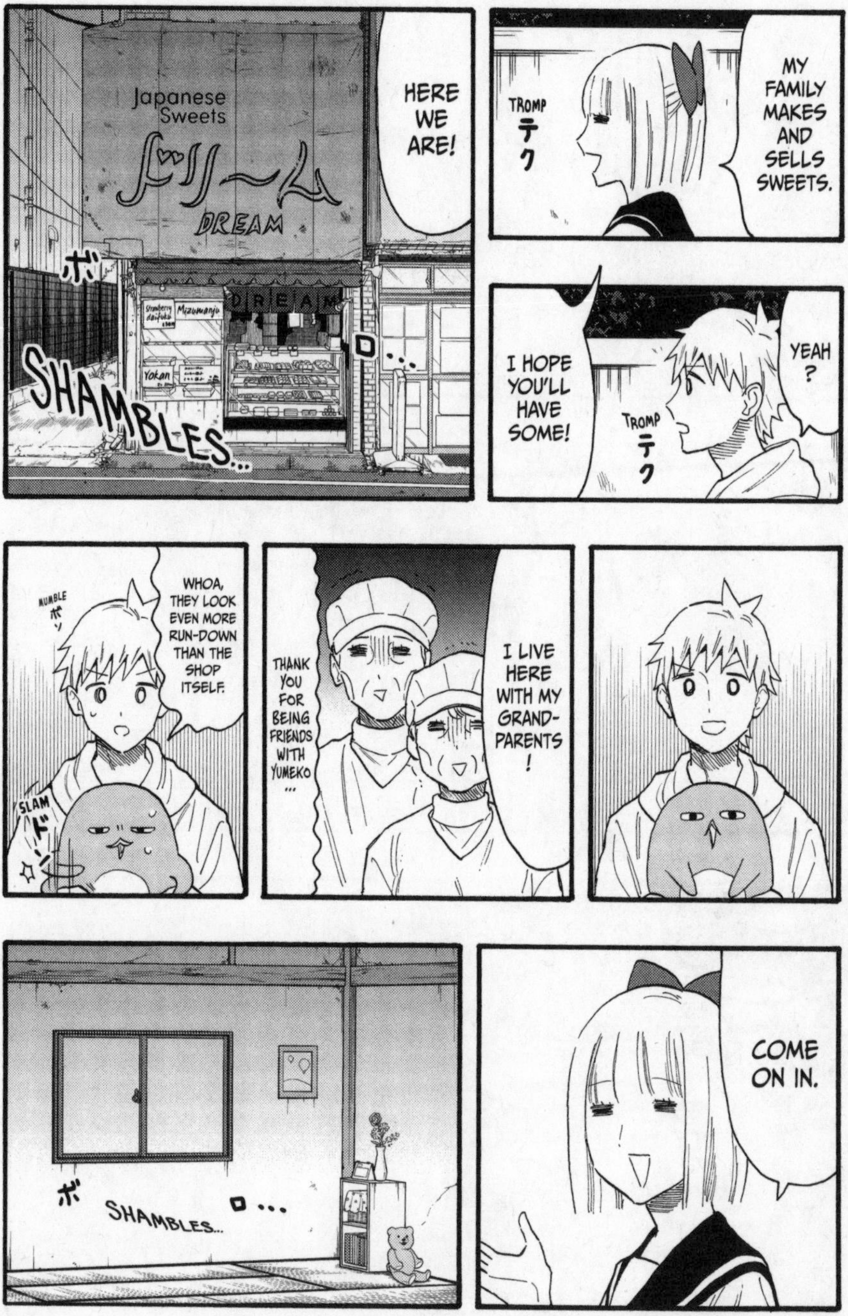
MY FAMILY MAKES AND SELLS SWEETS.
TROMP
テク
YEAH?
TROMP
テク
I HOPE YOU'LL HAVE SOME!
HERE WE ARE!
Japanese Sweets
ド♡リーム
DREAM
DREAM
Mizumanju
Yokan
ボ
SHAMBLES...
ロ...
I LIVE HERE WITH MY GRAND-PARENTS!
THANK YOU FOR BEING FRIENDS WITH YUMEKO...
WHOA, THEY LOOK EVEN MORE RUN-DOWN THAN THE SHOP ITSELF.
MUMBLE
ボソ
SLAM
ドン
COME ON IN.
ボ
SHAMBLES...
ロ...

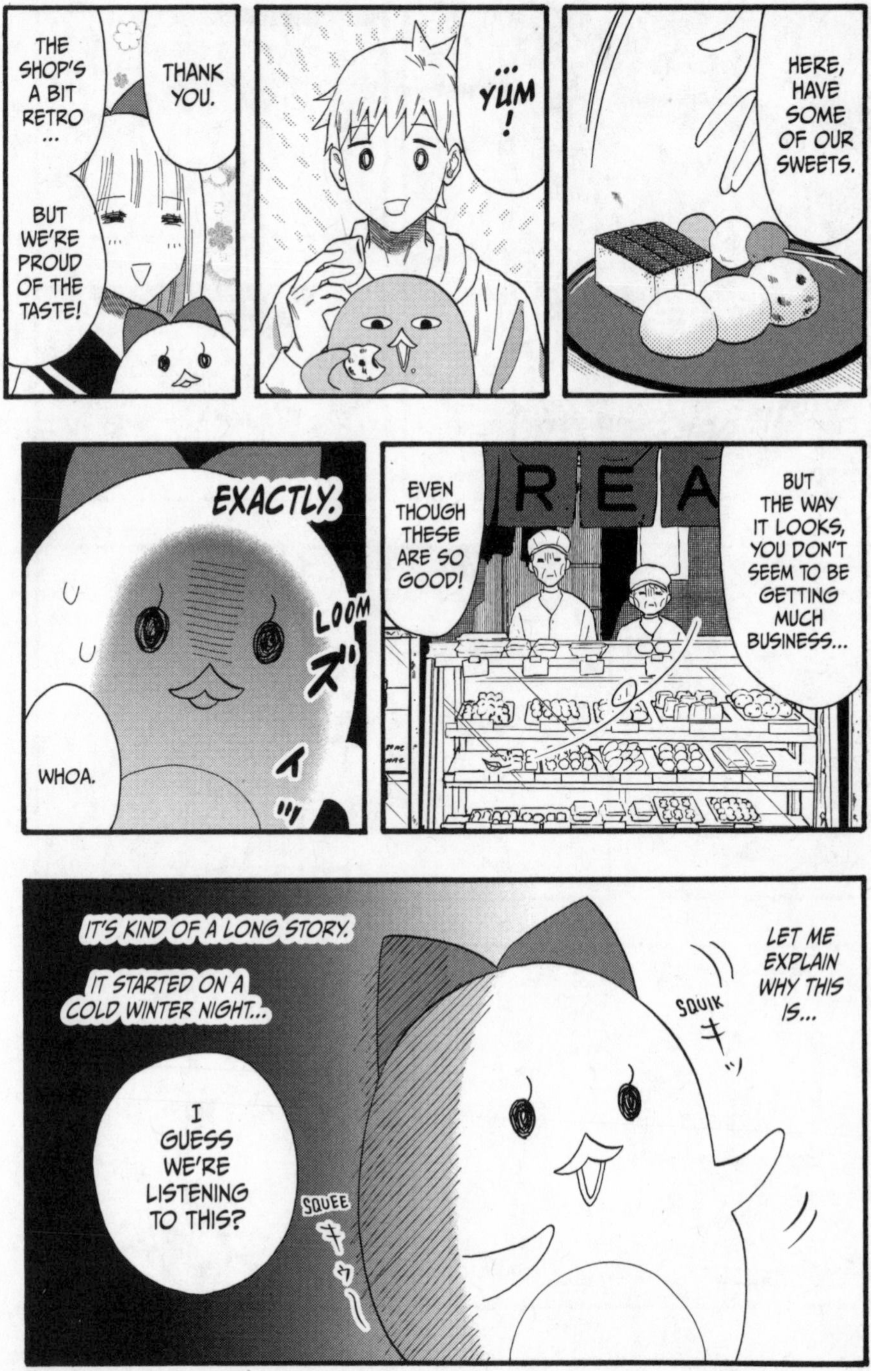
HERE, HAVE SOME OF OUR SWEETS.
...YUM!
THANK YOU.
THE SHOP'S A BIT RETRO...
BUT WE'RE PROUD OF THE TASTE!
BUT THE WAY IT LOOKS, YOU DON'T SEEM TO BE GETTING MUCH BUSINESS...
REA
EVEN THOUGH THESE ARE SO GOOD!
EXACTLY.
LOOM
WHOA.
LET ME EXPLAIN WHY THIS IS...
SQUIK
IT'S KIND OF A LONG STORY.
IT STARTED ON A COLD WINTER NIGHT...
I GUESS WE'RE LISTENING TO THIS?
SQUEE

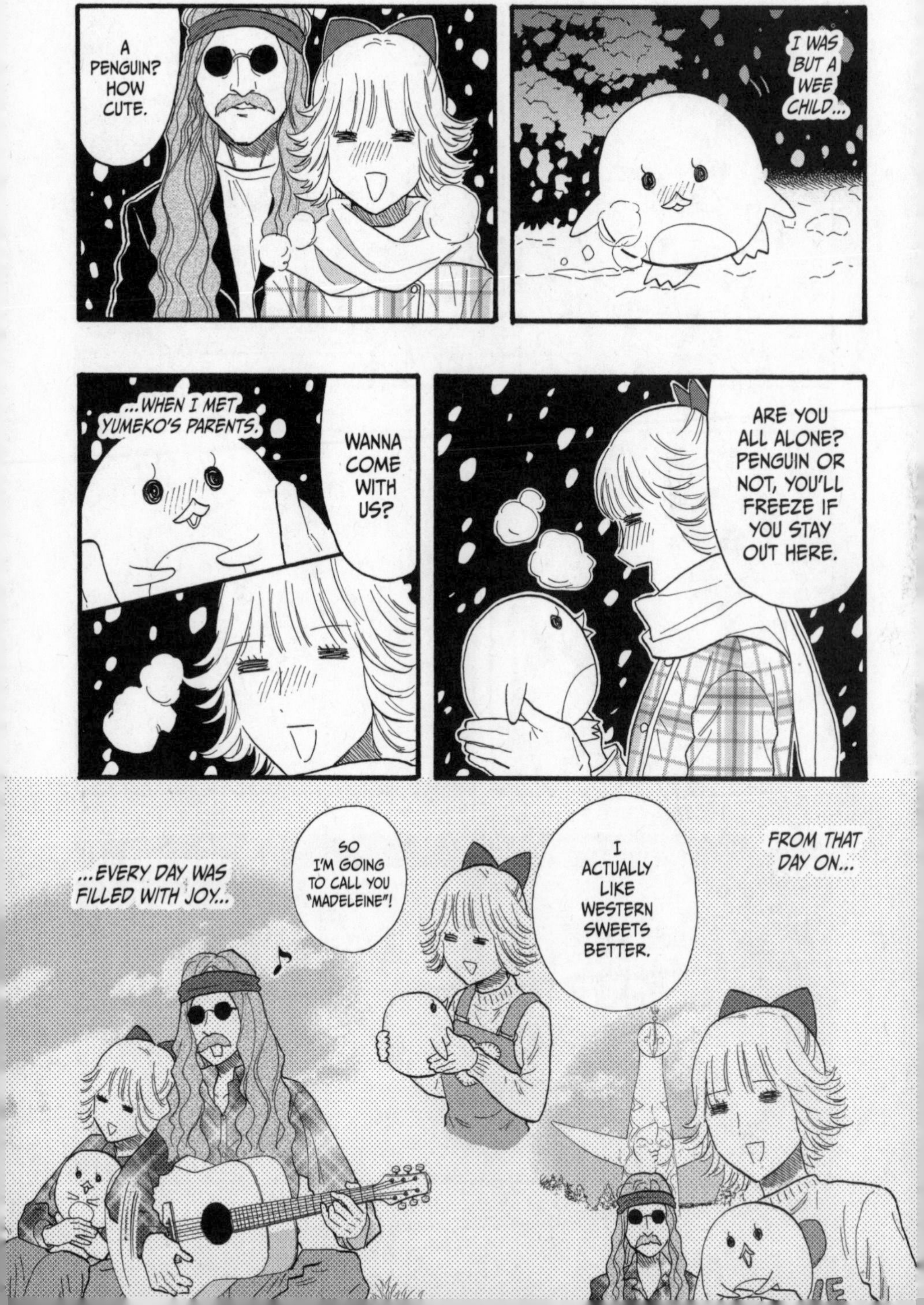
I WAS BUT A WEE CHILD...
A PENGUIN? HOW CUTE.
ARE YOU ALL ALONE? PENGUIN OR NOT, YOU'LL FREEZE IF YOU STAY OUT HERE.
WANNA COME WITH US?
...WHEN I MET YUMEKO'S PARENTS.
FROM THAT DAY ON...
I ACTUALLY LIKE WESTERN SWEETS BETTER.
SO I'M GOING TO CALL YOU "MADELEINE"!
...EVERY DAY WAS FILLED WITH JOY...

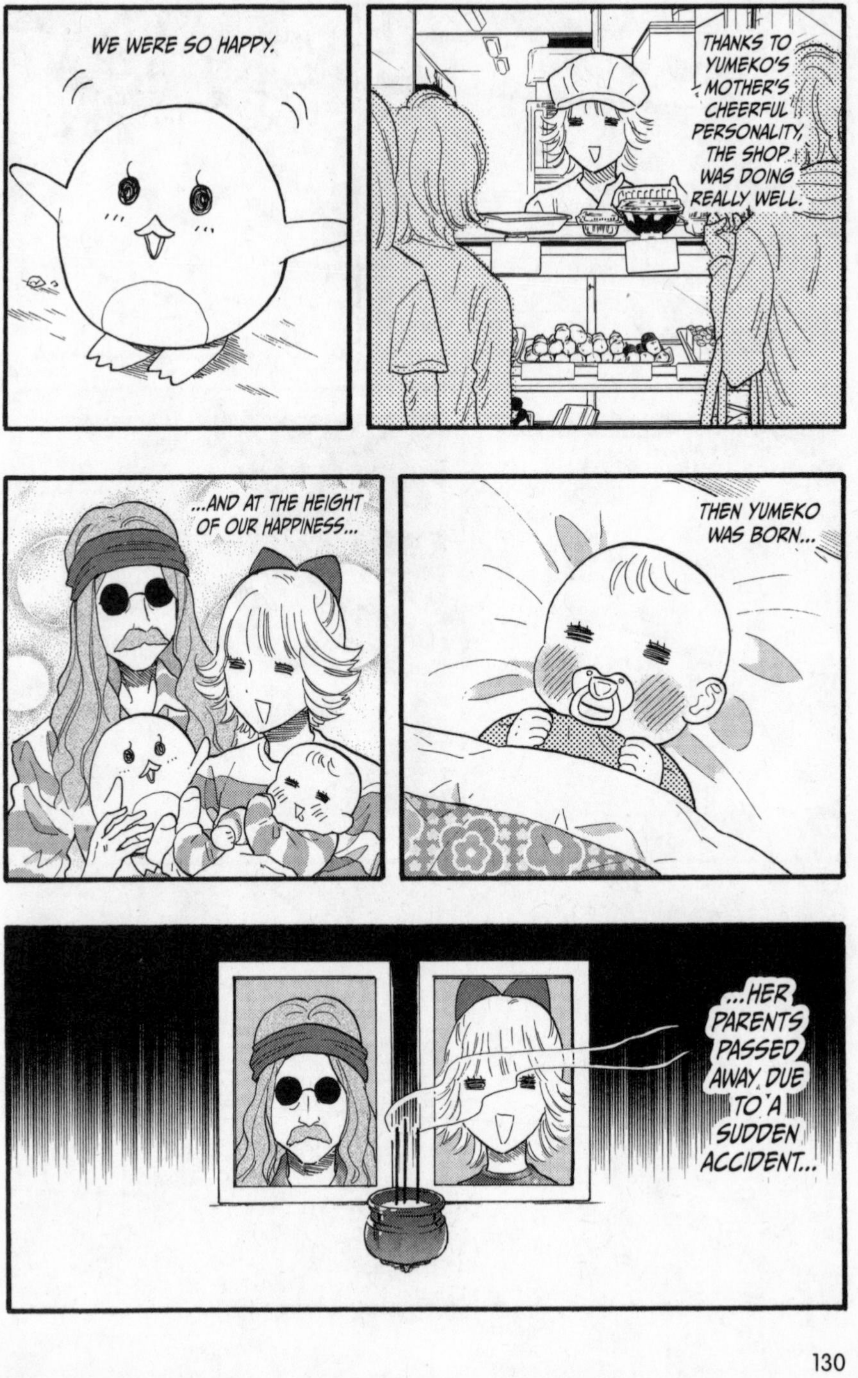
THANKS TO YUMEKO'S MOTHER'S CHEERFUL PERSONALITY, THE SHOP WAS DOING REALLY WELL.
WE WERE SO HAPPY.
THEN YUMEKO WAS BORN...
...AND AT THE HEIGHT OF OUR HAPPINESS...
...HER PARENTS PASSED AWAY DUE TO A SUDDEN ACCIDENT...

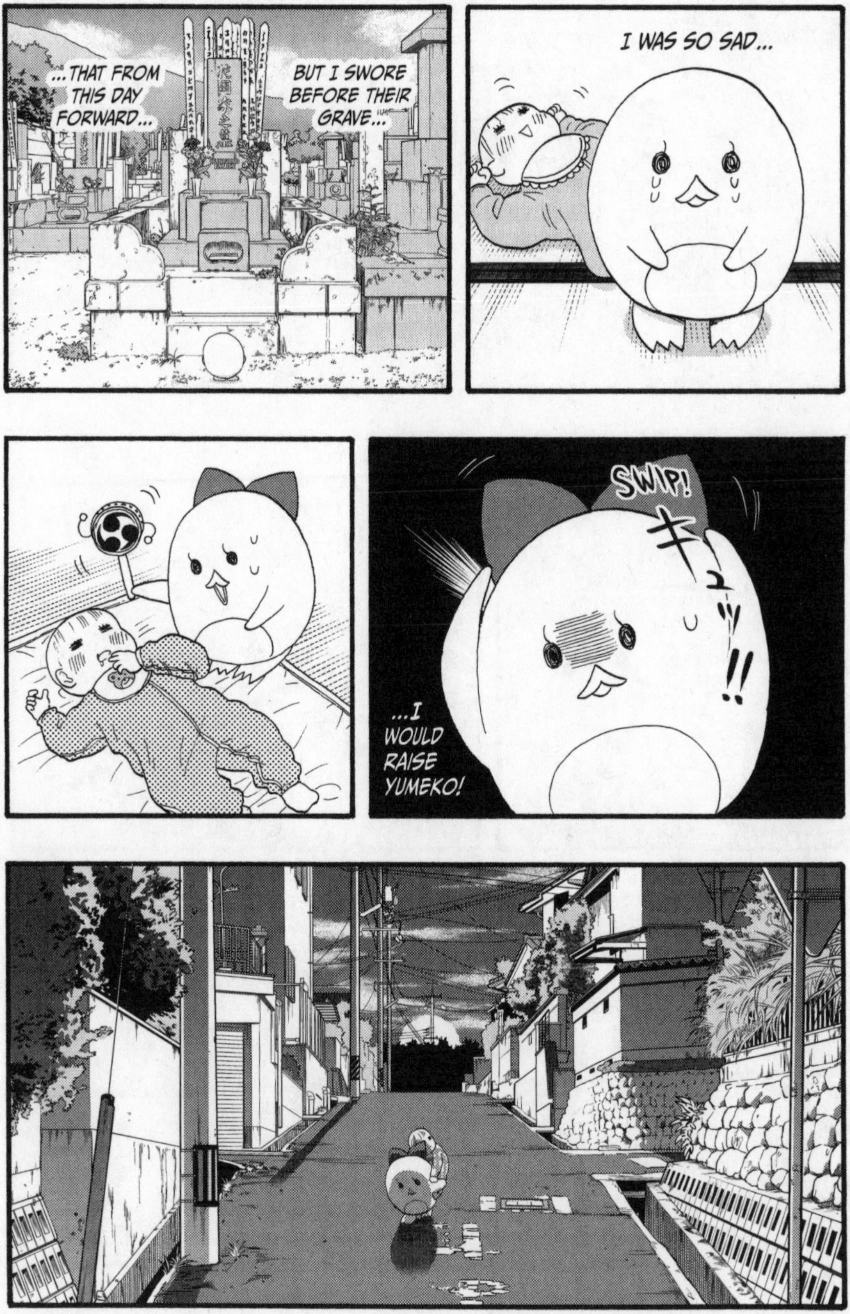
I WAS SO SAD...
BUT I SWORE BEFORE THEIR GRAVE...
...THAT FROM THIS DAY FORWARD...
SWIP!
キュッ!!
...I WOULD RAISE YUMEKO!

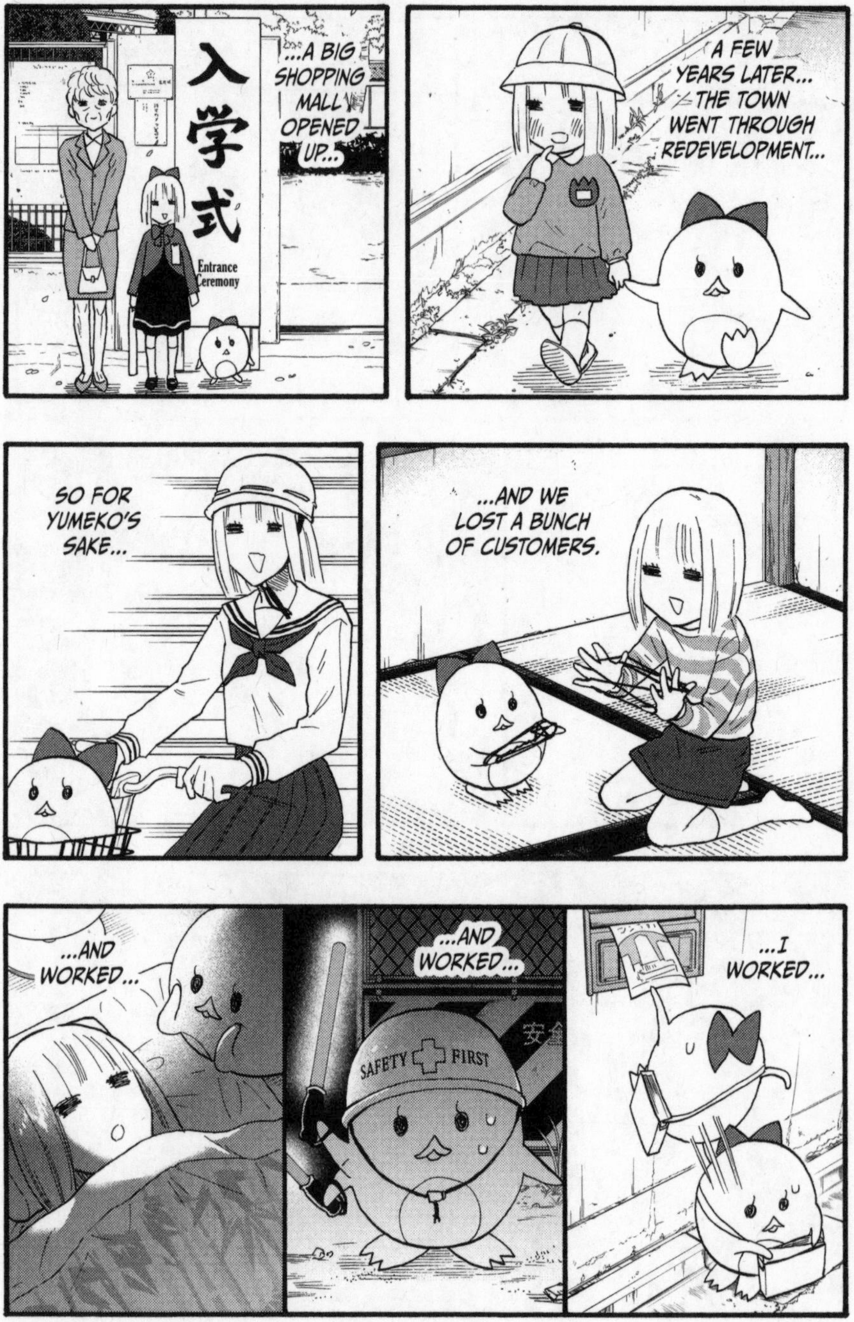
A FEW YEARS LATER... THE TOWN WENT THROUGH REDEVELOPMENT...
入学式
Entrance Ceremony
...A BIG SHOPPING MALL OPENED UP...
...AND WE LOST A BUNCH OF CUSTOMERS.
SO FOR YUMEKO'S SAKE...
...I WORKED...
...AND WORKED...
SAFETY FIRST
...AND WORKED...

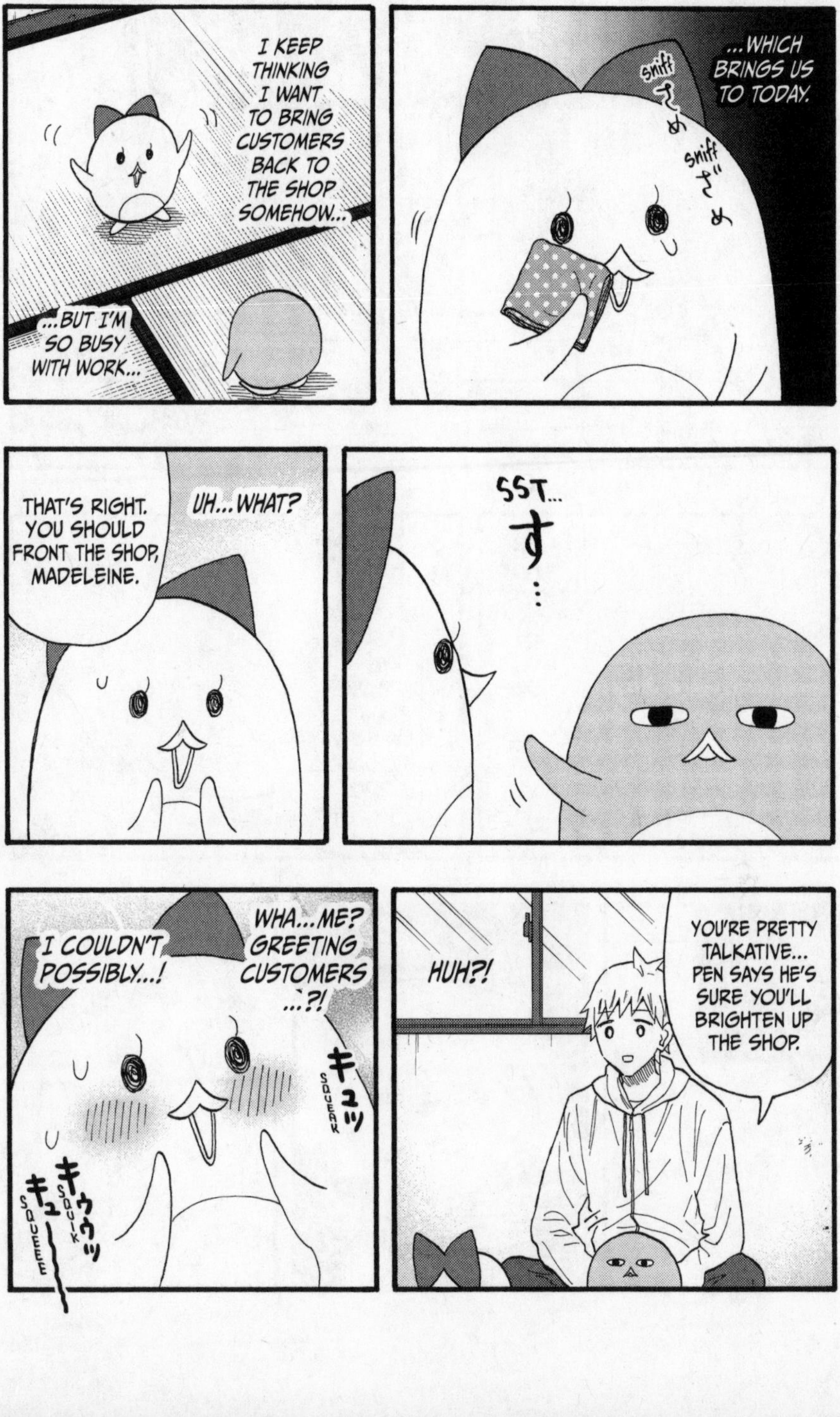
...WHICH BRINGS US TO TODAY.
sniff
sniff
I KEEP THINKING I WANT TO BRING CUSTOMERS BACK TO THE SHOP SOMEHOW...
...BUT I'M SO BUSY WITH WORK...
SST...
す…
UH...WHAT?
THAT'S RIGHT. YOU SHOULD FRONT THE SHOP, MADELEINE.
YOU'RE PRETTY TALKATIVE... PEN SAYS HE'S SURE YOU'LL BRIGHTEN UP THE SHOP.
HUH?!
WHA...ME? GREETING CUSTOMERS ...?!
キュッ
SQUEAK
I COULDN'T POSSIBLY...!
キウウッ
SQUIK
キュー
SQUEEE

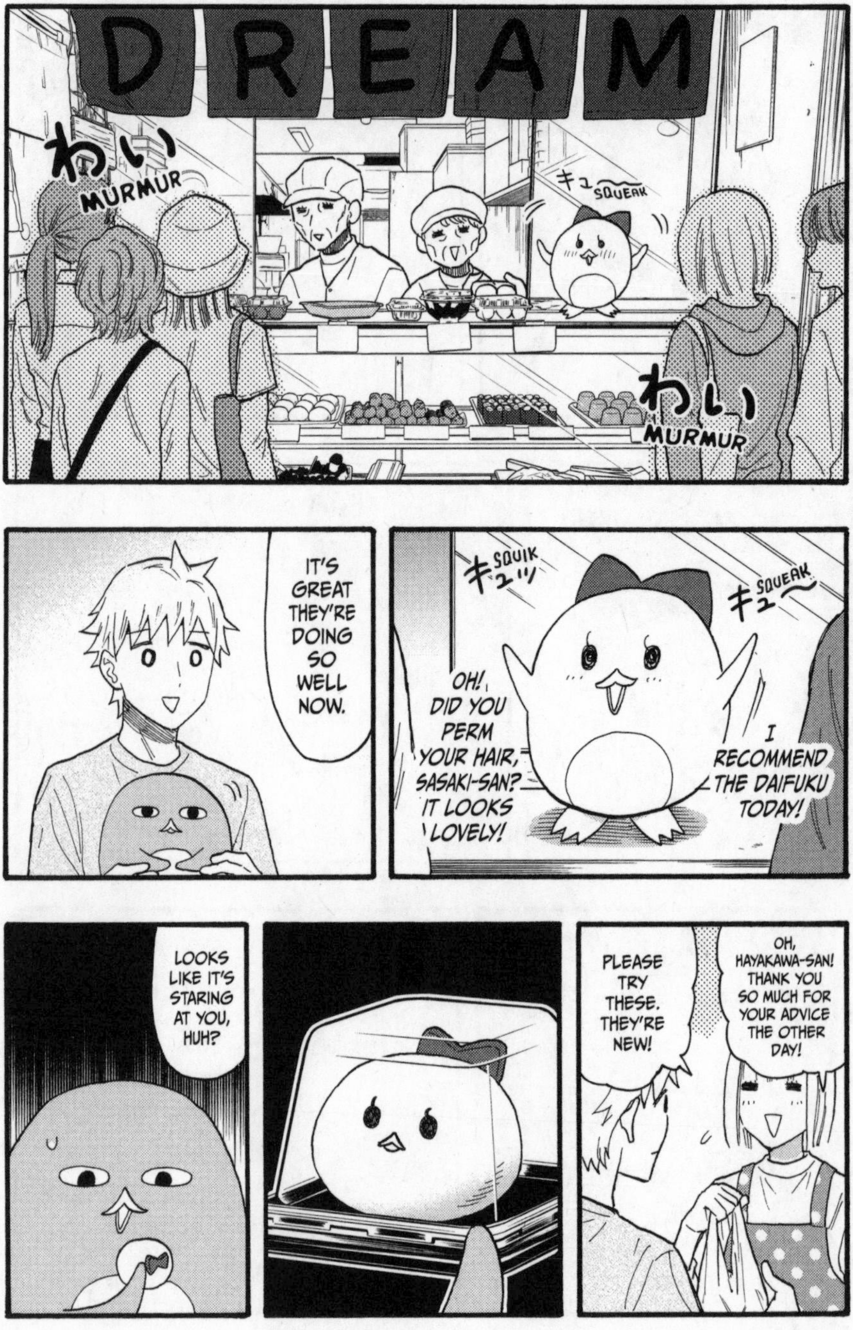
DREAM
キュ SQUEAK
わい MURMUR
わい MURMUR
キュ〜 SQUEAK
キュッ SQUIK
I RECOMMEND THE DAIFUKU TODAY!
OH! DID YOU PERM YOUR HAIR, SASAKI-SAN? IT LOOKS LOVELY!
IT'S GREAT THEY'RE DOING SO WELL NOW.
OH, HAYAKAWA-SAN! THANK YOU SO MUCH FOR YOUR ADVICE THE OTHER DAY!
PLEASE TRY THESE. THEY'RE NEW!
LOOKS LIKE IT'S STARING AT YOU, HUH?

#1 Penguin hairstyles

Loads of hair trends!

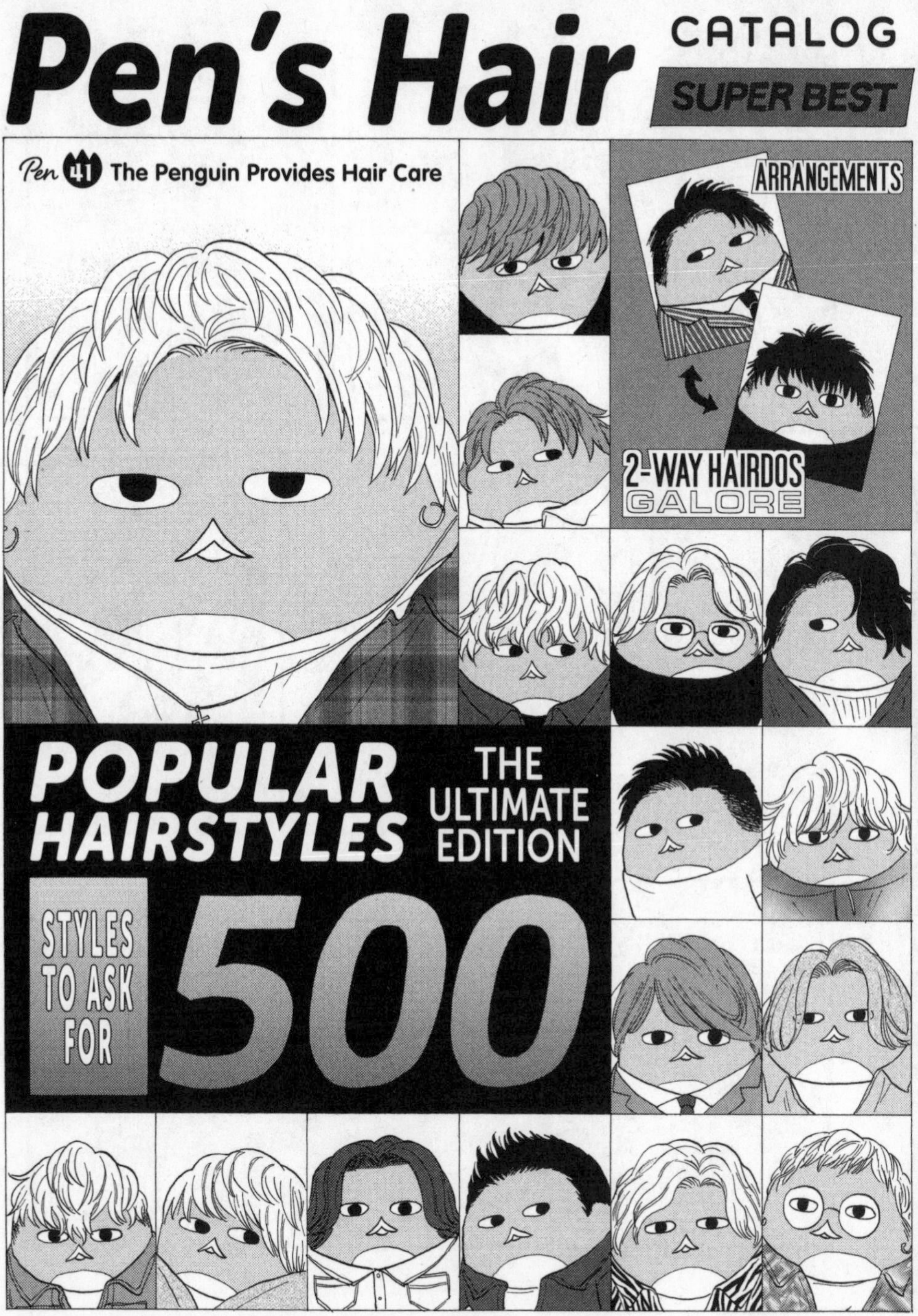
Pen's Hair
CATALOG
SUPER BEST
Pen 41 The Penguin Provides Hair Care
ARRANGEMENTS
2-WAY HAIRDOS GALORE
POPULAR HAIRSTYLES
THE ULTIMATE EDITION
STYLES TO ASK FOR
500

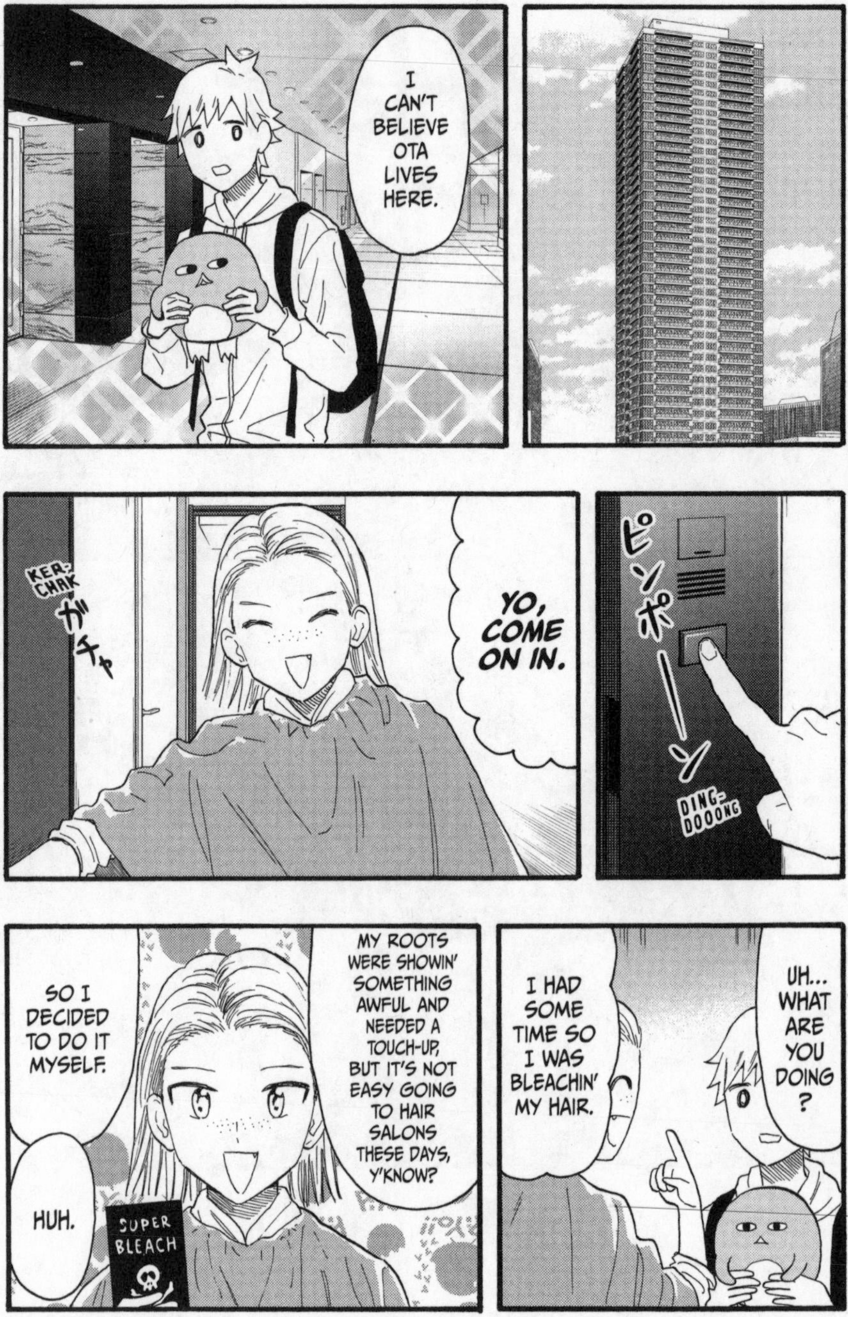
I CAN'T BELIEVE OTA LIVES HERE.
ピンポーン
DING-DOOONG
YO, COME ON IN.
KER-CHAK
ガチャ
UH... WHAT ARE YOU DOING?
I HAD SOME TIME SO I WAS BLEACHIN' MY HAIR.
MY ROOTS WERE SHOWIN' SOMETHING AWFUL AND NEEDED A TOUCH-UP, BUT IT'S NOT EASY GOING TO HAIR SALONS THESE DAYS, Y'KNOW?
SO I DECIDED TO DO IT MYSELF.
HUH.
SUPER BLEACH

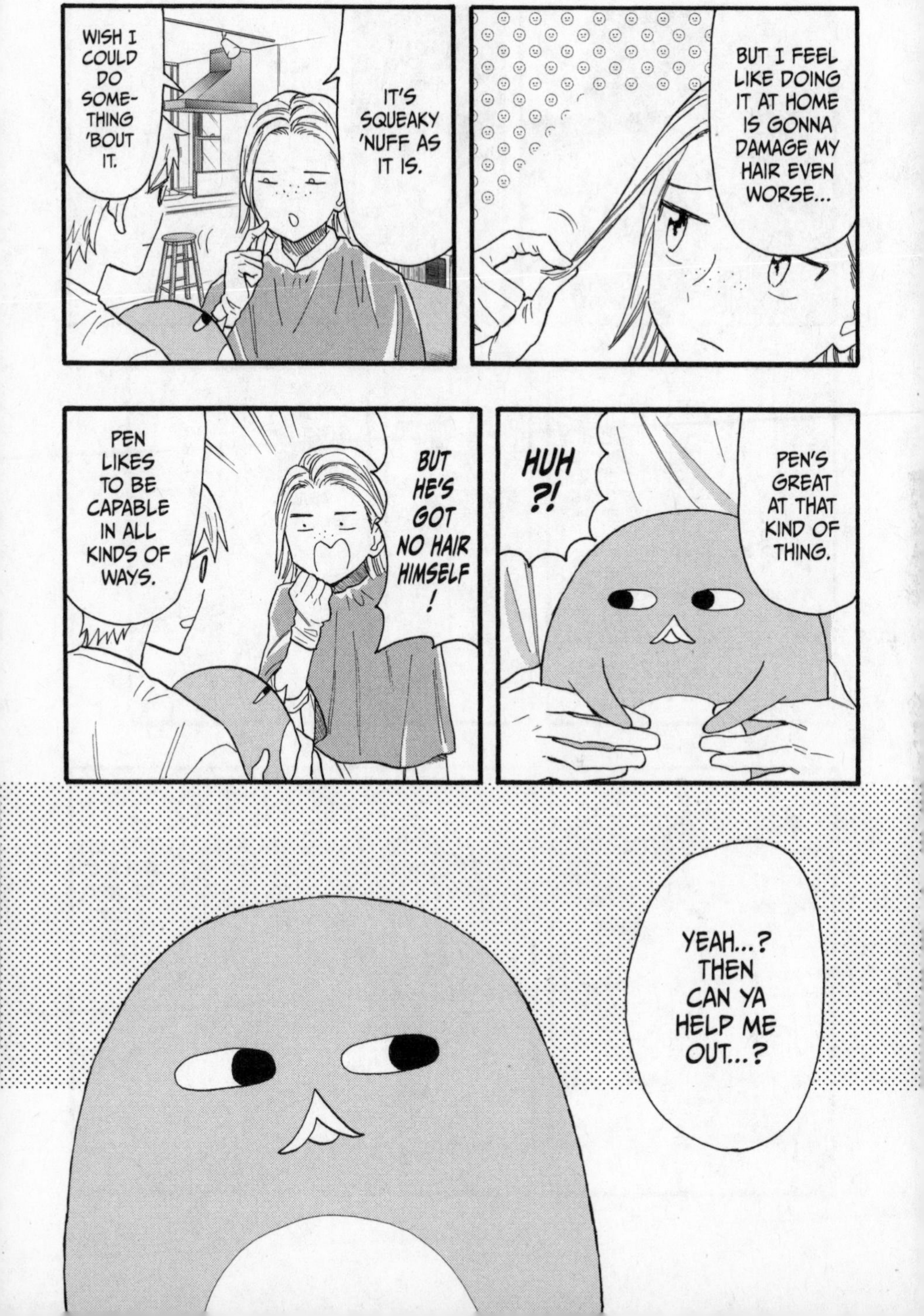

BUT I FEEL LIKE DOING IT AT HOME IS GONNA DAMAGE MY HAIR EVEN WORSE...
IT'S SQUEAKY 'NUFF AS IT IS.
WISH I COULD DO SOME-THING 'BOUT IT.
PEN'S GREAT AT THAT KIND OF THING.
HUH ?!
BUT HE'S GOT NO HAIR HIMSELF!
PEN LIKES TO BE CAPABLE IN ALL KINDS OF WAYS.
YEAH...? THEN CAN YA HELP ME OUT...?

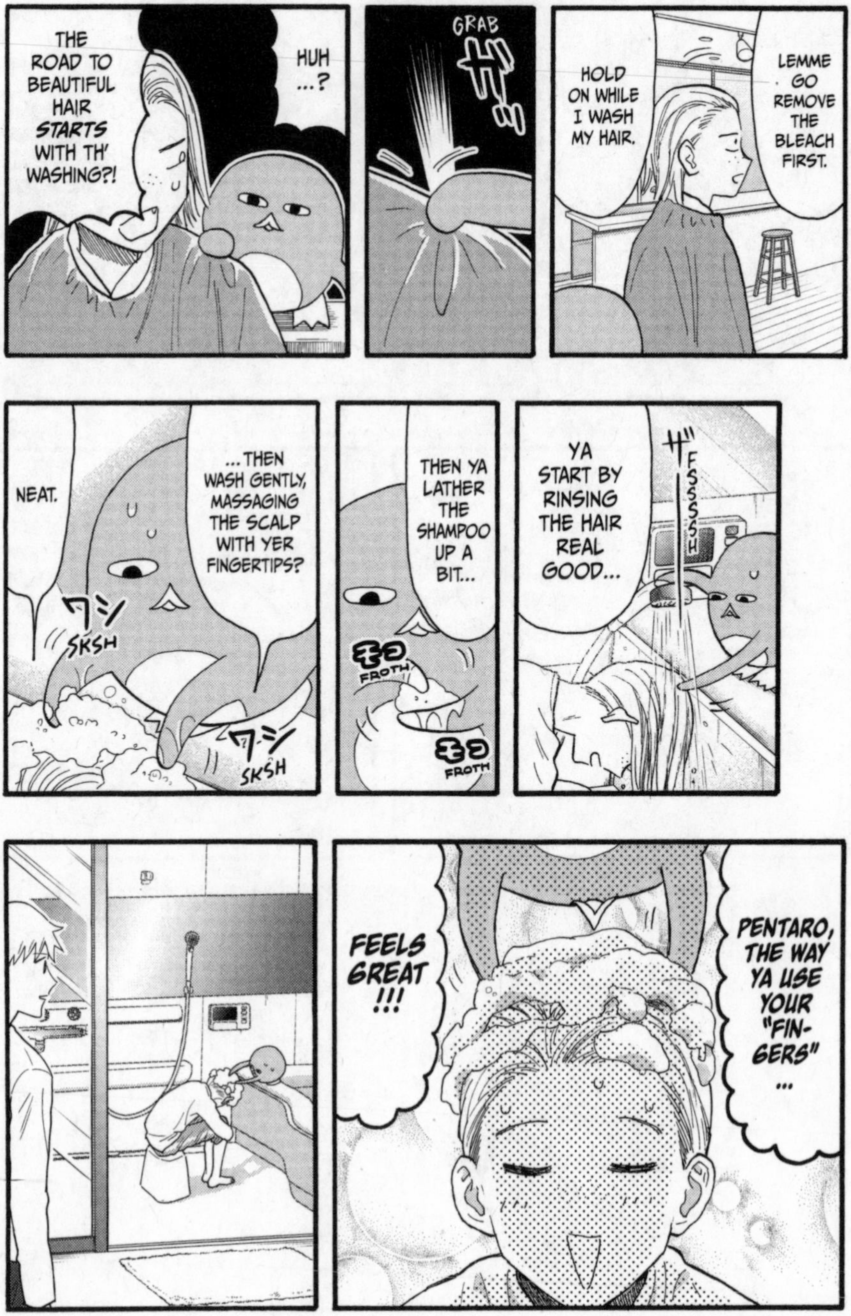
LEMME GO REMOVE THE BLEACH FIRST.
HOLD ON WHILE I WASH MY HAIR.
GRAB
ガッ
HUH ...?
THE ROAD TO BEAUTIFUL HAIR *STARTS* WITH TH' WASHING?!
ザ
FSSSSH
YA START BY RINSING THE HAIR REAL GOOD...
THEN YA LATHER THE SHAMPOO UP A BIT...
モコ
FROTH
モコ
FROTH
...THEN WASH GENTLY, MASSAGING THE SCALP WITH YER FINGERTIPS?
NEAT.
ワシ
SKSH
ワシ
SKSH
PENTARO, THE WAY YA USE YOUR "FINGERS" ...
FEELS GREAT !!!

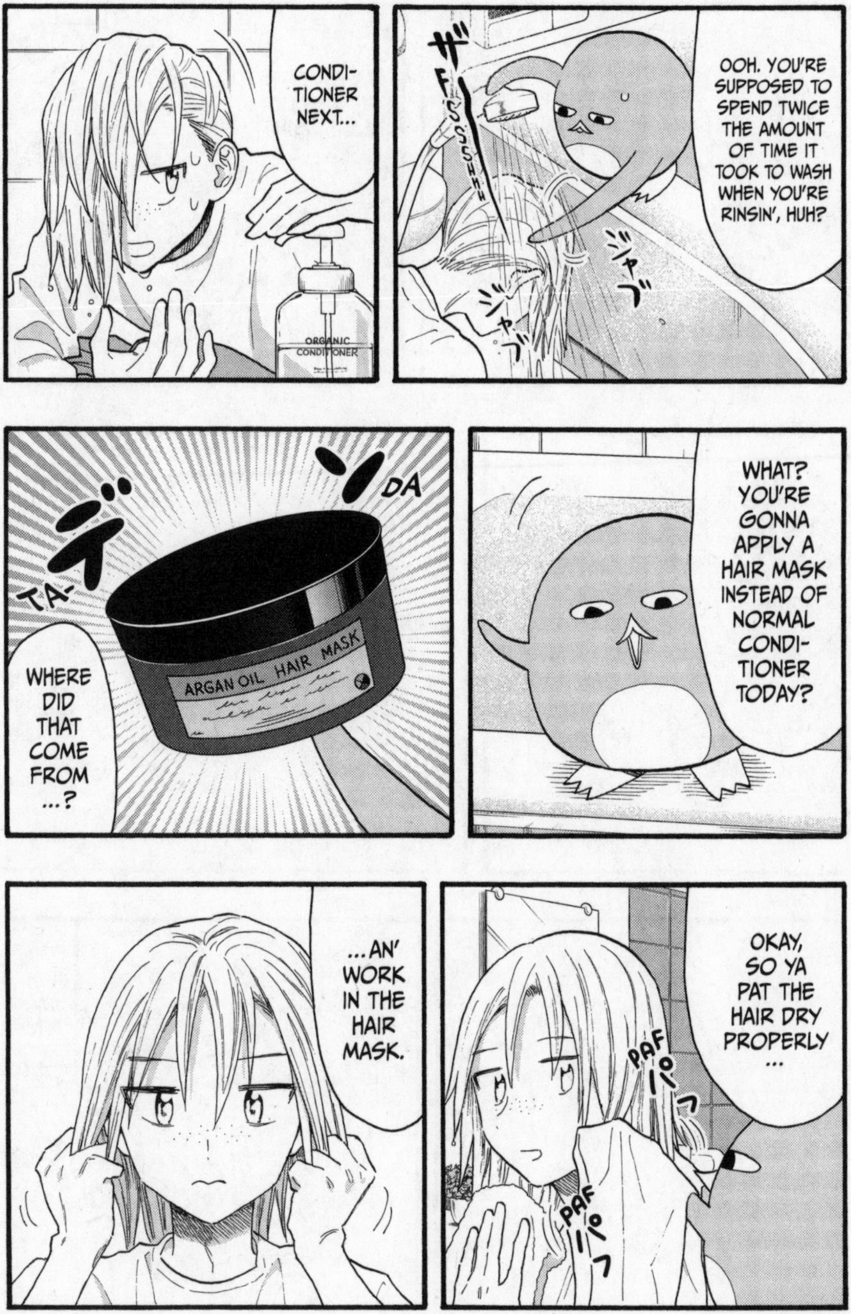
FSSSHHH
OOH. YOU'RE SUPPOSED TO SPEND TWICE THE AMOUNT OF TIME IT TOOK TO WASH WHEN YOU'RE RINSIN', HUH?
CONDI-TIONER NEXT...
ORGANIC CONDITIONER
WHAT? YOU'RE GONNA APPLY A HAIR MASK INSTEAD OF NORMAL CONDI-TIONER TODAY?
TA-DA
ARGAN OIL HAIR MASK
WHERE DID THAT COME FROM ...?
OKAY, SO YA PAT THE HAIR DRY PROPERLY ...
PAF
PAF
...AN' WORK IN THE HAIR MASK.

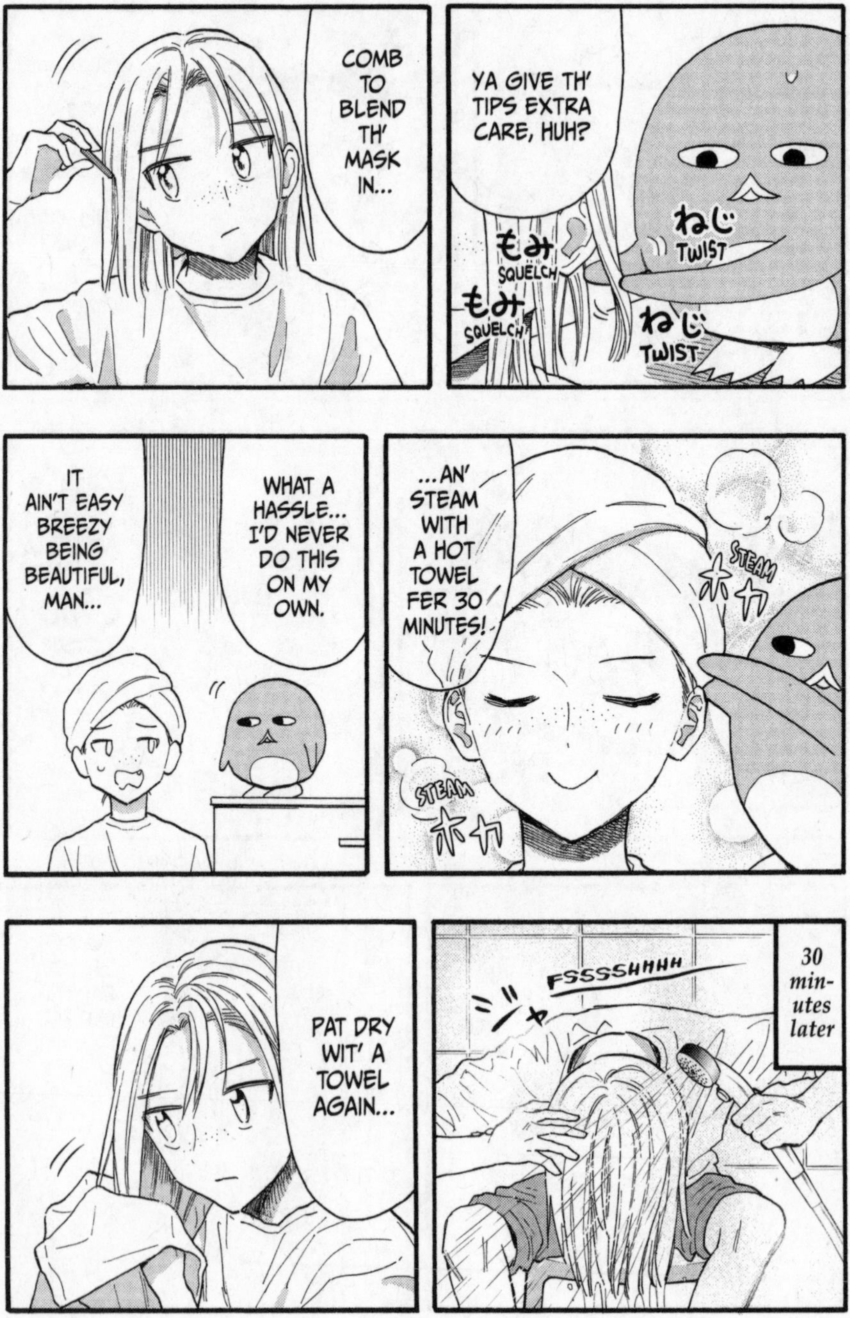
YA GIVE TH' TIPS EXTRA CARE, HUH?
ねじ TWIST
ねじ TWIST
もみ SQUELCH
もみ SQUELCH
COMB TO BLEND TH' MASK IN...
...AN' STEAM WITH A HOT TOWEL FER 30 MINUTES!
ホカ STEAM
ホカ STEAM
WHAT A HASSLE... I'D NEVER DO THIS ON MY OWN.
IT AIN'T EASY BREEZY BEING BEAUTIFUL, MAN...
30 minutes later
シャ FSSSSHHHH
PAT DRY WIT' A TOWEL AGAIN...

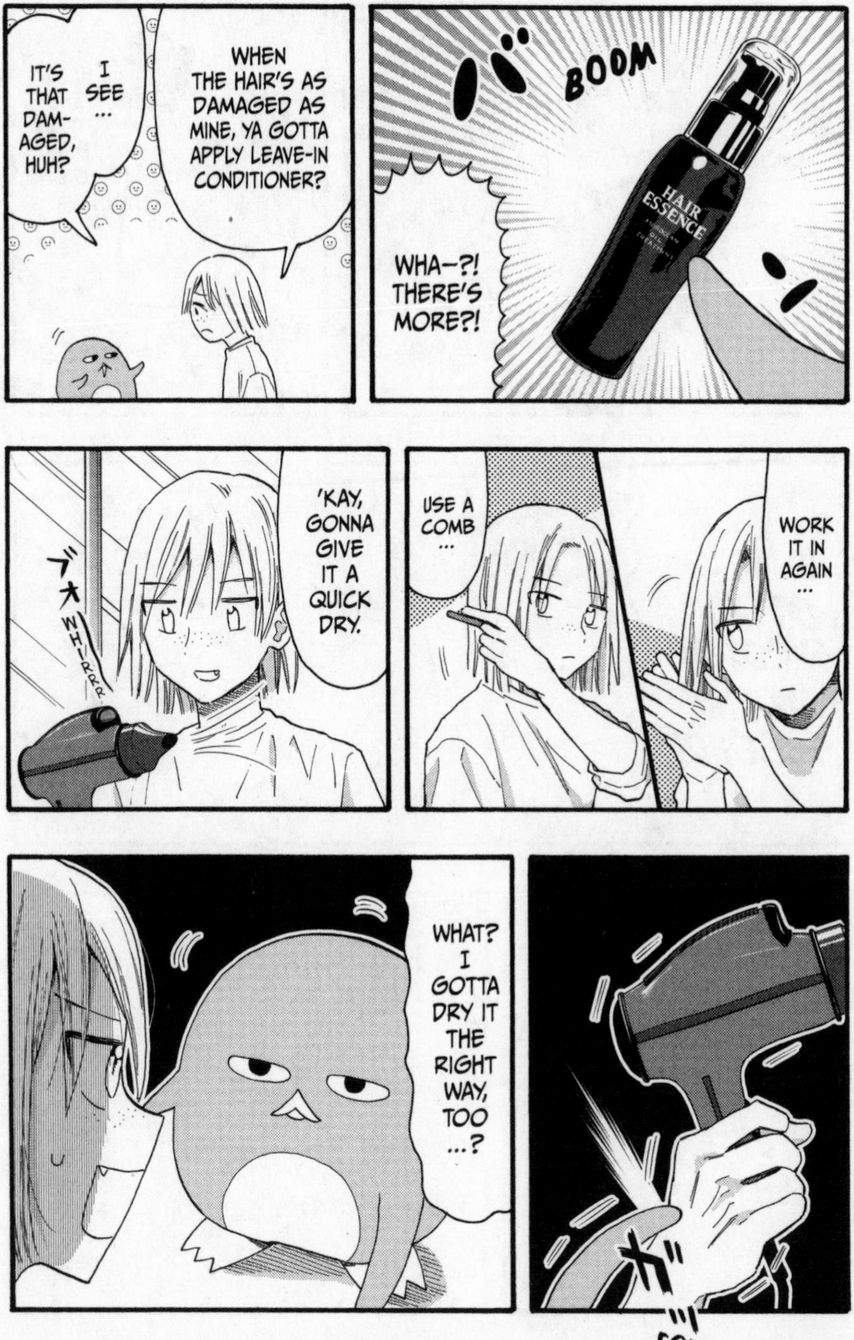
BOOM
WHA—?! THERE'S MORE?!
WHEN THE HAIR'S AS DAMAGED AS MINE, YA GOTTA APPLY LEAVE-IN CONDITIONER?
I SEE ...
IT'S THAT DAMAGED, HUH?
WORK IT IN AGAIN ...
USE A COMB ...
'KAY, GONNA GIVE IT A QUICK DRY.
WHIRRR
GRAB
WHAT? I GOTTA DRY IT THE RIGHT WAY, TOO ...?

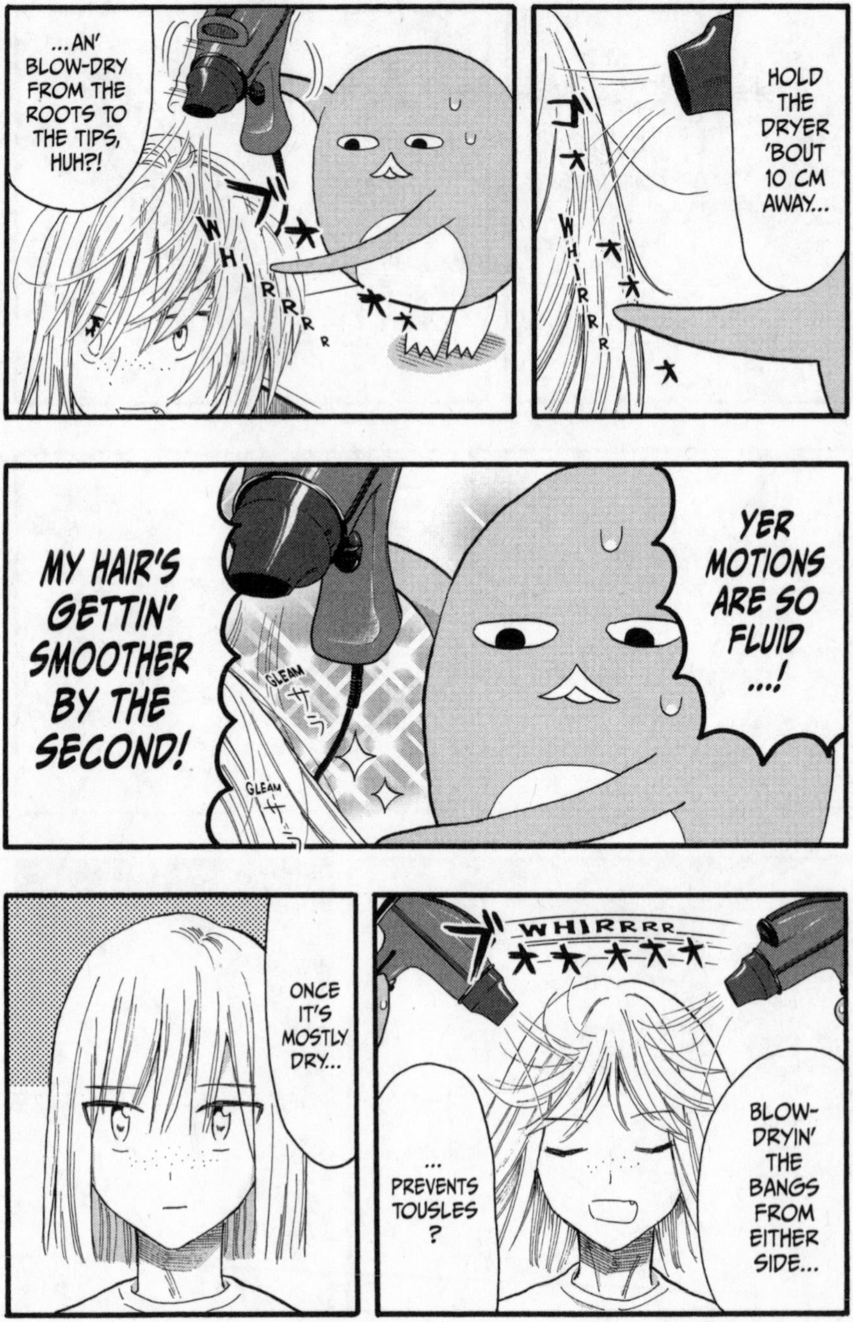
HOLD THE DRYER 'BOUT 10 CM AWAY...
WHIRRR
...AN' BLOW-DRY FROM THE ROOTS TO THE TIPS, HUH?!
WHIRRRR
YER MOTIONS ARE SO FLUID ...!
MY HAIR'S GETTIN' SMOOTHER BY THE SECOND!
GLEAM
GLEAM
WHIRRRR
BLOW-DRYIN' THE BANGS FROM EITHER SIDE...
...PREVENTS TOUSLES?
ONCE IT'S MOSTLY DRY...

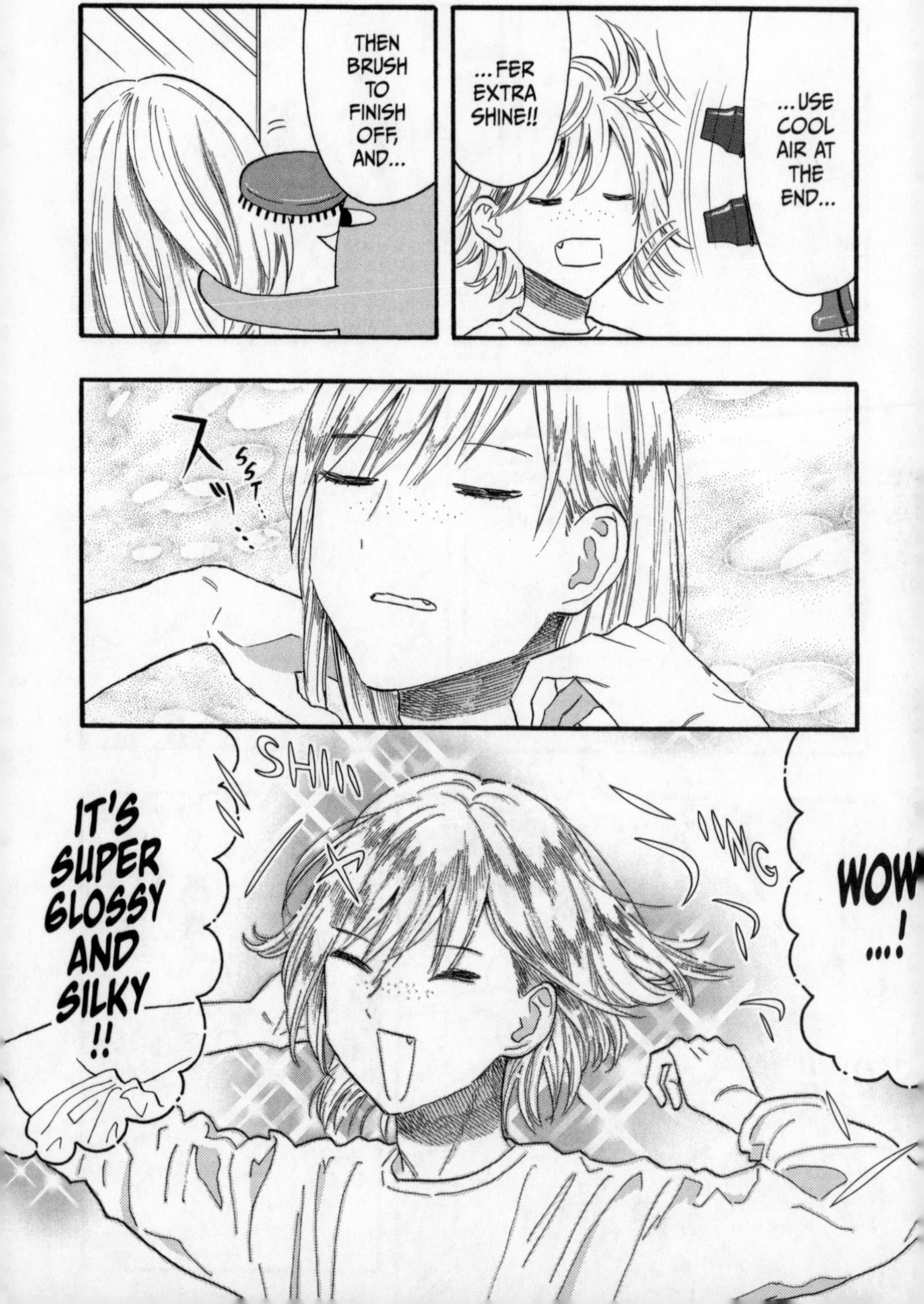
...USE COOL AIR AT THE END...
...FER EXTRA SHINE!!
THEN BRUSH TO FINISH OFF, AND...
SSST...
WOW...!
SHIIIIING
IT'S SUPER GLOSSY AND SILKY!!

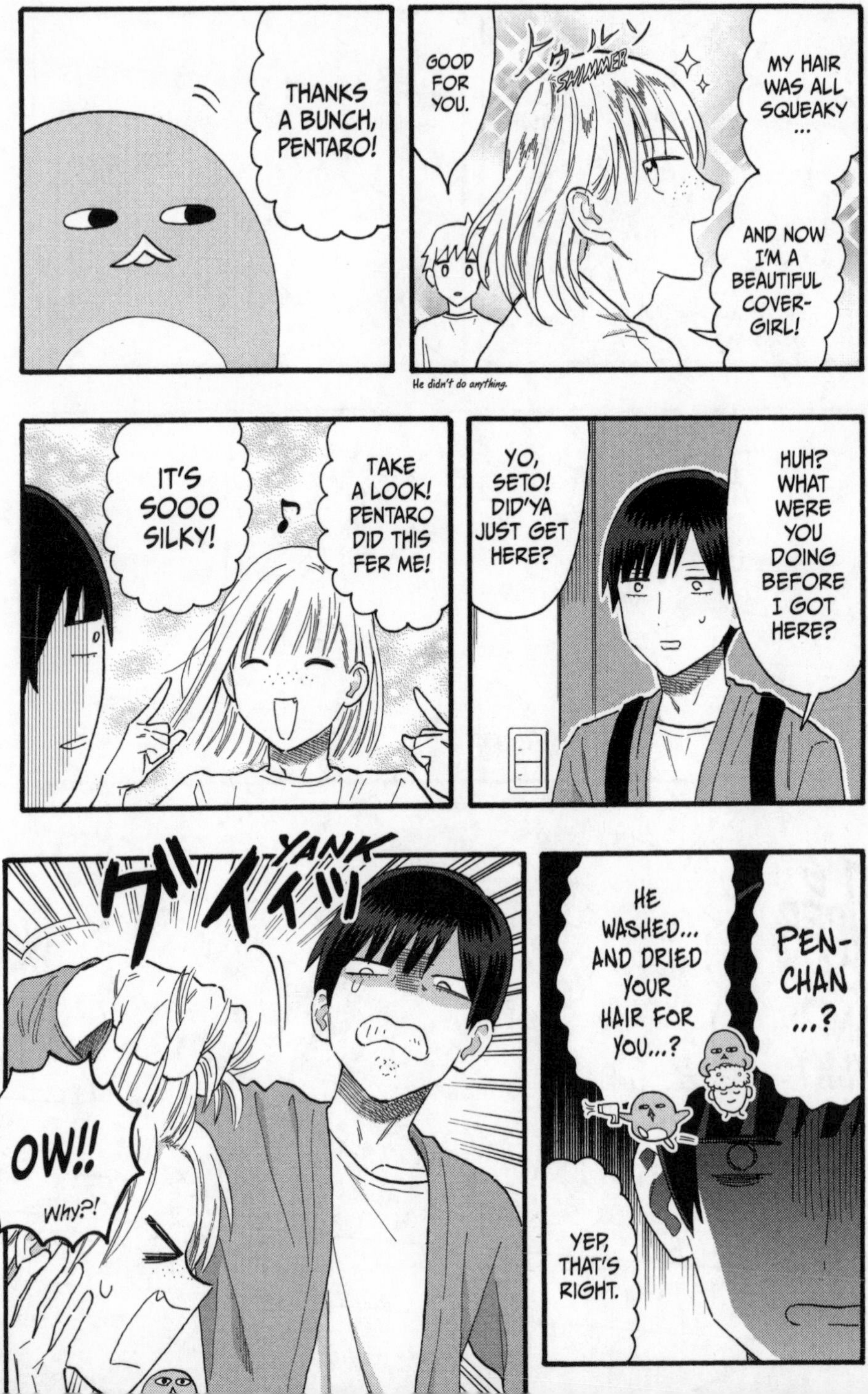
MY HAIR WAS ALL SQUEAKY ...
AND NOW I'M A BEAUTIFUL COVER-GIRL!
SHIMMER
GOOD FOR YOU.
THANKS A BUNCH, PENTARO!
He didn't do anything.
HUH? WHAT WERE YOU DOING BEFORE I GOT HERE?
YO, SETO! DID'YA JUST GET HERE?
TAKE A LOOK! PENTARO DID THIS FER ME!
IT'S SOOO SILKY!
PEN-CHAN ...?
HE WASHED... AND DRIED YOUR HAIR FOR YOU...?
YEP, THAT'S RIGHT.
YANK
OW!!
Why?!

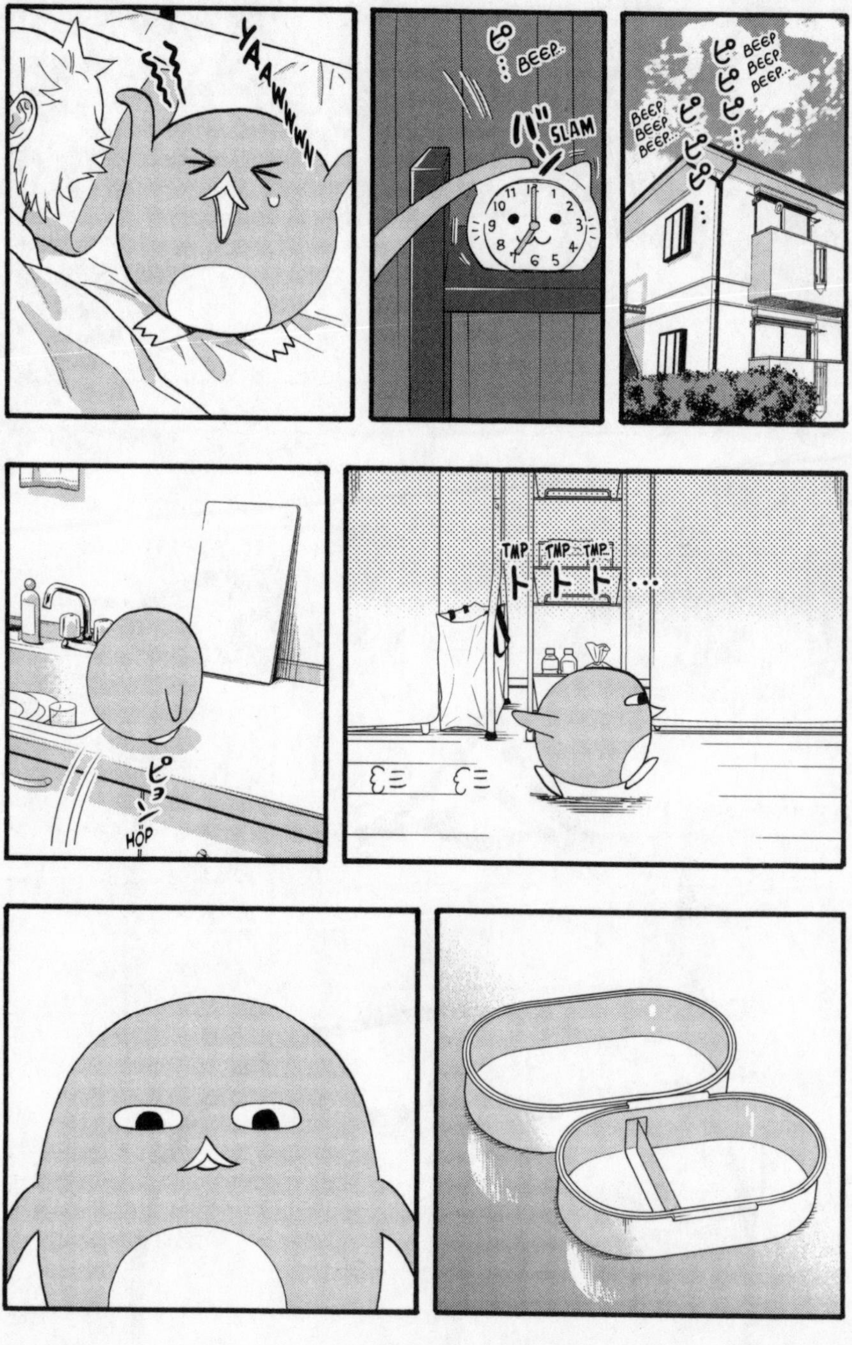
ピピピ… BEEP BEEP BEEP...
ピピピ… BEEP BEEP BEEP...
ピ… BEEP...
バ SLAM
YAAWWWWN
トトト… TMP TMP TMP
ピョン HOP

Pen 42 The Penguin Makes a Bento for His Owner

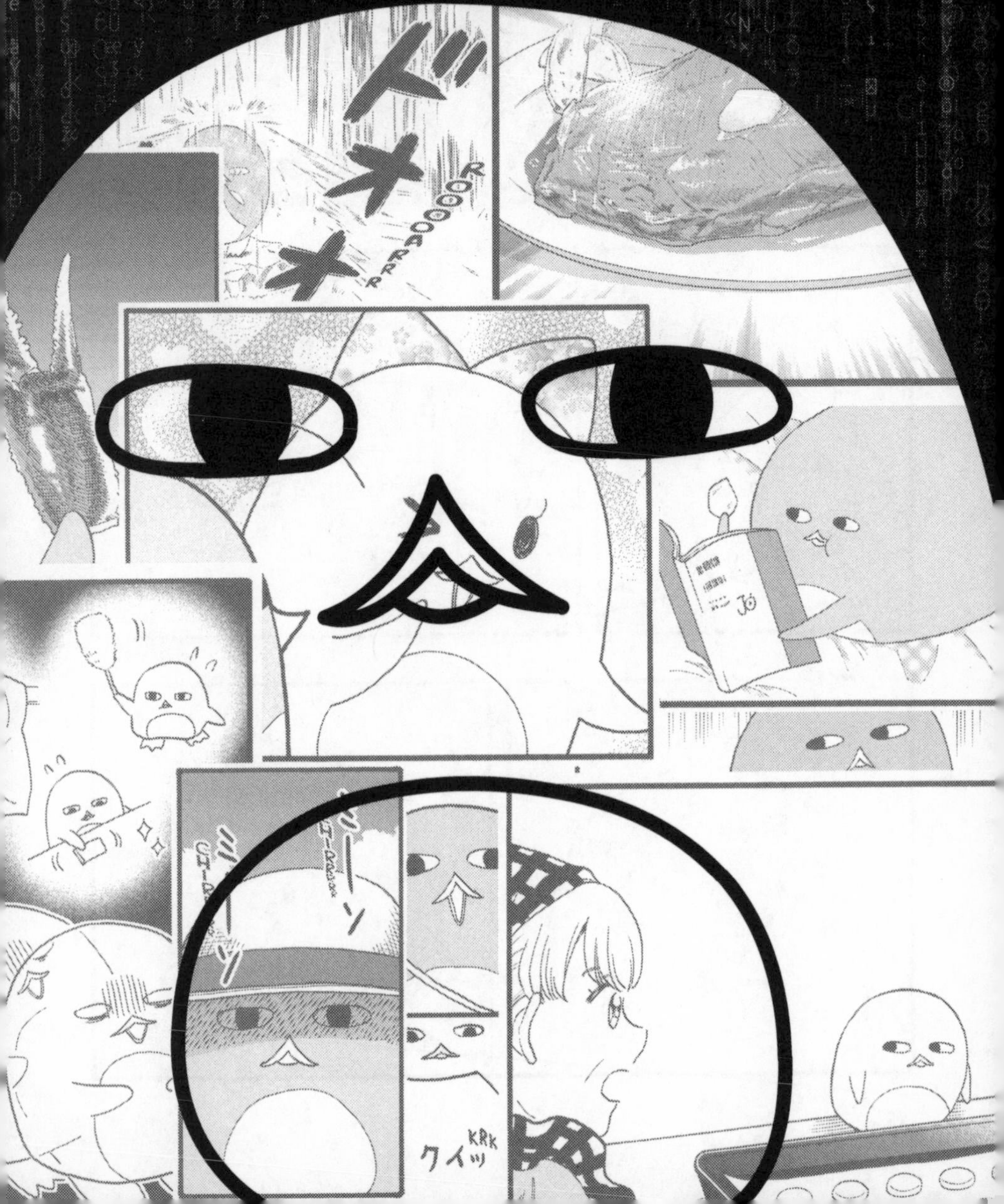
ROOOOARRR
KRK
クイッ

よそい SCOOP

よそい SCOOP

The rice needs to be cooled down because it can spoil if the lid is capped while still hot.

パ CLAK

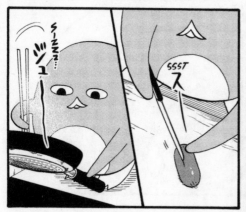

シーンン... ジュー

SSST ス

RUSTLE カサ

カサ RUSTLE

Red Sausages

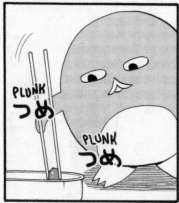

PLUNK つめ

PLUNK つめ

STEAM

STEAM

149

CLUNK
カッ
CLUNK
カッ
パ
CRACK
カ
チャッ
CLAK
チャッ
CLAK
チャッ
CLAK
チャッ
CLAK
テュ
TRICKLE...
SHK
パッ
Water
Salt
Sugar
パッ
SHK
S-ZZZ...
ジュウ...
クイッ
FWISH
クイ
FWISH-ッ
つめ
PLUNK
つめ
PLUNK

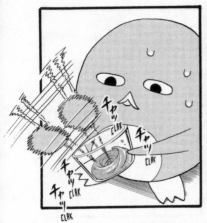

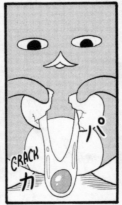

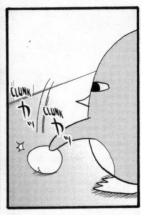

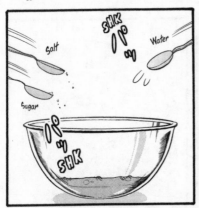

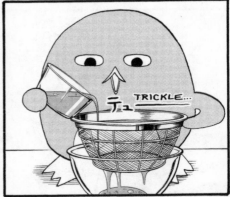

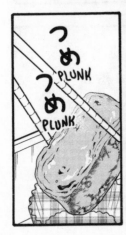

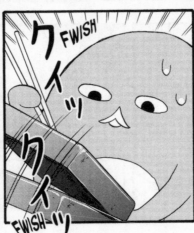

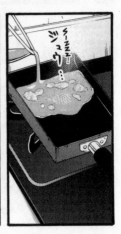

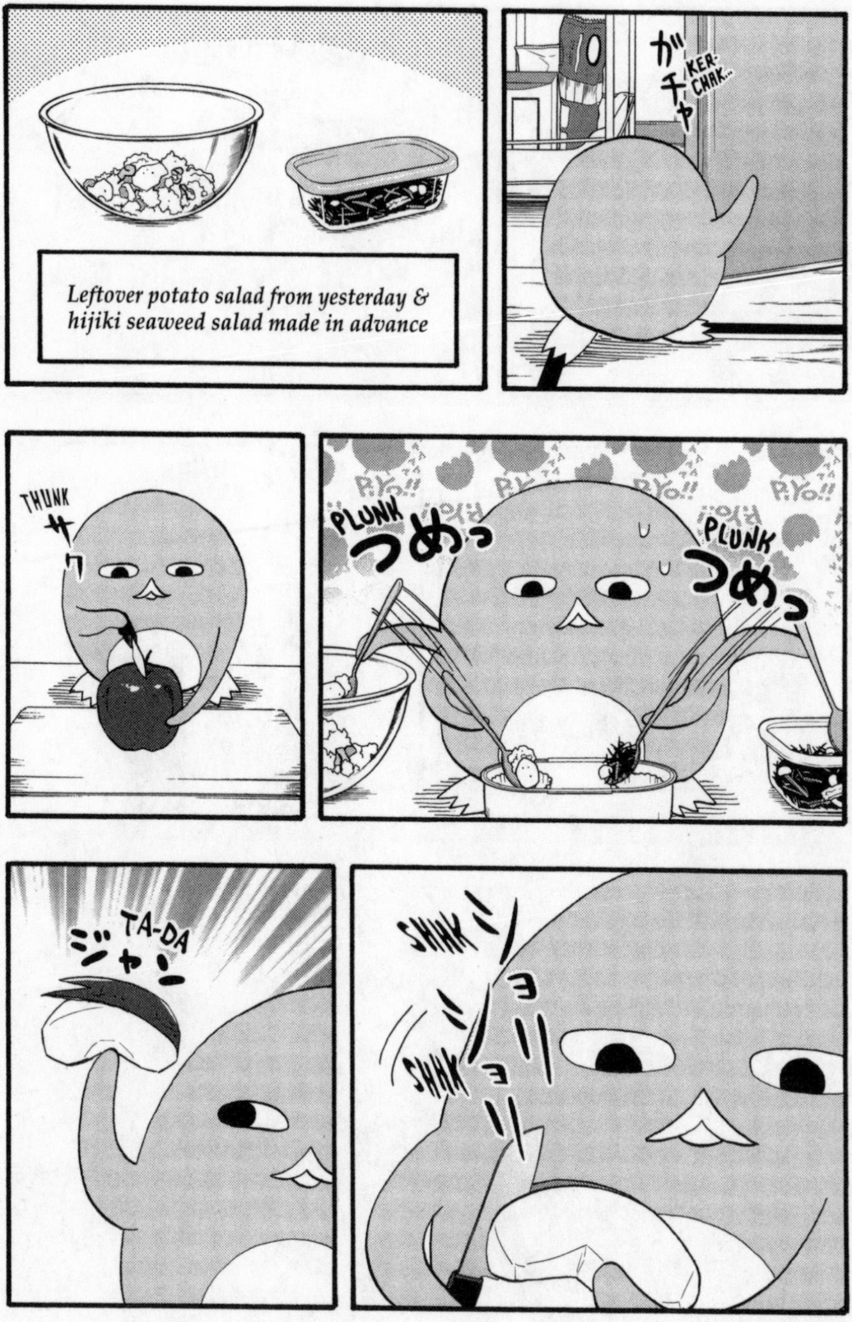
ガチャ
KER-CHAK...
Leftover potato salad from yesterday & hijiki seaweed salad made in advance
PiYo!!
PiYo!!
PiYo!!
PLUNK
つめっ
PLUNK
つめっ
THUNK
サク
SHHK
ショリ
SHHK
ショリ
TA-DA
ジャン

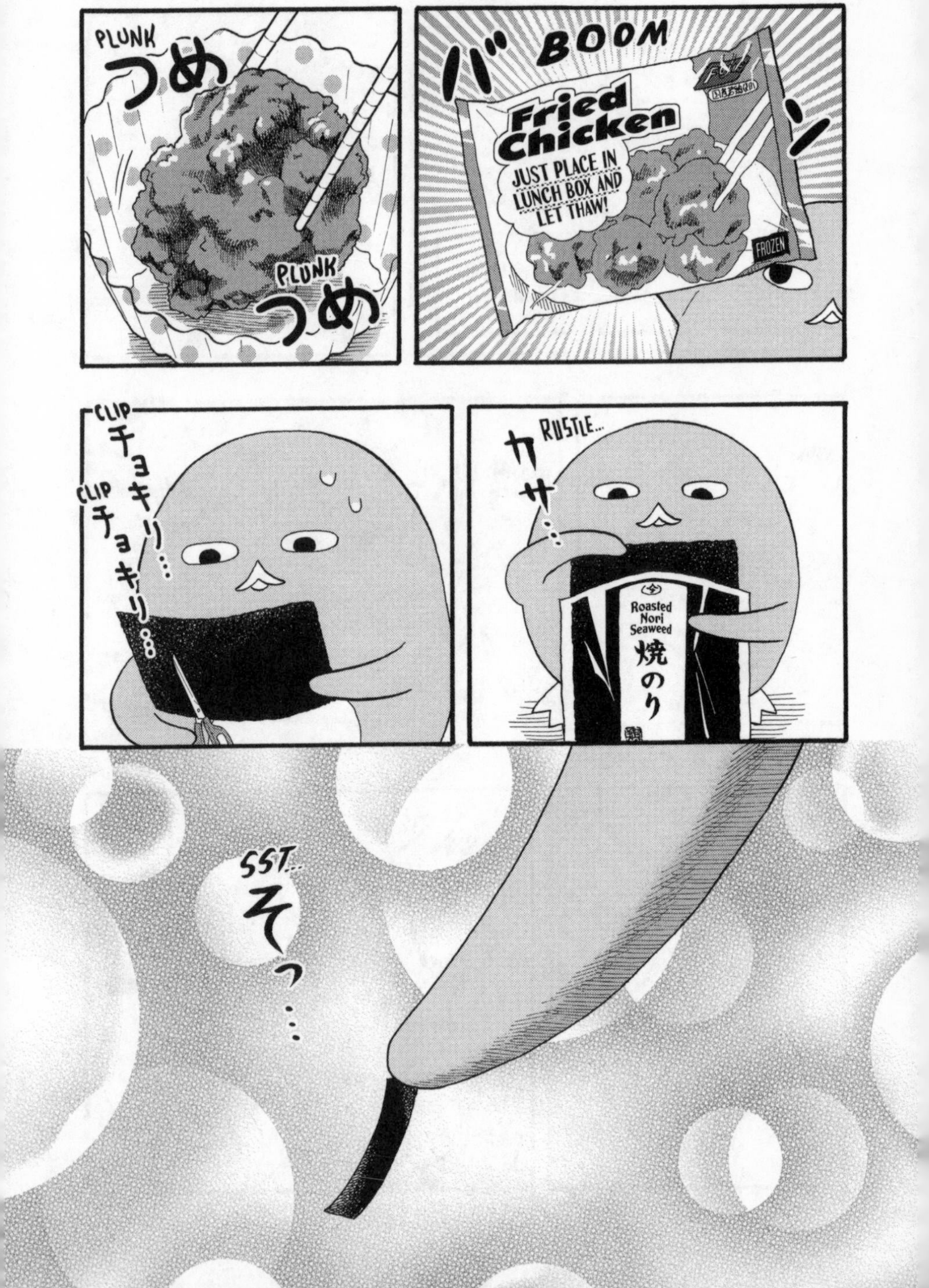
BOOM
バーン
Fried Chicken
JUST PLACE IN LUNCH BOX AND LET THAW!
FROZEN
PLUNK
つめ
PLUNK
つめ
RUSTLE...
カサ…
Roasted Nori Seaweed
焼のり
CLIP
チョキリ…
CLIP
チョキリ…
SST...
そっ…

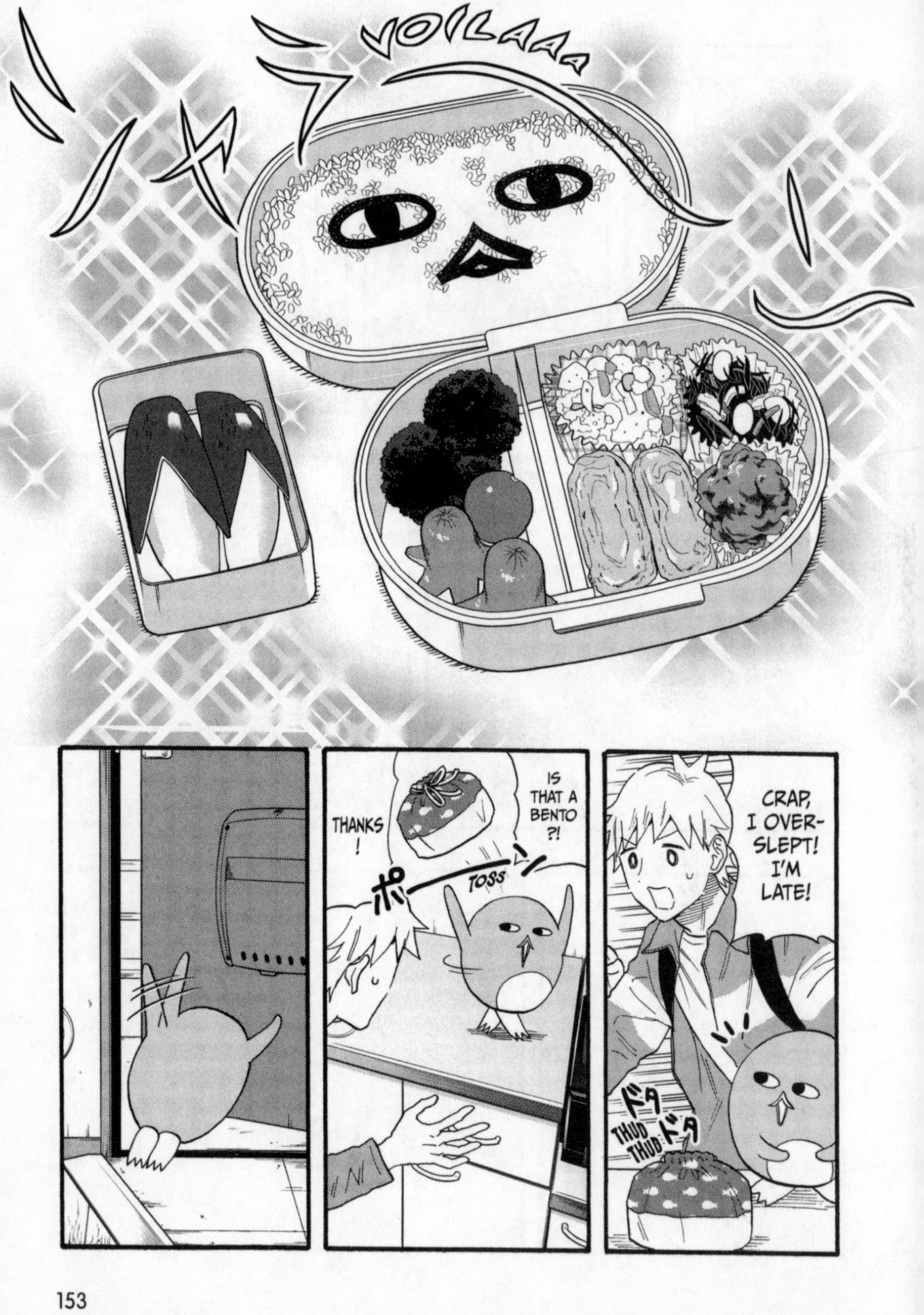
VOILAAA
CRAP, I OVER-SLEPT! I'M LATE!
THUD THUD
IS THAT A BENTO ?!
THANKS !
TOSS

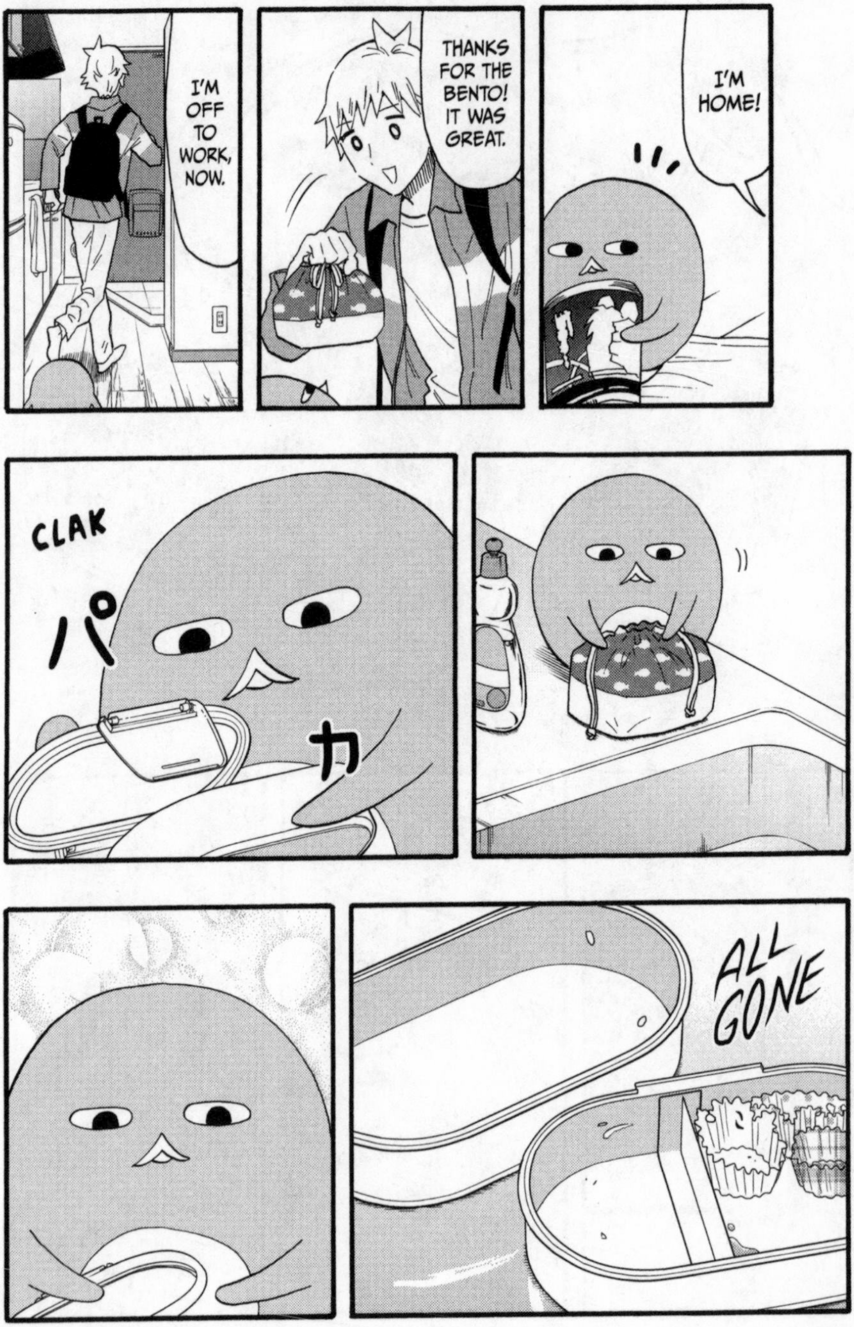
I'M HOME!
THANKS FOR THE BENTO! IT WAS GREAT.
I'M OFF TO WORK, NOW.
CLAK
パカ
ALL GONE

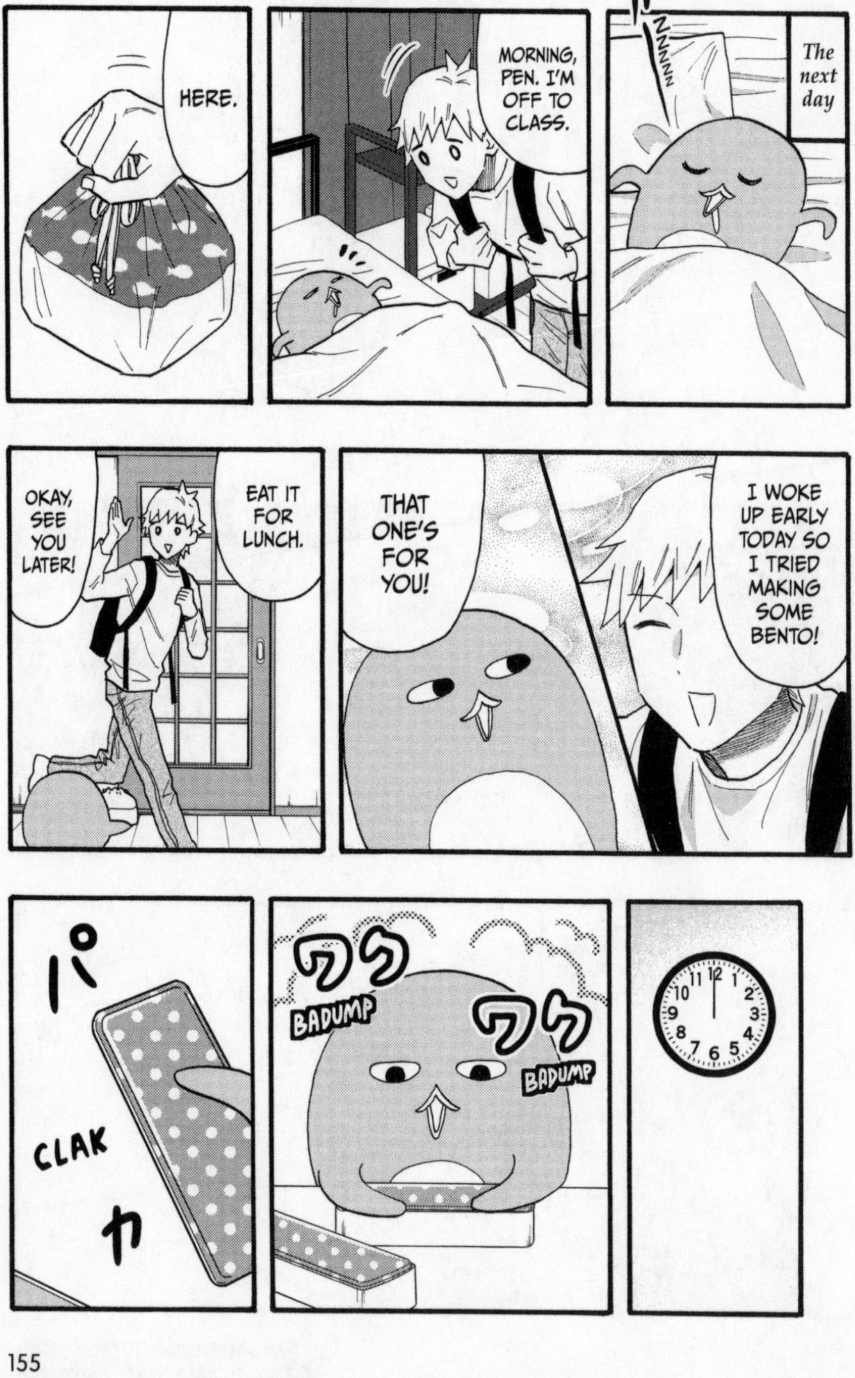
The next day
カ
ZZZZZ
MORNING, PEN. I'M OFF TO CLASS.
HERE.
I WOKE UP EARLY TODAY SO I TRIED MAKING SOME BENTO!
THAT ONE'S FOR YOU!
EAT IT FOR LUNCH.
OKAY, SEE YOU LATER!
ワク
BADUMP
ワク
BADUMP
パ
CLAK
カ

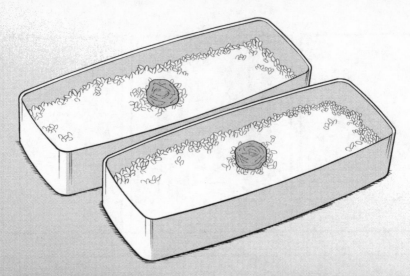

OOPS, ALL SIDES.

PENGUIN & HOUSE: THE END

He paired it
with all the things
that go with rice
and ate it all.

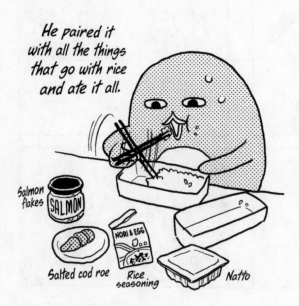

Salmon
flakes

SALMON

Salted cod roe

NORI & EGG

Rice
seasoning

Natto

Pentaro

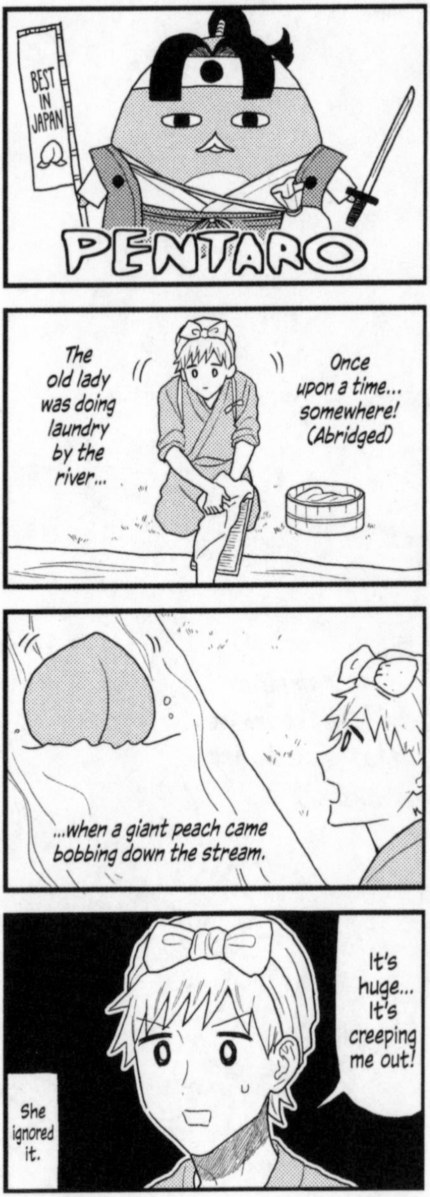
BEST IN JAPAN
PENTARO
Once upon a time... somewhere! (Abridged)
The old lady was doing laundry by the river...
...when a giant peach came bobbing down the stream.
It's huge... It's creeping me out!
She ignored it.

Penshima Taro

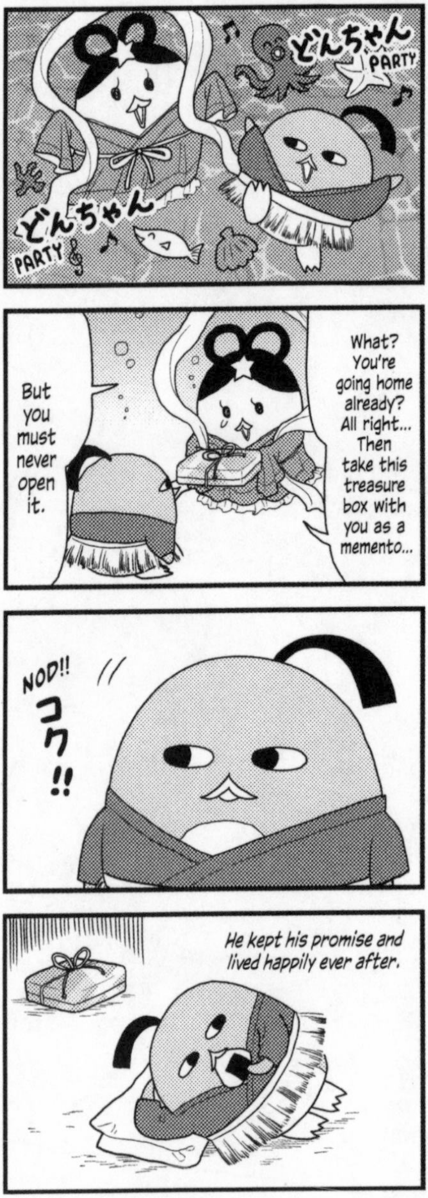
どんちゃん PARTY
どんちゃん PARTY
What? You're going home already? All right... Then take this treasure box with you as a memento...
But you must never open it.
NOD!! コク!!
He kept his promise and lived happily ever after.

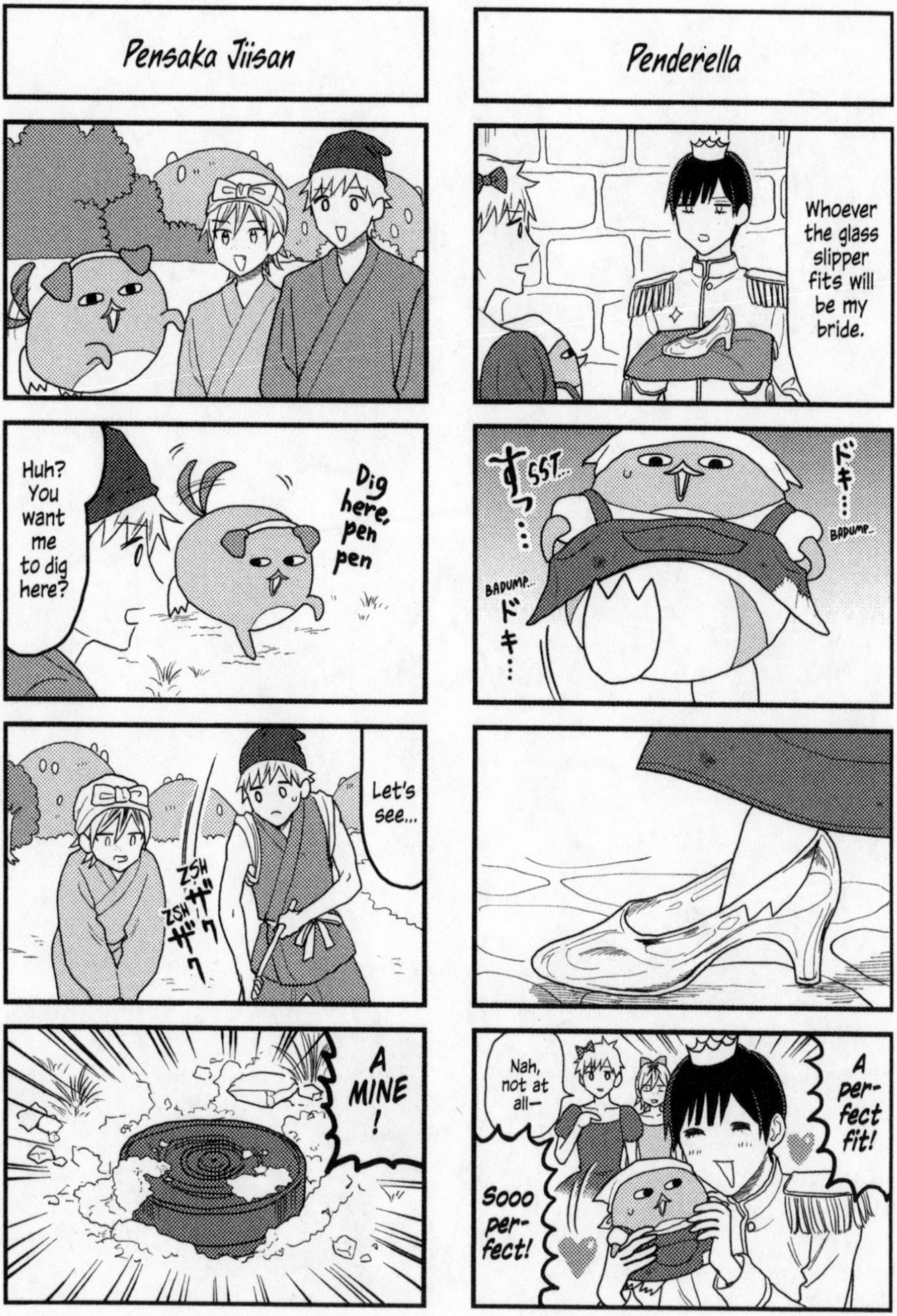
Penderella
Whoever the glass slipper fits will be my bride.
ドキ… BADUMP…
すっ… SST…
BADUMP… ドキ…
A perfect fit!
Nah, not at all—
Sooo perfect!
Pensaka Jiisan
Dig here, pen pen
Huh? You want me to dig here?
Let's see…
ZSH ザク
ZSH ザク
A MINE!

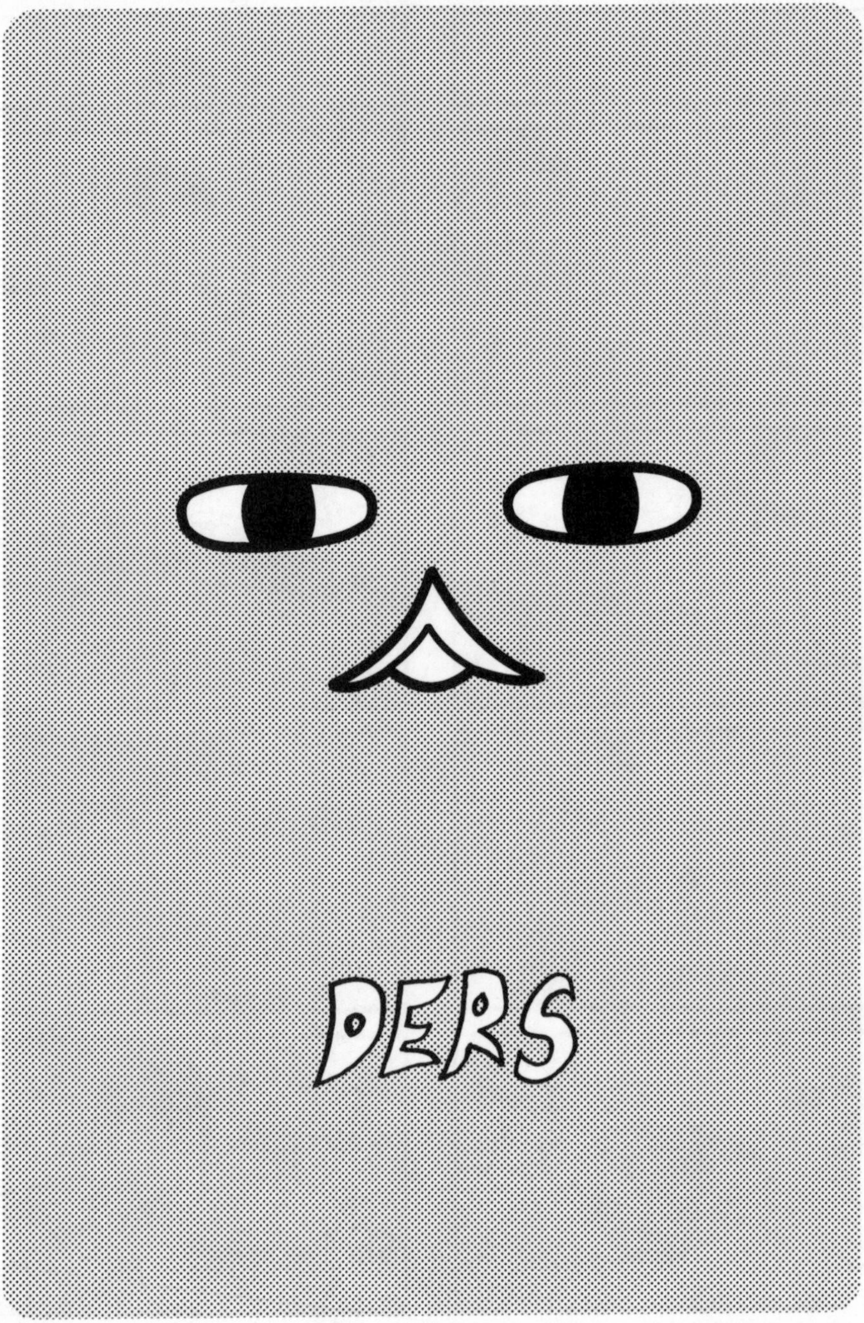
DERS

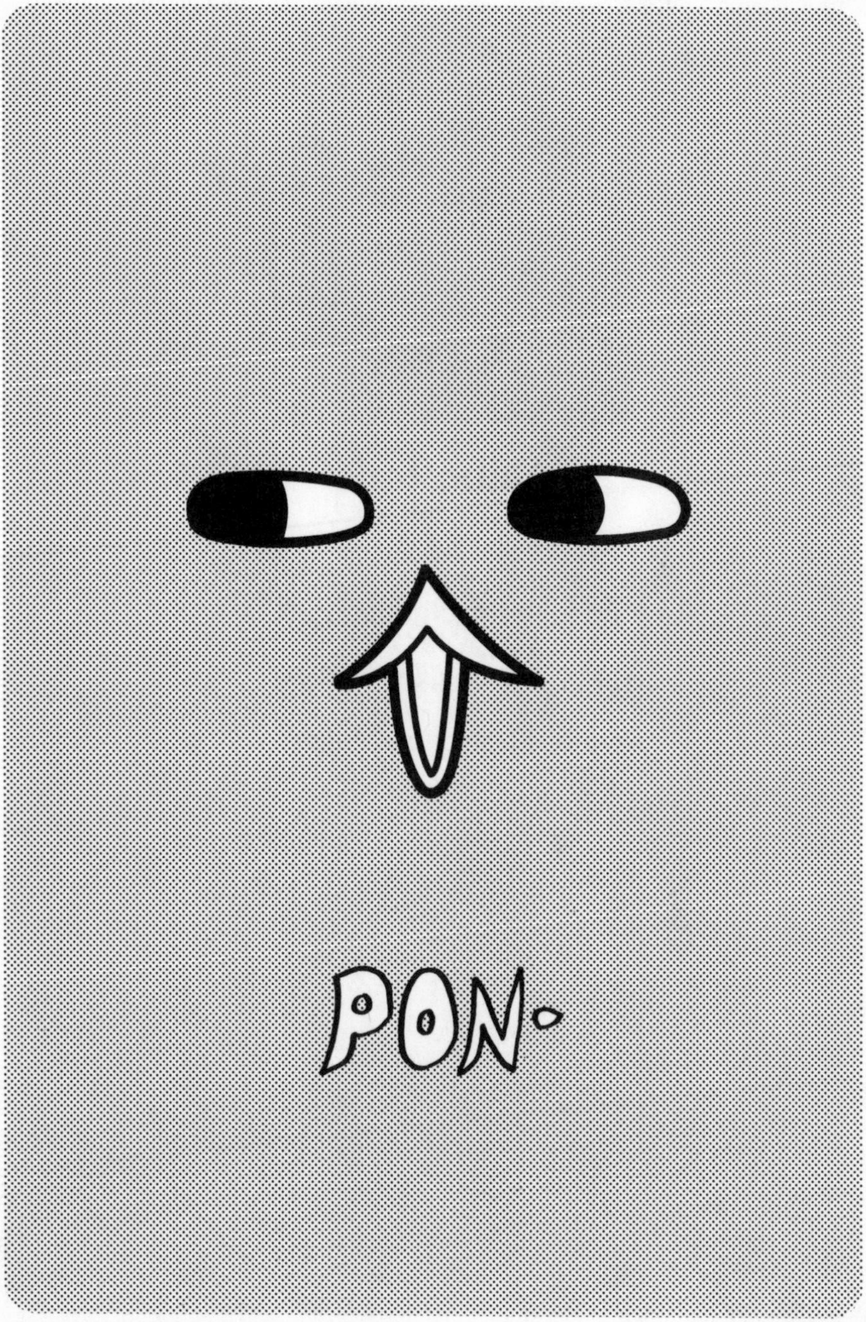
PON

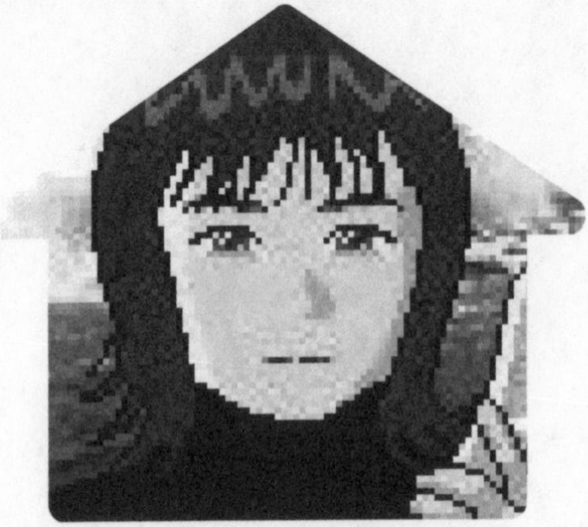

Akiho Ieda

家田明歩

I made this avatar of myself

using *Nigaoe Illust Maker*

(Avatar Illustration Maker).

Translation Notes

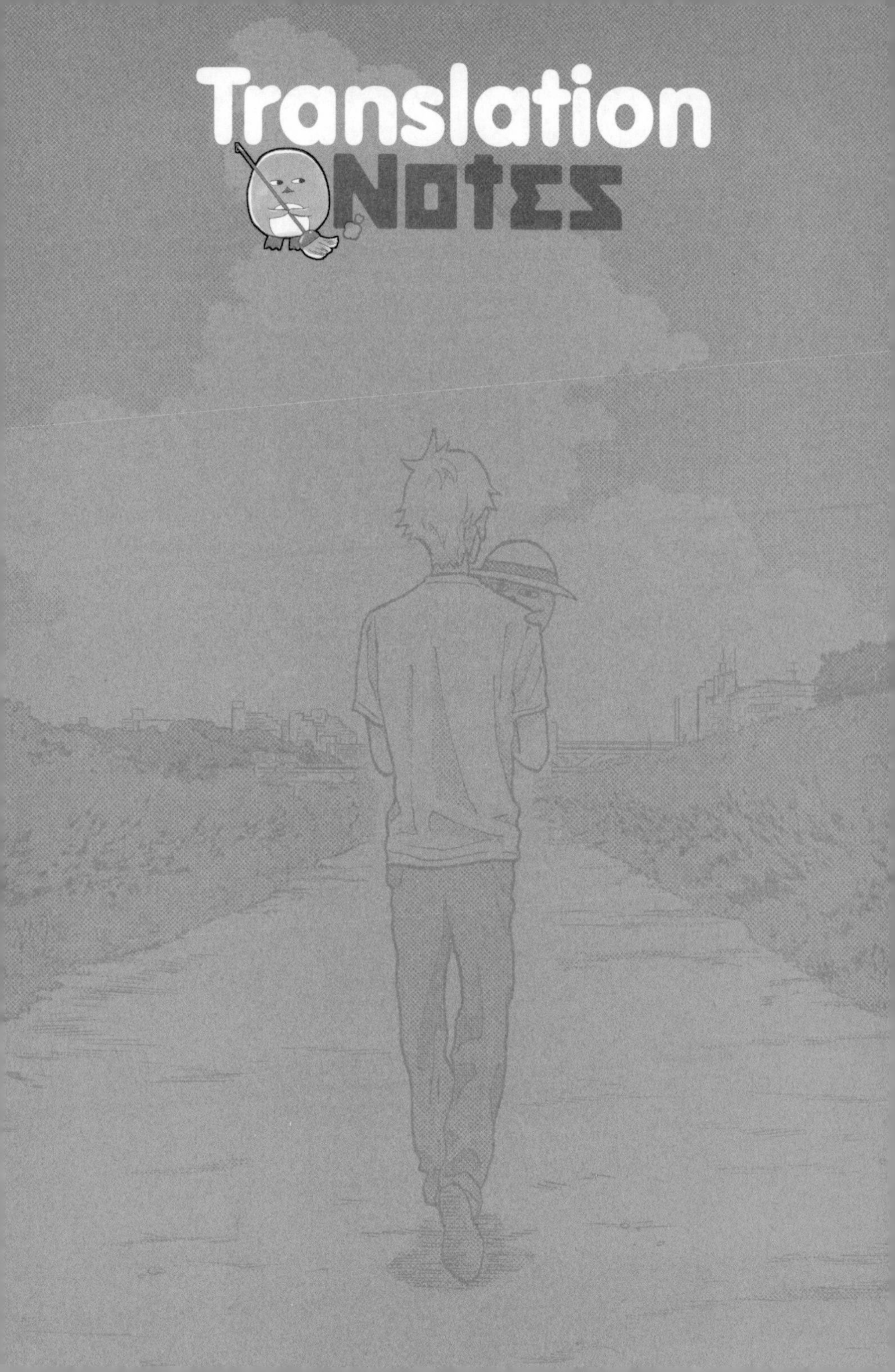

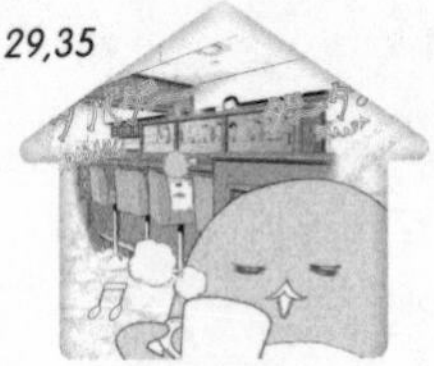

THE PENGUIN WHO KNOWS THE DIFFERENCE, DABADA

pg 29,35

References to ads for Nescafé Gold Blend Instant Coffee, which used the tagline, "For the man who knows the difference," and a special theme composed for the product that features scat singing with the syllables "dabada, dada." These ads, which ran for nearly 30 years, gave the impression that Nescafé Gold Blend was a luxury product fit for discerning tastes.

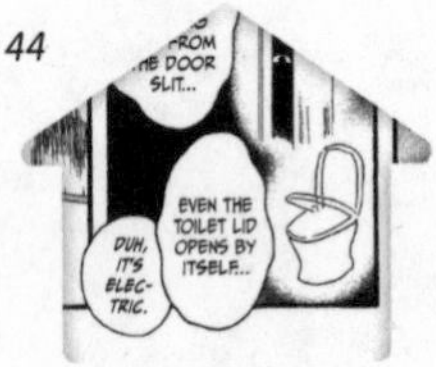
SLIT...
EVEN THE TOILET LID OPENS BY ITSELF...
DUH, IT'S ELEC-TRIC.

TOILET LID OPENS BY ITSELF

pg 44

Most toilets in Japan now have lids that open and close automatically.

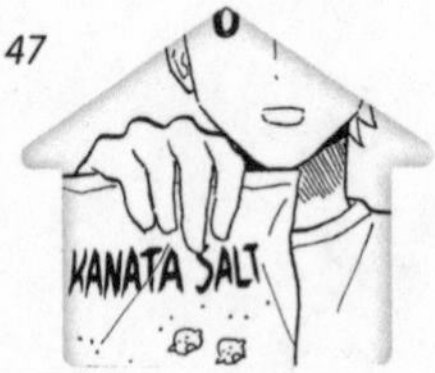
KANATA SALT

SALT

pg 47

In Japan, salt is traditionally believed to be purifying and an effective agent in purging ghosts and evil spirits.

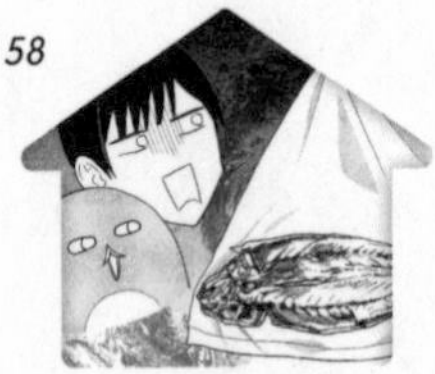

KUSAYA

pg 58

Salted, dried, fermented fish that smells so pungent, even its name literally means "stinky fish." The funk is so strong that it gets into everything around it, including laundry.

pg 61

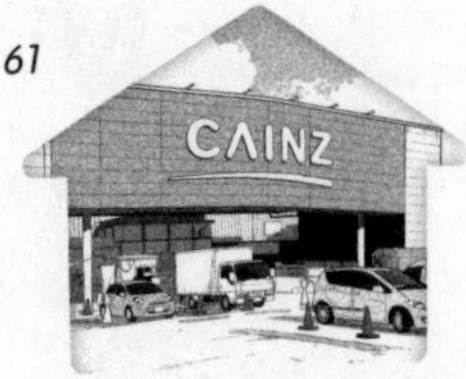
CAINZ

CAINZ

Cainz is a major home hardware chain that also sells homeware and lifestyle items.

pg 115

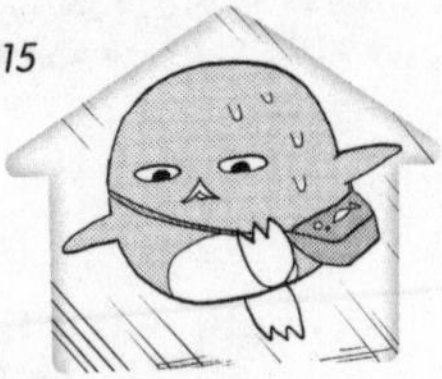

RUN, PENGUIN!

A reference to *Run, Melos!,* a short story by 20th-century author Osamu Dazai that is almost always read in Japanese schools. In the story, Melos is a shepherd who is sentenced to die after a failed assassination attempt on the tyrant king. He pleads to be allowed three days to return home for an important family event and leaves his friend Selinuntius as hostage, who will be executed in his stead should he fail to return by sundown on the third day. Melos is faced with multiple obstacles on the way back, such as an overflowing river and bandits. Utterly worn out, he almost gives up but rejuvenates himself with water from a clear spring, just like Pen, and makes it back just in time. The previously skeptical tyrant king is touched by the two men's bond of friendship and pardons Melos.

pg 126

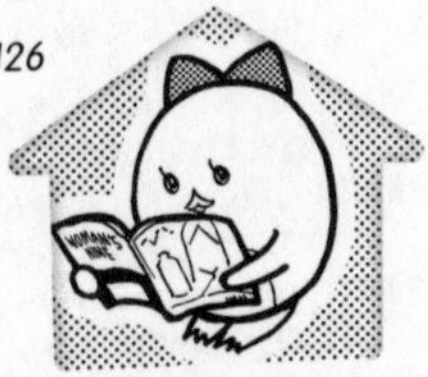

WOMAN'S NINE

A reference to the tabloid magazine *Women's Seven.*

pg 127

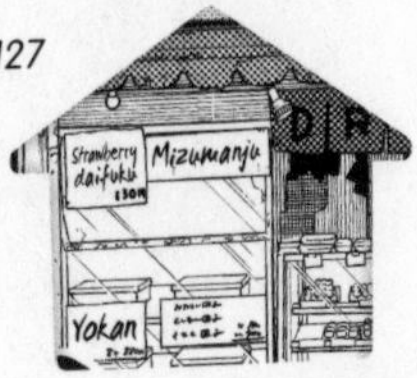
Strawberry daifuku
Mizumanju
Yokan

STRAWBERRY DAIFUKU, MIZUMANJU, YOKAN

These are all Japanese sweets with sweet bean paste.

pg 136

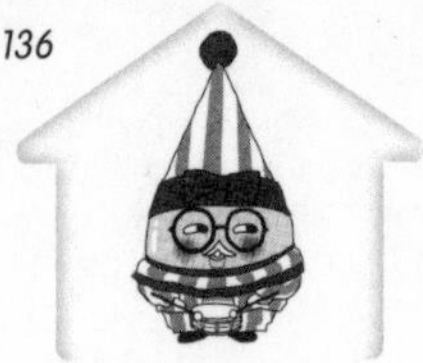

CUI-DAORÉ DOLL

Pen is dressed here as Cui-daoré Taro, the iconic advertisement doll that stood for 58 years in front of the Cui-daoré Restaurant in Osaka until it closed down in 2008. The doll came to represent Osaka's famous Dotonbori restaurant district and still continues to be a popular tourist attraction in a new location nearby.

pg 151

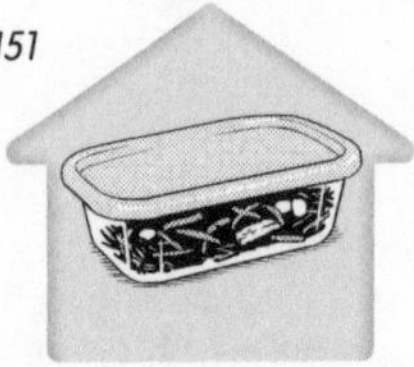

HIJIKI SEAWEED SALAD

A common bento item that involves stewing pieces of *hijiki* seaweed, *konnyaku* jelly, fried tofu, beans, and carrots in a sweet soy-sauce broth.

pg 158

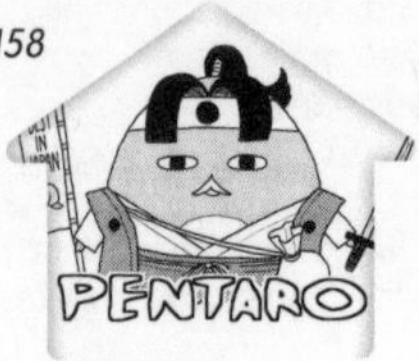
PENTARO

PENTARO

A parody of *Momotaro,* a folktale about a hero born from a giant peach. In the original, the old lady takes the peach home and discovers a baby in it.

pg 158

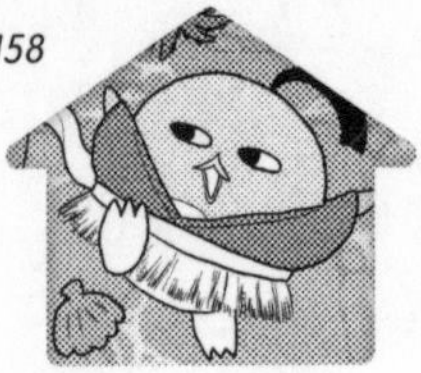

PENSHIMA TARO

A parody of *Urashima Taro,* a folktale about a young man who is invited to a palace under the sea for saving a sea turtle from some bullies. After three nights, he decides to return home, and the princess gives him a special box as a memento, which she says he must never open. When Urashima Taro returns home, many decades have gone by instead of three days, and when he opens the box in despair, smoke billows out of it and turns him into an old man.

PENSAKA JIISAN

A parody of the folktale *Hanasaka Jiisan,* or *The Old Man Who Made the Dead Trees Blossom,* in which a nice old man is rewarded and a jealous neighbor is punished for doing awful things to try and emulate the nice man's success. Towards the beginning, the nice old man's pet dog points to places to dig, where they find pots of gold.

pg 159

NIGAOE ILLUST MAKER

A free online service for making digital pixel avatars using pre-existing facial parts and accessories. A *nigaoe* is a "caricature" drawing in Japanese.

pg 162

The adorable new odd-couple cat comedy manga from the creator of the beloved *Chi's Sweet Home*, in full color!

Praise for Chi's Sweet Home

"Nearly impossible to turn away... a true all-ages title that anyone, young or old, cat lover or not, will enjoy. The stories will bring a smile to your face and warm your heart."

—School Library Journal

Sue & Tai-chan

Konami Kanata

Sue is an aging housecat who's looking forward to living out her life in peace... but her plans change when the mischievous black tomcat Tai-chan enters the picture! Hey! Sue never signed up to be a catsitter! *Sue & Tai-chan* is the latest from the reigning meow-narch of cute kitty comics, Konami Kanata.

KC
KODANSHA
COMICS

◄ KAMOME ►
SHIRAHAMA

Witch Hat Atelier

A magical manga
adventure for
fans of Disney
and Studio
Ghibli!

Witch Hat Atelier © Kamome Shirahama/Kodansha Ltd.

The magical adventure that took Japan by storm is finally here, from acclaimed DC and Marvel cover artist Kamome Shirahama!

In a world where everyone takes wonders like magic spells
and dragons for granted, Coco is a girl with a simple dream:
She wants to be a witch. But everybody knows magicians
are born, not made, and Coco was not born with a gift for
magic. Resigned to her un-magical life, Coco is about to
give up on her dream to become a witch...until the day
she meets Qifrey, a mysterious, traveling magician. After
secretly seeing Qifrey perform magic in a way she's never
seen before, Coco soon learns what everybody "knows"
might not be the truth, and discovers that her magical
dream may not be as far away as it may seem...

KC
KODANSHA
COMICS

SAINT ☆ YOUNG MEN

A LONG AWAITED ARRIVAL IN PREMIUM 2-IN-1 HARDCOVER

After centuries of hard work, Jesus and Buddha take a break from their heavenly duties to relax among the people of Japan, and their adventures in this lighthearted buddy comedy are sure to bring mirth and merriment to all!

"Brilliant...the physical comedy and facial expressions will make you literally LOL."
—Sam Humphries
(host of *DC Daily*; writer, *Green Lanterns*, *Legendary Star-Lord*)

Saint Young Men © Hikaru Nakamura/Kodansha Ltd.

Young characters and steampunk setting, like *Howl's Moving Castle* and *Battle Angel Alita*

Beyond the Clouds © 2018 Nicke / Ki-oon

A boy with a talent for machines and a mysterious girl whose wings he's fixed will take you beyond the clouds! In the tradition of the high-flying, resonant adventure stories of Studio Ghibli comes a gorgeous tale about the longing of young hearts for adventure and friendship!

Magus of the Library

Mitsu Izumi

MITSU IZUMI'S STUNNING ARTWORK BRINGS A FANTASTICAL LITERARY ADVENTURE TO LUSH, THRILLING LIFE!

Young Theo adores books, but the prejudice and hatred of his village keeps them ever out of his reach. Then one day, he chances to meet Sedona, a traveling librarian who works for the great library of Aftzaak, City of Books, and his life changes forever...

The beloved characters from *Cardcaptor Sakura* return in a brand new, reimagined fantasy adventure!

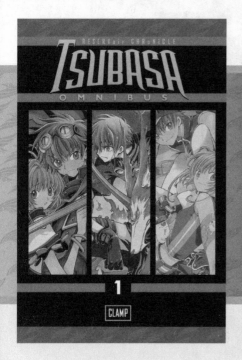

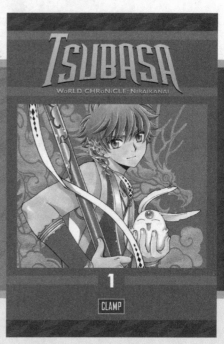

"[*Tsubasa*] takes readers on a fantastic ride that only gets more exhilarating with each successive chapter." —Anime News Network

In the Kingdom of Clow, an archaeological dig unleashes an incredible power, causing Princess Sakura to lose her memories. To save her, her childhood friend Syaoran must follow the orders of the Dimension Witch and travel alongside Kurogane, an unrivaled warrior; Fai, a powerful magician; and Mokona, a curiously strange creature, to retrieve Sakura's dispersed memories!

Princess Jellyfish

Akiko Higashimura

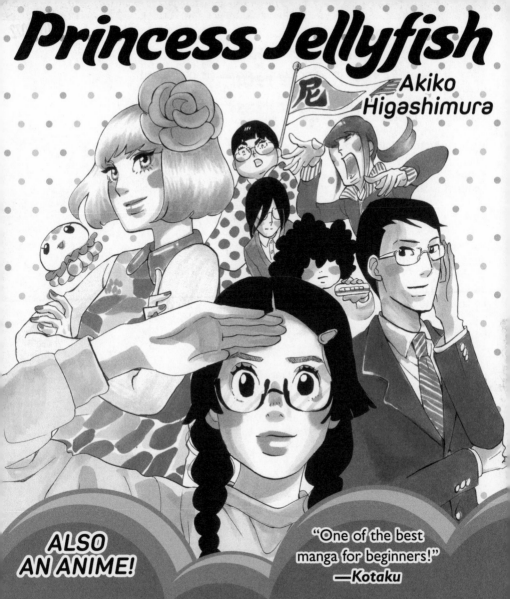

ALSO AN ANIME!

"One of the best manga for beginners!"
—*Kotaku*

Tsukimi Kurashita is fascinated with jellyfish. She's loved them from a young age and has carried that love with her to her new life in the big city of Tokyo. There, she resides in Amamizukan, a safe-haven for geek girls where no boys are allowed. One day, Tsukimi crosses paths with a beautiful and fashionable woman, but there's much more to this woman than her trendy clothes...!

KC KODANSHA COMICS

A Kodansha Trade Paperback Original

Penguin & House 3 copyright © 2020 Akiho Ieda
English translation copyright © 2022 Akiho Ieda

Published in the United States by
Kodansha USA Publishing, LLC, New York.

Publication rights for this English edition arranged through
Kodansha Ltd., Tokyo.

First published in Japan in 2020 by Kodansha Ltd., Tokyo
as *Pento House*, volume 3.

Original cover design by Airi Inoue (Nartis)

ISBN 978-1-64651-348-2

Printed in the United States of America.

9 8 7 6 5 4 3 2 1

Translation: Sawa Matsueda Savage
Lettering: Evan Hayden
Editing: Haruko Hashimoto
Kodansha USA Publishing edition cover design by Phil Balsman

Publisher: Kiichiro Sugawara

Director of Publishing Services: Ben Applegate
Director of Publishing Operations: Dave Barrett
Associate Director of Publishing Operations: Stephen Pakula
Publishing Services Managing Editors: Madison Salters, Alanna Ruse
Production Managers: Emi Lotto, Angela Zurlo

KODANSHA.US

KODANSHA